# CRITICAL EXCESS

## TRACKING POP

SERIES EDITORS: JOCELYN NEAL, JOHN COVACH, ROBERT FINK, AND LOREN KAJIKAWA

RECENT TITLES IN THE SERIES:

Critical Excess: *Watch the Throne* and the New Gilded Age
*by J. Griffith Rollefson*

Soda Goes Pop: Pepsi-Cola Advertising and Popular Music
*by Joanna K. Love*

*The Beatles* through a Glass Onion: Reconsidering the White Album
*edited by Mark Osteen*

The Pop Palimpsest: Intertextuality in Recorded Popular Music
*edited by Lori Burns and Serge Lacasse*

Uncharted: Creativity and the Expert Drummer
*by Bill Bruford*

I Hear a Symphony: Motown and Crossover R&B
*by Andrew Flory*

Hearing Harmony: Toward a Tonal Theory for the Rock Era
*by Christopher Doll*

Good Vibrations: Brian Wilson and the Beach Boys in Critical Perspective
*edited by Philip Lambert*

Krautrock: German Music in the Seventies
*by Ulrich Adelt*

Sounds of the Underground: A Cultural, Political and Aesthetic Mapping of Underground and Fringe Music
*by Stephen Graham*

Rhymin' and Stealin': Musical Borrowing in Hip-Hop
*by Justin A. Williams*

Powerful Voices: The Musical and Social World of Collegiate A Cappella
*by Joshua S. Duchan*

# CRITICAL EXCESS

## *Watch the Throne* and The New Gilded Age

J. Griffith Rollefson

UNIVERSITY OF MICHIGAN PRESS
Ann Arbor

Published in the United States of America by
the University of Michigan Press
Manufactured in the United States of America
Printed on acid-free paper

First published June 2021

A CIP catalog record for this book is available from the British Library.

ISBN 978-0-472-07487-7 (hardcover : alk. paper)
ISBN 978-0-472-05487-9 (paper : alk. paper)
ISBN 978-0-472-12889-1 (ebook)

# CONTENTS



Digital materials related to this title can be found on the Fulcrum platform via the following citable URL https://doi.org/10.3998/mpub.10170706

Audio, video, and other resources are posted on this book's companion website: www.criticalexcess.org

# ACKNOWLEDGMENTS

Writing this book has been a strange and uncanny journey. Since I first conceived of the argument in the disorienting wake of Donald Trump's election to the US presidency, I've drawn input and inspiration from a range of activists, artists, and scholars, both formal and informal, about how white resentment functions—about how white privilege can and must be dismantled. So, I first have to say thank you to the people of color—many of them queer and non-gender conforming—whose voices animate the pages of this book. My thanks to the activists, artists, scholars, organizers, students, and everyday people who could wait no longer. Thank you for pulling the curtain back—all the way back—on an unjust and unsustainable world. That struggle, while by no means new, will bear fruit. I thank you. And I have redoubled my efforts to do my part.

Thank you to Mary J. King, who, as ever, pushed my thinking—especially in the realm of intersectional and Black feminist activism and scholarship. Your challenges, your reading leads, and your support have enlivened my work—both on the page and in the community. Thanks for your detailed reading and conceptual leads. Thanks for your help with the musical examples in the book. Thanks for everything—for our journey together.

Thank you to my colleagues at University College Cork, National University of Ireland. Thanks to Alex Khalil, whose recent arrival has brought me a kindred spirit to bounce ideas off of. Thanks to Melanie Marshall, who is the quiet and ever-thoughtful center of a diverse and politically radical department. Thanks to Danijela Kulezic-Wilson, Emily Gale, Jools Gilson, Yvon Bonenfent, Tríona Ní Shíocháin, Jonathan Stock, Christopher Brown, Karl Kitching, Eileen Hogan, Amanullah De Sondy, the UCC chapter of Universities Studying Slavery, and all the other UCC colleagues who have proven so inspiring over these last years. Foremost among those, a special thanks goes to Graham Allen, who, on thinking back about where this book comes from, was probably the provocateur that planted the seed of such an absurd and necessary idea. Thanks, Graham. Here's to prophesy. Here's to Frankenstein!

Thanks to my colleagues in hip hop studies, among them my European Research Council CIPHER: Hip Hop Interpellation team of Maria Fitzgerald Houlihan, Warrick Moses, Jason Ng, Gustavo Souza Marques, David Browne, Steven Gamble, Ophelia McCabe, and the amazing advisory board for that project (please check out https://www.ucc.ie/en/cipher/ for more information). The ERC—and the European Union that funds it—has provided essential support for my work and this global hip hop knowledge-mapping project over the last year through their Consolidator Grant initiative.

Thanks to my colleagues on the editorial board of the new journal, *Global Hip Hop Studies* (*GHHS*), especially my critically incisive coeditor and relentless scholar-activist friend, Adam Haupt. Many thanks to the editorial team of Murray Forman, Sina Nitzsche, Karim Hammou, and Bettina Love. Special thanks to Murray, who—in addition to countless other solids—introduced me to Parisian hip hop impresario Bruno Laforestrie, who is a major focus of chapter 4. Speaking of which, thanks to Youssef Jaison Carter who first hipped me to the mind blowing political video I analyze in that chapter. Much love to the *GHHS* section editors Kendra Salois, Quentin Williams, Monique Charles, Justin Burton, Mark Campbell, Amy Coddington, Adam de Paor-Evans, A.D. Carson, and the journal's remarkable advisory board (please see the journal's page at https://www.intellectbooks.com/global-hip-hop-studies for more). Indeed, Kendra and Justin's work also appears front and center in the introduction that follows—and I owe them a special debt of gratitude for their comments on early drafts of this book.

Thanks to my colleagues farther afield in hip hop studies, African American studies, postcolonial studies, media studies, popular music studies, musicology, and ethnomusicology. Special thanks to Catherine Appert, Justin Williams, Sarah Hill, Nabeel Zuberi, Elliott Powell, John O'Flynn, Áine Mangaoang, Aileen Dillane, Danielle Sofer, Samy Alim, Jeff Chang, Joe Schloss, Mark Katz, Lauron Kehrer, Richard Bramwell, James Butterworth, Paul Gilroy, Lez Henry, Julian Henriques, Joy White, Tom Perchard, Byron Dueck, Jason Stanyek, Simran Singh, my colleagues in the Society for Musicology in Ireland (SMI), and so many others.

Thanks to the team at University of Michigan Press—to Mary Francis for bringing the project on board, Sara Cohen for shepherding it to publication, and Loren Kajikawa for immeasurable conceptual input in developing the manuscript (and I do mean immeasurable).

Thanks to Jacques Attali and Tricia Rose, who inspired the central heuristic frame for this book—the combined historical frame of rupture captured in the dyad *Black/Noise.*

Thanks to all the artists who have inspired this book—and especially to those with whom I've worked in the past years. Thanks to Garry McCarthy and the Kabin Studios in Cork City, to Stevie G, Spekulativ Fiktion, 0phelia, JusMe, Ross, OutsiderYP, Rusangano Family, Mankyy, Danny Deepo, and—as ever—Juice Aleem and Rico Pabón, whose musical wisdom is always ringing in my ear. Indeed, to prepare yourself for this book's analysis of white resentment of BIPOC success, I encourage you to check out Rico's track "No Thin Line" at RicoPabon.com or this book's companion site, CriticalExcess.org. Thanks also to another type of hip hop artist—my man, Gabe Urist, the illest hip hop jeweler alive (flip back to the cover of this book and check the method).

A final thanks to Jay-Z and Kanye West, artists with whom I might not always agree, but nonetheless value deeply for their commitment to hip hop ways of knowing and being—for their *prophesy.*

# Introduction

## *Death Dance for Capitalism:* Watch the Throne *as Prophetic Critique*

> Music is prophecy. Its styles and economic organization are ahead of the rest of society because it explores, much faster than material reality can, the entire range of possibilities in a given code. It makes audible the new world that will gradually become visible, that will impose itself and regulate the order of things; it is not only the image of things, but the transcending of the everyday, the herald of the future. For this reason musicians, even when officially recognized, are dangerous, disturbing, and subversive; for this reason it is impossible to separate their history from that of repression and surveillance.
>
> —JACQUES ATTALI, *NOISE: THE POLITICAL ECONOMY OF MUSIC* (1977/1985)

Jay-Z and Kanye West's 2011 *Watch the Throne* is a self-avowed "luxury rap" album centered on Eurocentric constructions of nobility, artistry, and race. Notably, it is also an album about the *excess* associated with royalty. In this book, I perform a close reading of the album's sonic and social commentary while placing it in its social, cultural, and political contexts across the Black Atlantic. In particular, I examine how the album alternately performs and critiques the mutually reinforcing ideas of *Europe, nobility, old money, artistry*, and their standard bearer, *whiteness.*

In 1920 W. E. B. Du Bois wrote of this very network of white privilege in "The Souls of White Folk," chapter 2 of his *Darkwater: Voices from within the Veil.*

> Here it is that the comedy verges to tragedy. The first minor note is struck, all unconsciously, by those worthy souls in whom consciousness of high descent

> brings burning desire to spread the gift abroad,—*the obligation of nobility to the ignoble.* Such sense of duty assumes two things: a real possession of the heritage and its frank appreciation by the humble-born. So long, then, as humble black folk, voluble with thanks, receive barrels of old clothes from lordly and generous whites, there is much mental peace and moral satisfaction. But when the black man begins to dispute the white man's title to certain alleged bequests of the Fathers in wage and position, authority and training; *and when his attitude toward charity is sullen anger rather than humble jollity; when he insists on his human right to swagger and swear and waste,—then the spell is suddenly broken.*[1]

It is in the connections between Jay and Ye's boastful luxury rap and this 100-year-old premonition of "swagger" that this book finds its *raison d'être.*

In this study, I argue that this system of racial privilege that has undergirded the global capitalist economy for the past 400 years is now in its death throes—that Black swagger has revealed the racial underpinnings of capitalism and broken the spell of capitalist hegemony. More specifically, I suggest that if we listen closely to this "dangerous, disturbing, and subversive" album we can hear, as Jacques Attali put it, that it "makes audible the new world that will gradually become visible, that will impose itself and regulate the order of things." While much remains unclear at this time of global precarity, tumult, and realignment, I argue with certainty that Jay and Ye's Obama-era album—and its well-publicized fallout—can be shown to "herald the future." It prophesies nothing less than the end of capitalism. *Watch the Throne* is capitalism's death dance.[2]

In this book, I show how Jay and Ye seem to *accede* to Eurocentric signifiers of *Kultur,* but through a strategy that I dub "critical excess," performatively *exceed* the logics of Europe, nobility, and artistry and break "the spell" of white supremacy. Articulating the Black Atlantic, postcolonial, and critical theory of Du Bois, Houston Baker, Frantz Fanon, Tricia Rose, Paul Gilroy, Daphne Brooks, Fred Moten, Stuart Hall, Cedric Robinson, and Kimberlé Crenshaw to Jacques Attali's theorizations about the prophetic nature of music in his *Noise: The Political Economy of Music,* I argue that the album brings the idea of Europe to its logical conclusion and heralds the final stage of late capitalism—our current one-percenter era, "the New Gilded Age."[3]

Further, through their performative Blackness and conspicuous consumption—their *critical excess*—on the luxury rap album, I show how Jay and Ye fashion a move directly from the subhuman to the superhuman.

Indeed, this move draws simultaneously on postcolonial technologies of "strategic essentialism" and critical excess, moving effortlessly from the jungle and the ghetto to the penthouse and the throne. While all of the following chapters work in and through the well-documented theory of strategic essentialism and elaborate my related theory of critical excess, the individual chapters are structured, respectively, around the compounding heuristic frames of essentialism (especially chapters 1 and 2), anti-essentialism (especially chapters 2, 3, and 4), and anti-anti-essentialism (especially chapters 3, 4, and 5)—and accordingly track, respectively, the categories of subhuman, human, and superhuman. In this way, the book analyzes the Jay and Ye album in all its maddening complexity while introducing us to the fundamental conceptual layers that the music is working through and against. Indeed, following Houston Baker's entreaty for the critically attuned scholar to "heat up the observational space" in reading Black cultural performances and artifacts, this book follows leads far and wide to engage this album and its contexts in a manner befitting that complexity—and adding to it.[4]

As Justin D. Burton—author of the landmark study *Posthuman Rap*—writes in his double review of *Watch the Throne* and the Roots' *Undun*, Jay and Ye's album revels in duplicity, living a "double life of fun, sophomoric tracks juxtaposed with biting social critique"—usually in the same track. Most importantly, he writes, the album presents "a salient critical agenda hidden inside a collection of catchy tunes built from the debris of greatest hits past."[5] Indeed, Burton's analysis continues a long line of hip hop scholarship that illustrates the critical complexities of a seemingly blunt musical instrument.

Hip hop's lifeblood of storytelling, playful allusion, and striking metaphor is, of course, a long- and well-established fact in the literature on Black music—stretching back from funk, rock and roll, and blues innuendo to "the dozens" and the slave spiritual codes. Yet in its *always already* racialized state of crisis, hip hop is also uniquely capable of getting people to forget about those poetic, sonic, and rhetorical hallmarks of Afrodiasporic performance cultures—to forget that this music is *music*. Scholars from Tricia Rose and Robin Kelley to Eithne Quinn and Loren Kajikawa have established in sonic and social detail how gangsta rap—the most glaring example—has been widely misunderstood in its decontextualizing crossover into the mainstream of popular culture and its familiar fixations.[6]

In his groundbreaking book, *Race Rebels*, Kelley underscores this foundational paradox of hip hop—that "the primary purpose" of this often violent form of social critique "is to produce 'funky dope rhymes' for our listening pleasure."[7] He writes:

> Unfortunately, much of this debate [around gangsta rap], especially in the media, has only disseminated misinformation. Thus, it is important to clarify what gangsta rap is *not*. First, gangsta rappers have never merely celebrated gang violence, nor have they taken a partisan position in favor of one gang over another. Gang bangin' (gang participation) itself has never even been a central theme in the music. Many of the violent lyrics are not intended to be literal. Rather, they are boasting raps in which the imagery of gang bangin' is used metaphorically to challenge competitors on the microphone.[8]

As we begin to interrogate the music, lyrics, images, and rhetorics of this album, it will be key to keep this foundational analysis in mind. Like most hip hop albums, *Watch the Throne* plays with genre expectations to enact its cultural critique. As Kelley explains, "Some gangsta rappers—Ice Cube in particular—are especially brilliant at showing how, if I may paraphrase Marx, young urban black men make their own history but not under circumstances of their own choosing."[9]

Echoing Burton's assessment, the scholar of North African hip hop, Kendra Salois, expands on Jay and Ye's "critical hidden agenda" on *Watch the Throne* in a published roundtable, "Religion and Hip Hop." Commenting on the knee-jerk reactions that might immediately pigeonhole and shut down hip hop that demonstrates such critical play in the context of commercial catchiness, she counters:

> But it's also important to remember that, in some contexts, celebrating yourself in the way that I think you're referring to [ . . . ] can be a form of critique. You remember Jay-Z and Kanye's song "Otis." I used to use it in my classes a lot, because if you were not attuned to the potential for critique inside even the most commercial of hip hop, then you would see it as just crass materialism, a complete celebration of wealth. But then you have to think about what they're sampling, and how that changes how you have to read the lyrics, and you have to think about the history of systematic dispossession of black Americans, to recognize that what Jay-Z and Kanye are doing is saying, "In your face! We did this. We made it to this point that no one could imagine for us, including ourselves, in spite of you." And that's a really powerful critique, even if we don't

necessarily personally agree that anyone should have that much money. That's a really powerful form of critique.[10]

This "double life"—of entertainer *and* artist; of fun *and* critique; of "In your face! We did this"—is central to this book's analysis.

## PROPHESY AND POSTHUMANISM

It is here that Jacques Attali's political economy and proto-sound studies will prove foundational for our understanding of the album and this book's most outrageous claim—that, on *Watch the Throne,* Jay and Ye prophesied Donald J. Trump. That, in many ways, they saw him coming. Indeed, in this book I support the claim that, through this "critical excess," they willed him into being; *they made him.*

In the first chapter of Attali's *Noise: The Political Economy of Music,* the economic and social theorist lays out the "double game" of the musician in society. It will be important to cite him at length here, as he writes:

> The musician, like music, is ambiguous. He plays a double game. He is simultaneously *musicus* and *cantor,* reproducer and prophet. If an outcast, he sees society in a political light. If accepted, he is its historian, the reflection of its deepest values. He speaks of society and he speaks against it. This duality was already present before capital arrived to impose its own rules and prohibitions. The distinction between musician and nonmusician—which separates the group from the speech of the sorcerer—undoubtedly represents one of the very first divisions of labor, one of the very first social differentiations in the history of humanity, even predating the social hierarchy. Shaman, doctor, musician. He is one of society's first gazes upon itself; he is one of the first catalyzers of violence and myth. I will show later that the musician is an integral part of the sacrifice process, a channeler of violence, and that the primal identity *magic-music-sacrifice-rite* expresses the musician's position in the majority of civilizations: simultaneously *excluded* (relegated to a place near the bottom of the social hierarchy) and *superhuman* (the genius, the adored and deified star). Simultaneously a separator and an integrator.
>
> In the civilizations of antiquity, the musician was often a slave, sometimes an untouchable. Even as late as the twentieth century, Islam prohibited believers

> from eating at the same table as a musician. In Persia, music was for a long time an activity restricted to prostitutes or, at least, considered shameful. But at the same time, the ancient religions produced a caste of musician-priests attached to the service of the temple, and mythology endowed musicians with supernatural and civilizing powers.[11]

Central to the structure of this book's argument is the premise that, through their performance of "critical excess" on *Watch the Throne*—through their "double game"—Jay and Ye constantly move back and forth between the categories of "excluded subhuman" and "adored superhuman," thus eschewing the normative category of "human."

In the pages that follow, I argue that through this doubled sub- and superhumanity and performed denial of humanity, they render the latter category a played-out remnant of individualized bourgeois capitalism. That is, in exercising their "human right to swagger and swear"—but doing so as unapologetically rich Black men—Jay and Ye undermine the racially coded language of "humanity," break "the spell" of white supremacy, and bring the enlightenment/colonial idea of Europe to an end.

Though I will add detail and substance to this argument in the pages to come, to give you a sense of what I mean by "humanity" up front, I encourage the reader to think "All Lives Matter" when confronted with the category of the human. Indeed, in recent years it has become increasingly clear that humanism and its universalist ideology is, as Etienne Balibar has argued, a trick.[12] And further, that universalism and its "free market" ideology are little more than good cover for a centuries-old system of maintaining European (white) supremacy. Indeed, in his *Posthuman Rap*, Burton uses the category of "neoliberal humanism" as a foil for his inquiries, a clarifying term that collapses the category of Western Enlightenment subjectivity with the context of its capitalist emergence (and most commonplace practice today).[13] As I show through close musical, textual, and visual analysis, *Watch the Throne* performs for us the reality that white supremacy *is* capitalism.

Indeed, recent global events have clearly indicated the limits of capitalism's supposedly colorblind ideology. As Ye puts it on track 9, "Who Gon Stop Me," "Heard Yeezy was racist? / Well I guess it's on one basis / I only like green faces." The line is the ultimate critique of neoliberalism—an ideology and world system that reduces human value to monetary value. Importantly, however, neoliberalism is also ostensibly an ideology that denies white privilege—green faces are the only ones that matter. As we are seeing currently in our global political realignments, white people will not abide this privileging of green faces at the expense of white ones—and especially not where Black faces are involved.

Yet, as Cedric Robinson has convincingly argued in his *Black Marxism: The Making of the Black Radical Tradition*, capitalism has never been truly colorblind. Indeed, the first chapter, "Racial Capitalism: The Non-Objective Character of Capitalist Development," is a sweeping historical overview and masterful reading of capitalism's tribalist underpinnings, and racialized blossoming over the 18th and 19th centuries. Far from ever having been colorblind, Robinson begins:

> The historical development of world capitalism was influenced in a most fundamental way by the forces of racism and nationalism. This could only be true if the social, psychological, and cultural origins of racism and nationalism both anticipated capitalism in time and formed a piece with those events that contributed directly to its organization of production and exchange.[14]

He concludes: "Feudal society is the key."

In his detailed and incisive reading, Robinson shows how capitalism was not a distinct break from the premodern feudal, aristocratic, and religious order, but emerged as a reordering of particular ethnic peasant groups into racialized wage and slave labor classes. He writes: "The bourgeoisie that led the development of capitalism were drawn from particular ethnic and cultural groups; the European proletariats and the mercenaries of the leading states from others; its peasants from still other cultures; and its slaves from entirely different worlds." As such, capitalism was built through racial differentiation.

> The tendency of European civilization through capitalism was thus not to homogenize but to differentiate—to exaggerate regional, subcultural, and dialectical differences into "racial" ones. As the Slavs became the natural slaves, the racially inferior stock for domination and exploitation during the early Middle Ages, as the Tartars came to occupy a similar position in the Italian cities of the late Middle Ages, so at the systemic interlocking of capitalism in the sixteenth century, the peoples of the Third World began to fill this expanding category of a civilization reproduced by capitalism.[15]

In this way capitalism was built in and through white supremacy. While its ideology cloaks this truth in meritocratic, naturalizing, and "free market" universalist language, capitalism has always been powered by racial differentiation. Indeed, we might say that "racial capitalism" is a redundant term. From its roots in premodern feudalism through today's postmodern neoliberalism, capitalism developed through the systematic definition and subordination of racialized ethnic underclasses.

In addition to his theories about the prophecy and critical duality of music's social function, Attali's *Noise* is important for how it also traces that social function back to the *jongleur* of Europe's premodern societies. I'd never put it together that the medieval-looking musician on the cover art for *Noise* was meant as a play on the cultural figure of the precapitalist *jongleur* that the author theorizes as both prophet and historian in the text. The well-chosen image, it turns out, is a detail from one of Pieter Brueghel the Elder's lively village scenes titled *Carnival's Quarrel with Lent* (1559). It is something of a diptych, depicting the duality of human pleasure and excess on the left and human piety and abstinence on the right, via a range of images associated with this pivotal moment in the Christian calendar. The image thus focuses our attention not only on the "ambiguous" (and doubled) *jongleur* figure, but on this ambiguous moment in the liturgical year. Further, we might suspect, this close-up was chosen to focus the reader on the pivotal early modern sea change from feudal and guild economic systems to early capitalism—a major focus of Attali's analysis.

In her afterword to the 1985 English translation of *Noise*, Susan McClary suggests that the then-lively New Wave movement might rise to serve a similarly prophetic social function with its "compositional" grassroots, DIY critique. The "compositional" is Attali's hopeful shorthand for a community-centered music that will emerge from the ashes of capitalism—or, rather, a musicking that predicts and models, for us, the economic order to come after capitalism. We'll have to forgive McClary for her nonprophesy there, because she does go on to write insightfully about the transformative social function of hip hop later in the decade. Although New Wave never gained the globally socially transformative power of hip hop, it is worth recognizing that hip hop grew out of the same 1970s and 80s milieu in New York City that produced punk and New Wave—and was intricately interwoven with those subcultural communities, their parties, and their forms, an entanglement captured in the collaborations between

Blondie and Grandmaster Flash and the punk–to–hip hop maturation process of the Beastie Boys, among others.

In his recent *Dead Precedents: How Hip Hop Defines the Future*, Roy Christopher examines these continuities, building them into the thesis that hip hop—as a future-oriented culture rooted in the experimental tenets and counterhistories of Afrofuturism and cyberpunk—invented the twenty-first century. Recalling his first hearing of the remixed, recomposed mash-up of AC/DC and hip hop on Boogie Down Productions' "Dope Beat" (1987), Christopher reminisces "That moment was a door opening to a new world. I didn't realize it then, but that new world was the twenty-first century, and hip-hop was its blueprint."[16] As we will see, the argument aligns nicely with Attali's theory of "composition" and its interest in technological progress. Indeed, it aligns nicely with my argument about *Watch the Throne's* prophecy.

More importantly, for anyone in hip hop studies today, Attali's mention of "prophet *and* historian," "shaman, doctor, musician" will instead instantly call up the figure of the West African *griot*—to whom countless hip hop MCs and DJs look as forbear today.[17] Attali writes: "before the advent of recording and modern sound tools, the jongleurs were the collective memory, the essential site of cultural creation, and the circulation of information from the courts to the people."[18] The characterization perfectly captures the culture-bearer quality of the *griot*, a figure who "sings the people." Further, Attali's understanding of the jongleur also suggests the linkage between the *griot* and hip hop's much-heralded function as an information technology—what Chuck D famously called "the Black CNN": "informing people, connecting people, being a direct source of information."[19] Indeed, Attali terms his first heuristic category in *Noise* "sacrifice"—a premodern "ritual code" central to the griot's cultural function—which shares the community centeredness of "composition" but based its buy-in on fear (of sacrifice, of music's ritual power). The second is the modern category of "representation," a musical code centered on exchange and functional harmony that Attali claims predicted the age of revolution and representative democracy—and also capitalism.[20] The third is "repetition," the age of sign exchange typified in the culture industry's popular music and its prophesy of fascism from the 1930s to late capitalism's reality-TV reality.

On the surface, nothing could qualify as nicely for Attali's dystopian musical category of "repetition" as hip hop—a popular genre structured on samples, loops, and repeated chants. Mirroring Adorno's infamous critique of "jazz"—though we might dispute what he understood that musical praxis to be—hip hop too would seem like a nicely "predigested" form built on the repetition of signs of the global culture industry, a commodity well-suited to satiate (but further alienate) the tired, working masses. Notably, however, where Attali defines the code of "repetition" as a *code of normality* and one-sided "speech without response," hip hop, like its Afrodiasporic musical forbears, is premised on call and response, on the musical community, be it the congregation, juke joint, or hip hop cipher. Indeed, as we will see in the coming pages, hip hop refigures those signs, those cultural inheritances, to subvert our late capitalist hegemony from within and create a new community. Hip hop is a fitting pivot from the normative age of "repetition" to the community-responsive age of "composition"—a disruption of the code of repetition, revolutionary "noise" as Attali (and, later, Tricia Rose) would have it. It is thus my contention that *Watch the Throne* represents a tipping point in the exchange of the signs and codes of capitalist hegemony.

Following Tricia Rose's titular frame in *Black Noise* that hip hop's repetition represents a revolutionary break from the code of repetition—that "rap music uses rhythmic forces that are informed by mass reproduction technology, but it uses it in ways that affirm black cultural priorities that sometimes work against market forces"[21]—I suggest that *Watch the Throne* exceeds twentieth-century codes of mechanical reproduction, both musically and discursively. In Attalian terms, it exceeds music and emerges as disruptive "noise," portending the code of composition and heralding our current age of political realignment. It is a performance that lays bare the emptiness of the capitalist sign economy and *critically exceeds* the age of "repetition," marking the return of the *jongleur/griot* with a signal difference: freedom. A storyteller that tells the stories of people rather than the stories of power, of "a single totalitarian code."[22]

Indeed, the *jongleur*, we might say, is the particular European inheritance of what is, in fact, a global history of bards and oral historian-prophets that stretches from ancient Ireland and pre-Homeric Greece to West Africa, China, Native America, Aotearoa, and beyond.[23] More than European commitments to abstract (and thus, uneven) universalism, it is the storytelling traditions around the world that provide us with a glimpse of the truly universal, a network of deeply entangled, distinct-but-same archetypes.[24] While McClary's focus on New Wave was surely apropos in 1985, Attali's 1977 *Noise* is instead prophetic of hip hop's grassroots, DIY culture. Indeed, just as Rose would come to theorize the music and culture as *Black* Noise, Imani Perry would elaborate hip hop's own "double game" of heraldic dualities—such as the "prophet/profit" figuration that animates her *Prophets of the Hood*.[25] This is the critical trajectory that I pick up in the present study.

Before we move on, I also want to call attention to Rose's implication that not all hip hop works against the capitalist system. In suggesting that "rap music uses rhythmic forces that are informed by mass reproduction technology, but . . . in ways that affirm black cultural priorities that *sometimes* work against market forces" (my emphasis), Rose is working against a totalizing vision of all hip hop as politically resistant.[26] She is gesturing—rightly, I think—to the fact that hip hop is not simply a "resistance vernacular," but is also an increasingly valuable commodity and integral part of the global culture industry. The bifurcated discourse separating good, "underground" hip hop from bad, "commercial" hip hop has become accepted as common sense since Rose wrote her foundational text at the end of hip hop's much lauded "golden age" in 1994.[27]

While I agree with Rose's careful qualification, I want to suggest that hip hop's political economy is more complex than this good hip hop/bad hip hop binary might suggest. This music is deeply influenced by, indeed, premised on, "mass reproduction technology." While there are hip hop forms, subcultures, and communities that work at the margins of capitalist culture—and are often vocally critical of that culture—they nonetheless circulate in a capitalist global economy. Their possibilities are conditioned by capitalism and its technologies (think: the internet, the mp3, the microphone, the turntable). Some iterations of hip hop are critical of capitalism, while other forms seem to celebrate capitalist consumption, materialism and wealth accrual. But recalling our frame of the (im)possibility of Black humanity—subhuman/superhuman—I want to suggest that the good hip hop/bad hip hop binary presents us with a similarly bifurcated and *middle-less* discourse.

A central premise of this book's theory of critical excess is that, as an African American and highly racialized art form, hip hop is subject to the same racialized political economy. Just as humanity is systematically denied to Black people, so too is the category of "normal" denied to hip hop. In mainstream discourse it has to be underground or commercial, conscious or crass. As such, commercial hip hop is put in an odd spot. Commercial hip hop is, in many ways, as nonnormative as underground hip hop—and with most commercial hip hop's reliance on outrageous bling, sex, and violence, it often flouts bourgeois values even more than its underground doppelgänger. But unable to hide behind the *whiteness* of bourgeois values—and evade the fact that nothing is more capitalist than bling, sex, and violence—hip hop is rendered marginal despite its capitalist compliance.

The point is this: hip hop can never be *just* pop music. By performing capitalist excess so forthrightly and offensively on *Watch the Throne*, Jay-Z and Kanye West meet and exceed the limits of even hip hop's excesses. By mashing up Martin Luther King, Nina Simone, and Fidel Castro with Rollies, threesomes, and murder in such an arrogantly unabashed manner they complicate the good hip hop/bad hip hop binary and complicate the subhuman/superhuman tropes that still dominate our bifurcated discourses of Blackness. As we will see, in so doing they drive racially essentialist notions right through the unmarked race-free, anti-essentialist dreams of capitalist pop and emerge in the realm of anti-anti-essentialism.

Gayatri Chakravorty Spivak addresses just this paradox-laden double bind around "the popular" in her essay, "Scattered Speculations on the Subaltern and the Popular," from *An Aesthetic Education in the Era of Globalization* (2012). She writes:

> I have insisted throughout this book that Gramsci's attitude toward the state sees it as both medicine and poison and leads to a permanent educative activism . . . Subaltern is to popular as gender is to sex, class to poverty, state to nation. One word inclines to reasonableness, the other to cathexis-occupation through desire. "Popular" divides between descriptive (as in presidential or TV ratings) and evaluative (not "high," both a positive and a negative value, dependent on your "politics") and contains "people," a word with immense range, from "just anyone" to the "masses" (both a positive and a negative political value, depending on your politics).[28]

Echoing Gramsci, she suggests that the way forward through the term's contradictions is to "sabotage the Enlightenment."

In a 2016 New York Times interview, she explains how such "sabotage" must master Western systems of oppression in order to undo them.

> I used the term "affirmative sabotage" to gloss on the usual meaning of sabotage: the deliberate ruining of the master's machine from the inside. Affirmative sabotage doesn't just ruin; the idea is of entering the discourse that you are criticizing fully, so that you can turn it around from inside. The only real and effective way you can sabotage something this way is when you are working intimately within it.
>
> This is particularly the case with the imperial intellectual tools, which have been developed not just upon the shoulders, but upon the backs of people for centuries.[29]

As we will see, this subversive affirmation of the "master's machine" is Gramsci's "war of position." This is critical excess.

Like its continuation of the binary-complicating work of Tricia Rose's (*Black*) *Noise* and Imani Perry's *Prophets* (Profits) *of the Hood*, this book is also intended as a follow-up and complement to my 2017 monograph *Flip the Script: European Hip Hop and the Politics of Postcoloniality.*[30] In that study, I examine how the children and grandchildren of immigrants from the former colonies and peripheries of Europe employ the iconic African American model of musical protest, while simultaneously infiltrating and instrumentalizing the global culture industry—to various ends. A central claim of that book is that by studying European hip hop—and its communities that are on the front lines of history—we can hear US hip hop anew. This book flips the script on that claim, examining instead how this African American cultural artifact has much to teach us about the European inheritance. Indeed, this close reading of *Watch the Throne* offers a musically savvy and geopolitically attuned look at one hip hop artifact that places the cultural inheritance of Eurocentrism in the US at the center of its critique—touching on everything from the Socratic method, Christian hegemony, and feudalism to colonialization, slave capitalism, social Darwinism, Parisian *haute couture*, and museumized art.

## EXCEEDING EUROPE, EXCEEDING WHITENESS

Indeed, in this book I show how European patrimony not only casts a long shadow on the album's lyrics, music, images, and performativities, but how its (impossible) inheritance is absolutely fundamental to *Watch the Throne*'s conceptualization and realization—and to Jay and Ye's critique thereof. While African American artists and scholars have musically negotiated the idea of Europe since even before W. E. B. Du Bois first committed his thoughts on the Afro-European mingling audible in the "sorrow songs," this book shows how this musical artifact from the recent past marks a turning point, undermining the very logic of Europe by laying bare and then exceeding its commitments to race—to whiteness.[31]

To be sure, Josephine Baker, Sidney Bechet, Paul Robeson, Ralph Ellison, Dexter Gordon, James Baldwin, Nina Simone, Don Cherry, and countless other Black American expats would be drawn to the idea of Europe "After They've Seen Paree"; many reconciled themselves to the idea of Europe and its cultural *patrimoine*; and many also provoked, undermined, and altered that Eurocentric hegemony. Ironically, what these African Americans all had in common was that they helped to create the lion's share of cultural wealth over the course of their century but pocketed a mere fraction of that wealth. Jay and Ye, on the other hand, have broken that trend in a most disruptive—and, for many, unacceptable—fashion. As Du Bois predicted, "when the black man begins to dispute the white man's title to certain alleged bequests of the Fathers in wage and position, authority and training; *and when his attitude toward charity is sullen anger rather than humble jollity; when he insists on his human right to swagger and swear and waste,—then the spell is suddenly broken.*"[32]

In this book, I argue that on *Watch the Throne*, Jay-Z and Kanye West—with their collaborators, from Beyoncé and Frank Ocean to Mr. Hudson—stand on the shoulders of twentieth-century Black American artists and "Lift Off" (track 2) from the idea of Europe by exceeding the "excellence, opulence, decadence" (track 10, "Murder to Excellence") of the white royalty that resides at the heart of the idea of Europe—the "nobility" and "high descent" of Du Bois's "lordly and generous whites." Indeed, recalling Cedric Robinson's historical elaboration of the feudal order's reconstitution in early capitalism, Du Bois was not the first to understand race as a sort of inheritor of feudal nobility. As early as the 1840s, "The Liberator," Ireland's famed anticolonial activist Daniel O'Connell, referred to the emergent racial order as "the filthy aristocracy of skin."[33] To be sure, the invention of race was a way to ensure and enshrine the acquired affordances of European supremacy—of white supremacy—in the increasingly entangled era of (capitalist) colonial expansion.

Notably, in escaping the thrall of this most elevated form of white supremacy—European aristocracy—Jay and Ye also flatten Langston

Hughes's infamous "Racial Mountain." As Jay-Z puts it on the (secret) final track "Illest Motherfucker Alive" (track 13):

> When I say it then you see it, it ain't only in the music
> Basquiats, Warhols serving as my muses
> My house like a museum so I see 'em when I'm peein'
> Usually you have this much taste, you European
> That's the end of that way of thinking, nigga never again.[34]

Just as he seems to accede to the museumized logic of Western ideologies of high art, Jay exceeds the logic thereof by placing these icons in his bathroom. In just a few lines of verse—and a few bars of urgent sonic swagger—he undermines the ideology of art, nobility by birth, and Europe's *sine qua non*, whiteness. With poignant irony, however, he does so both artfully and passionately—as he does with countless other conceptual and performative gems throughout the album.

Similarly, on track 4, "Otis," Kanye West undermines the race and class logics of the racial mountain with his line, "Luxury rap, the Hermès of verses / Sophisticated ignorance, write my curses in cursive"—engaging aristocratic brands of luxury capitalism and literally flipping the "script" from a signifier of visual *élégance* (cursive) to sonic *vulgarité* (curses). On track 3, "Niggas in Paris," Kanye lays bare and further elaborates the ways that class and language work to uphold the fallacy of race and its entanglement with the received ideas about Europe and/as nobility, spitting the infamous lines:

> *Bougie* girl, grab my hand
> Fuck that bitch; she don't wanna dance
> Excuse my French, but I'm in France, I'm just sayin'
> Prince Williams ain't do it right if you ask me
> 'Cause I was him I would have married Kate and Ashley

In the first two couplets, Ye plays on the idiom "excuse my French," directing the listener towards the ear-catching, misogynistic red flag: "bitch." Yet all the while, he is slyly playing on the only French word in the lyric: "*bougie*"—a subversive bit of wordplay for his listeners patient enough to abide the apparent sexism.

Indeed, to use the new (digital) vernacular, the whole album seems to have been conceptualized as a chance for these Black millionaires to "*troll*" white America, alternately gaslighting its familiar fixations, stoking its racial anxieties, and toying with its misguided "bougie" commitments to political correctness. As we will see, these affronts seem almost systematic in their totality—part of a performative strategy to attract mainstream ire and simultaneously shrug off the resentment directed their way. In the very next couplet Ye goes on to drag the beloved British Prince William (here rendered with the studied malapropism of "Prince Williams") down to the gutter level of pop culture with his proposal for a polygamist arrangement with TV's Olsen twins. In so doing, however, he also reminds the listener that both the royal and the B-list celebs exist in their truest form in *the tabloid press*—a fact that, today, is manifestly obvious in Brexit-era England.

The above are just a few examples of an album that systematically defaces and destabilizes the received idea of Europe—an idea that, today, is considerably changed since the Fisk Jubilee Singers first performed before Queen Victoria and since jazz's royalty of *Dukes* and *Counts* first took on the mantle as the world's most influential artists. Indeed, we can trace Jay and Ye's Black American usurpation of white thrones back to those subversive yet ubiquitous naming practices that elevated Joseph Nathan Oliver to "King" Oliver and Bessie Smith to "Empress of the Blues." Like Duke Ellington, Count Basie, and Lady Day, these noble European titles claimed Black musical superiority in an era of universal white appropriation of Black popular styles. Yet, in thinking about African American Kings, Empresses, Dukes, Counts, and Ladies, we must remember that these inversional discursive practices arose in an era when such gestures of Black nobility were premised on the cognitive dissonance they would engender. Compounded by the irony of Americans doing Euro-drag, these performances of eliteness were gestures of spell-breaking swagger playing on the perceived irony of Black excellence in a white supremacist society. As Jay and Ye—and, as we'll see, Queen Bey—know, such performances remain subversive ones. There is still plenty of spell breaking to do.

In addition to the lyrical rhetorics and visual performances on *Watch the Throne*, this book also focuses on the swing, swag, and other sonic performative legacies of Black American musical excellence evident on the album. As just one noteworthy sonic example, the book performs a musical and political economy analysis of "Otis" centered on the track's resignification of Otis Redding's classic soul tune, "Try a Little Tenderness"—a song about the role of materialism in a love economy and the value of love in a materialistic society. (Take, for instance, Redding's line "things that she'll never, never, never, never possess.") Indeed, on the track "Otis," the priceless soul tune (and costly sample thereof) is itself treated like a gem that is cut, refashioned, and polished, just as a pricey Maybach German automobile is cut, refashioned, and polished in the recombinatory narrative of the track's video. That both are commodities seems all too clear to Jay and Ye. That much has changed in the fifty years since the release of Redding's "Tenderness," too, seems clear. Nonetheless, on the Jay and Ye track, the vocal power and pure affect of the wordless climax to Redding's 1966 classic is beautifully recomposed, *acceding* to the aristocratic ideology of the European artistic tradition but *exceeding* that regal ethos to emerge into the domain of Du Bois's "swagger"—and Jay's boastful "swag." "In your face! We did this," as Salois puts it.[35]

While close reading and musical analysis are at the heart of this album-centered book, I also incorporate ethnomusicological and cultural historical methodologies to situate the album in its transatlantic, new millennium context. The book's visual, sonic, and social analysis of "Niggas in Paris," for instance, is also informed by Yasiin Bey's cutting parody, "Niggas in Poorest," and an interview-based examination of François Hollande's tone-deaf use of the hit track in his "unofficial" 2012 campaign video "48H avec FH" as part of his minority outreach strategy in the Parisian *banlieues*. As the French-language Swiss news site, 20min.ch, put it, "Pas sûr que ce soit de cette façon là que François Hollande souhaite devenir célèbre aux Etats-Unis" (Not sure that this is how François Hollande wants to become famous in the United States).[36] The book thus tracks the reception of "Niggas in Paris," drawing on work with artists, media accounts, and personal interviews with the Parisian duo *Blackara* and the founder of Paris's hip hop Radio *Génération*, Bruno Laforestrie.

In sum, in this book I look to the realm of music to explain nothing less than the unprecedented inequality of our "New Gilded Age" and its ongoing geopolitical realignment, from Trumpism, to Brexit, to the global resurgence of fascism—from Orbán to Bolsonaro to Duterte to Modi—and, notably, to the destabilization of the EU. As evidenced by Euro-American politics being reduced to the unsustainable poles of neoliberal globalization vs. ethnonational protectionism in the wake of Brexit and Trumpism, it seems we need to take seriously the prophetic force of hip hop—even, or maybe especially, luxury rap. For Jay and Ye's *performative* and *critical excess* seems to exceed the limits of conspicuous consumption and usher in an age of deeply ambivalent hypercapitalism—a late stage that finally looks primed to eat itself.

Thus, I argue that the critical excess performed on *Watch the Throne* is a consumption so conspicuous that it amounts to a critique of capitalism; that Jay and Ye's unashamed Black "excellence, opulence, and decadence" (track 10, "Murder to Excellence") amounts to a full-circle, anti-anti-essentialist critique of *whiteness and/as capitalism*—a doubled critique exemplified in Kanye's construction, "I adopted these niggas / Phillip Drummoned 'em" (track 4, "Otis"). As we will see, this is critical excess. Indeed, the gilded album art for *Watch the Throne* would fit comfortably in 45's Trump Tower penthouse (as might Kanye himself as we've seen).

As recent political events have made abundantly clear, long-promised freedoms for some have been perceived as existential threats for others. This was true in the wake of the Emancipation Proclamation in 1863 as Reconstruction fanned the flames of racial violence; it was true during and after the fight for the Civil Rights Act in 1964 as Jim Crow fell, kicking and screaming, burning and lynching; and it has been increasingly true since the election of the nation's first Black president as the edifice of white privilege succumbed to the greatest structural impropriety: Barack Hussein Obama and his African American family living in the White House—a Black man sitting on the throne.[37]

As we have already seen in the ironies of recent geopolitical realignments, once Black and Brown people gain a foothold and begin breaking the glass ceiling, capitalism's racialized underpinnings will begin to erode because, to borrow a phrase from Ta-Nehisi Coates, the "people who think themselves white" will cease their buy-in to the capitalist hegemony and its globalist, free-market ideology.[38]

"What's a mob to a king?" (track 1, "No Church in the Wild"). We're finding out right now. Will we "make it out alive?" If we listen closely we might find some answers.

* * *

Was Jay and Ye's luxury rap swag instrumental in these political developments? I think so. Was Barack Obama's presidency instrumental in the mobilization and politicization of anti-Black racism? Absolutely. Indeed, between the gilded excess of *Watch the Throne*'s album art and the thug-

Fig. 1. Album cover art for *Watch the Throne* (2011) and *To Pimp a Butterfly* (2015). *Watch the Throne* is a "luxury rap" album and is packaged accordingly. In contrast, the cover art for *To Pimp a Butterfly* represents the contradicting frames of Black excellence and Black poverty.

gish stereotypes (camped out in front of the White House) on Kendrick Lamar's 2015 album art for *To Pimp a Butterfly*, we have a powerful rhetorical encapsulation of the bifurcation of subhuman and superhuman that echoed throughout the Obama presidency. (Here, I encourage you to visit this book's companion website, www.criticalexcess.org, to examine these and associated media artifacts—images, musical recordings, music videos, and other accompanying materials arranged by chapter—in more detail). Where the cover art for *Watch the Throne* revels in the gilded bling of Black excellence, opulence, and decadence, *To Pimp a Butterfly* presents us with the image of *unrespectable* young Black men and boys celebrating shirtless in front of the White House, brandishing stacks of money, gold chains, and bottles. The thuggish stereotypes loom over the dead body of a white politician, eyes exed-out at the bottom left of the album cover. Indeed, the cover art renders a stark contrast with Obama's expression of respectable Black excellence.

Where Jay-Z was, in fact, a welcome and highly visible supporter of Obama, the cover art for *To Pimp a Butterfly* calls to mind the line from Kanye's 2010 "Power": "They say I was the abomination of Obama's nation / Well, that's a pretty bad way to start the conversation."

## HOW DO YOU SOLVE A PROBLEM LIKE KANYE?

Before I continue this introduction, I must attend to the MAGA-hatted elephant in the room—if only briefly and provisionally. When I first proposed this book in the early days of the Trump regime, Kanye West was already a celebrity provocateur. Indeed, he'd already been called a (talented) "jackass" by fellow Chicagoan Barack Obama.[39] That said, Ye finding his "dragon energy" soul mate in Donald J. Trump is as scary and disconcerting to me as anyone—all the more so, now that I run the risk of being seen to defend his indefensible "off the rails" behavior.[40] How he went from speaking truth to power on live television in the heartbreaking aftermath of Hurricane Katrina ("George Bush doesn't care about black people") to seemingly being in thrall to alt-right power in Trump's White House, I can't exactly say.

Yet, perhaps we all should have been prepared. His work had grown increasingly dark, conspiratorial, and megalomaniacal after the trilogy of his first three albums—Grammy-nominated albums which, it warrants mention, were all finalists for, *but never winners* of Album of the Year. Always the bridesmaid, never the bride. Indeed, on the chorus to his 2008 "Amazing" from the album *808s & Heartbreak*, Ye pre-empts our Trump-era questions rather forthrightly, singing: "I'm a problem / That'll never ever be solved." In the following chorus, his self-assessment grows prophetic.

> I'm a monster, I'm a maven
> *I know this world is changing*
> Never gave in, never gave up
> I'm the only thing I'm afraid of[41]

In setting himself up as a "monster" that would come to bow before Trump's throne, the lines anticipate Ye's well-founded fear that even he doesn't know what he's capable of. Certainly, our "world is changing"—and we still haven't solved the Ye problem.

While I can't say how Kanye ended up palling around with Trump—gleefully hovering over Resolute with Old Hickory looking on—it is a foregone conclusion that both men have fragile egos. Perhaps that's the "dragon energy." Or perhaps Kanye has contracted a particularly virulent strain of white fragility. My guess is that those mounting Grammy snubs have something in common with Obama's roasting of Trump about his "birtherism" at the 2011 White House Correspondent's Dinner—a public humiliation widely credited as activating Trump's interest in seeking the presidency.[42] In my reading, 2011 had a profound effect on 2016. But as we can see in these 2008 lines, the writing was already on the wall for Ye.

In any case, Kanye's prophetic posture and increased noncompliance with the racial orthodoxies of US party politics in particular does seem to augur what I'm suggesting here—that we are in a time of great social upheaval and political realignment and do not know how this fast-changing world will turn out. Whether ultimately for good or ill, I won't pretend to know. We got some preliminary answers in the 2018 midterms when (nondisenfranchised) Americans went to the polls, but in the wake of the Mueller Report and dismantling of the Department of Justice, we have learned that our "nation of laws" is, instead, remarkably overreliant on "political norms" and "legal memos." As such, the US seems to be sliding into a fascist dystopia. But as a respected colleague of mine recently suggested, because of this global upheaval, socialism is back on the table. Indeed, it is. Again, I won't pretend to know how to read the tea leaves—I am not, myself, a prophet.

One widely read take may provide some answers (and a modicum of hope) in this regard. In her article for *the Nation*, "Time's Up for Capitalism. But What Comes Next?," Astra Taylor writes: "The resurgence of interest in traditional left-wing politics is a sign that times have changed. . . . In a remarkable reversal for citizens of the country that brought the world Coca-Cola, Ford, and Amazon, more American millennials now say they would prefer to live in a socialist society than a capitalist one, and this preference has helped send a new generation of self-described democratic socialists to office at the local and state levels."[43] Perhaps my colleague was right—if this global realignment means that even the "s-word" is becoming less taboo in American politics, anything is possible.

So how do you solve a problem like Kanye?[44] You don't. You just listen. I'm not terribly interested in Kanye's personal reality-TV reality—and this book will stay as far away as practicably possible from personal hijinks, social media buzz, and influencer culture.[45] But suffice it to say that the evidence of this once-unimaginable turn of events is scattered throughout the 2011 album. For instance, on track 6, "New Day," Ye raps about his son: "I mean, I might even make him be Republican / So everybody know he love white people." And, as we'll see, those couplets about transgressing US racial-political orthodoxies are delivered over a Nina Simone sample—lines from her signature track, "Feeling Good," in which Nina sounds *hell-bent on revenge* rather than simply "good."

Of course, Nina is one of countless African American women and men who have struggled with mental health—what Frantz Fanon would call a healthy response to a racially sick society.[46] Indeed, the subject of trauma and Black "madness" as trope, strategy, and social construction will be an important point of reference for us to consider as we look into Black celebrities and Black capitalism.[47] I'll save that consideration—of Nina, of Kanye, of Audre, of Lauryn—for later.[48]

Enough Prognostication. Now, let us turn to the past.

## WHITENESS AND/AS POWER

"It's the economy, stupid!" So goes the conventional wisdom that has ruled ever since James Carville made it a mantra for Arkansas governor Bill Clinton's 1992 presidential campaign. It was, of course, Thatcher and Reagan who first began to implement Milton Friedman's deregulating and privatizing economic theories. But it was Clinton's tacit acceptance of this worldview—and his own reduction of politics to economics and continuing liquidation of state assets—that consolidated the power of this ideology, known as "neoliberalism," and established it as the new common sense on both sides of the American political duopoly. Since the early '90s, neoliberalism has thus taken the day. As Clinton himself put it in 1996, "the era of big government is over."

I remember, firsthand, the utter befuddlement of liberal common sense in the 1990s, the apoplectic reaction to working-class whites "voting against their interests." "Can't they see," went the refrain, "that by voting for anti-welfare, anti-Medicare, anti–Social Security Republican candidates, poor whites are just shooting themselves in the foot!" But as Attali himself writes, "Music, as a mirror of society, calls this truism to our attention: society is much more than economistic categories, Marxist or otherwise, would have us believe."[49]

What was missing was the language—and thus the understanding—now widespread, of how white privilege works. Of course, some people had an understanding. Republicans had gained a very strong understanding of the politics of white privilege and white supremacy after the success of Nixon's Southern Strategy and had learned to hone a dog-whistle politics centered on fear of Black advancement and racial resentment.[50]

Clinton's win seemed to prove neoliberalism right—if only temporarily. Economics seemed to predict politics. No more.[51] Today, culture rules. And as this book will argue, music *predicts*.

When Jay-Z and Kanye West released their "luxury rap" album in 2011 in the depths of the Great Recession, commentators agreed that it was a bad look.[52] We didn't need millionaires boasting about their Rollies and "other, other Benzes" while the nation—and the globe—suffered the worst economic downturn since the Great Depression. As we will see, the album was indeed widely resented. But it was also the biggest album of 2011, ultimately selling over two million copies in the US alone.

This book tracks this paradoxical story of the widely successful musical artifact that also epitomized a favorite target of white resentment: the entertainment industry and its rich African Americans. Indeed, this book will center on this African American cultural artifact from the music industry, but in the process of reading this album we will also come across other Black artists, entertainers, athletes, and media moguls—figures who are now, in the age of Trump and Brexit, favorite targets of conservative think tanks, alt-right media, their emboldened talking heads, and their Proud Boys and Coulter Girls.

Jay-Z and Kanye West's 2011 chart topper, *Watch the Throne*, not only epitomized how Black people had won the famed culture wars of the 1990s, it was proof positive for millions of Americans that this victory augured the end of decent, hard-working, middle-American values—from Nixon's silent (white) majority to Newt Gingrich's (white) nuclear family and its way of life.[53] The rise and ultimate victory of the Tea Party was dedicated to "taking back our country" and "not being replaced"; the ultimate aim to "Make America (~~White~~) Great Again."

Community organizers, white liberals, Blacks, Jews, Muslims, and immigrants, along with their funders such as George Soros and their "antifamily" projects such as Planned Parenthood and Acorn were eroding the USA and its God-given freedoms. Was anybody going to protect the American way of life? And more to the point, was anybody going to protect the white womanhood at the center of those morally upright Christian values that made America great?[54]

Of course, recent activism, journalism, and scholarship have claimed with increasing vigor that it was slave capitalism and immigrant labor that made America great (for some), not the boot-strap ingenuity that is central to the story that Americans (mostly white) like to tell about themselves.[55] Not surprisingly, however, these "revisionist" arguments have essentially been nonstarters for generations of white Americans deeply invested in the American Dream and its myth of meritocracy.

In 2015, Ta-Nehisi Coates put it thus: "the Dream rests on our backs, the bedding made from our bodies."[56] But Martin Luther King had already eloquently detailed the unfulfilled promise of this dream back in 1967, almost fifty years earlier.

> America freed the slaves in 1863 through the Emancipation Proclamation of Abraham Lincoln, but gave the slaves no land or nothing in reality, as a matter of fact, to get started on. At the same time, America was giving away millions of acres of land in the West and the Midwest, which meant there was a willingness to give the white peasants from Europe an economic base. And yet it refused to give its black peasants from Africa—who came here involuntarily, in chains, and had worked free for 244 years—any kind of economic base. And so emancipation for the negro was really freedom to hunger. It was freedom to the winds and rains of heaven. It was freedom without food to eat or land to cultivate and therefore it was freedom and famine at the same time. And when white Americans tell the negro to lift himself by his own bootstraps, they don't look over the legacy of slavery and segregation.
>
> Now, I believe we ought to do all we can and seek to lift ourselves by our own bootstraps, but it's a cruel jest to say to a bootless man that he ought to lift himself by his own bootstraps.[57]

Surely, King's economic argument would have gained traction some fifty years on? Surely this well-documented story describing the wholly discrepant experiences between "white peasants from Europe" and "black peasants from Africa" would find some purchase, allow us to recover some historical memory, and do something to undermine the exceptionalist myth of American equality?

But surely too, would this "revisionist history" threaten to expose the privileges many held dear. Even if it meant "voting against their economic interests," lifting the veil from this history would threaten something many held much more dear, something intimately related to but even more valuable than *economic* privilege. As it turns out, those voters knew *exactly* what was at stake. Increasingly, with the rise of the Tea Party movement, they took the long view and voted against the immediate economic gains—of a welfare state, of access to low-cost health care, of a solvent Social Security system—to maintain the much more valuable (in the long run) sociocultural edifice of white privilege, of white *power.*

In her 2015 book, *Strangers in Their Own Land: Anger and Mourning on the American Right,* Arlie Russell Hochschild offers a piercing insight into this mindset. Based on long-term ethnographic research with right-wing communities in Louisiana, she found that every nonwhite success is viewed as "cutting in line."[58] And far from denying the *longue durée* of American history, she found that these white Americans conceived of their place at the front of the line—their entitlement—on the basis that their forbears, Dr. King's "European peasants," *were here first* (and forgetting, for instance, that the first Africans had been brought to Virginia Colony over a decade before the chaste and freedom-loving Mayflower "Pilgrims" at the heart of the American myth).

While we might disagree with the logic of entitlement at play here, it is hardly irrational. It is rooted in 400 years of history, 400 years of structural racism. It is, to use a now-familiar term, quite "transactional." This is how we've gotten to Trump. If it ain't broke don't fix it.

In this book, I argue that a close look at the creative work of these Black millionaires on *Watch the Throne* confirms Hochschild's thesis—that Black and Latino success is hateful to conservative whites and will have repercussions. And while Obama's rise to power surely played a politically pivotal role here, I want to look at the cultural firmament that would enable such a fervent backlash against a moderate president who focused, unlike any before him, on reconciliation and rapprochement. "There are no blue states and red states" indeed.

Of course, this politics of white resentment may have been perfected in the crucible of American racial ideology, but it is proving quite transferrable and localizable in European contexts (indeed, around the world). Recalling my befuddlement with "voting against your interests" in the US context, Nigel Farage famously bet that white Brits would also vote against their economic interests—as long as they did it on their own terms. Again, of course, that's the point: they're not wrong. They are voting in their interest—the interest of whiteness, of white privilege, of white power.

Indeed, Du Bois wrote with just this insight as early as 1935—fifteen years after his analysis of "The Souls of White Folk." As the specter of a reinvigorated white power grew out of the ashes of Germany's post–Great War economic disaster, Du Bois wrote presciently of his own national context, post–Civil War, in *Black Reconstruction in America*,

> It must be remembered that the white group of laborers, while they received a low wage, were compensated in part by a sort of public and psychological wage. They were given public deference and titles of courtesy because they were white. They were admitted freely with all classes of white people to public functions, public parks, and the best schools. The police were drawn from their ranks, and the courts, dependent on their votes, treated them with such leniency as to encourage lawlessness.[59]

As Du Bois rightly suggests, this "psychological wage" of "public deference" and "courtesy"—of humanity—was worth far more than a few more cents for an hour's work. And, sadly, Du Bois's structural critique of racialized policing and white impunity sounds all too familiar in twenty-first century America.

In this book, I thus argue that on *Watch the Throne*, Jay and Ye devalued this supplemental wage of whiteness and purposefully stoked white resentment—a resentment that would ultimately spill over into public life, make audible right-wing dog whistling, and embolden white supremacists to come out from under their rocks. It is this well of resentment, of course, that led to the unlikely election of Donald J. Trump as the forty-fifth president of the United States.[60] While I will not claim that the election of an inarticulate, narcissistic, and openly racist oligarch is in any way a positive development, I will argue that this unthinkable development has shown the United States of America who it really is.[61]

In this book, I argue that *Watch the Throne*, as a high-profile and deliberate provocation, was pivotal in this development. Through the strategy that I dub "critical excess" on the album, Jay and Ye have drawn the worst elements of American society—those most entrenched realities of American history—out into the light of day. And while I don't mean to suggest that their prophesy is of the literal Nostradamus variety, I do suggest that, recalling Attali, this "dangerous, disturbing, and subversive" album "makes audible the new world that will gradually become visible, that will impose itself and regulate the order of things." From the mainstream outing of "white privilege" to the reassessment of neoliberalism and resurgence of socialism, the new order of things is now becoming visible.

In the chapters that follow, I track how *Watch the Throne* heralds the future; how it prophesies nothing less than the end of capitalism; how it is capitalism's death dance.

## "CAN'T NOBODY TELL ME NUTHIN'"

In the spring of 2019, me, my university students from Ireland, the UK, the wider EU, the US, and listeners around the world reveled in the absurd brilliance of (and rubberneck-inducing discourse around) Lil Nas X's "Old Town Road." The story of the track is a rather too spot-on case study in white privilege, racial resentment, and the "you will not replace us" meme of the (global) Right. What's more it offers a chance to substantiate how structures of white privilege connect the cultural superstructure to the economic base.

The track itself was a short country-and-western track, inflected with hip hop imagery and swagger (notably, a song, not a rap), that might have been dismissed as pure camp were it not so über-catchy. In March 2019, the banjo-suffused track by the Atlanta hip hop artist Lil Nas X went viral and debuted on the *Billboard* Hot Country Songs chart.[62] When country tastemakers and the Billboard charts realized that it was by a hip hop artist, they manufactured a case against its inclusion on the country charts and "*Billboard* quietly removed 'Old Town Road' from Hot Country Songs," lest it overshadow more purely country acts.[63]

For our purposes here, the lesson is: hip hop artists could easily *replace* country artists at the top of their own charts if not for the gatekeepers and structures that keep country, country (i.e., white).[64] Indeed, while white country artists regularly fiddle with hip hop sounds, the interpenetration of trap beats and country twang in the music of a Black artist here seemed to foster resentment and betray an underlying fear of sonic miscegenation in this episode of industry-policed resegregation.[65] While there's more to the story (much more . . . the father of the industry-sanctioned Black appropriator, Miley Cyrus, ultimately recorded a country-approved "remix" of the track), this basic outline should suffice for reference.

If this all weren't enough, it's also worth noting that the hook for "Old Town Road" is, itself, a microcosm of the ensuing scandal. After describing the accoutrements of his hip hop–inflected country style on the track's verse (horse tack, boots, and of course, the brilliantly country bling of "Cowboy hat from Gucci / Wrangler on my Booty"), Lil Nas X sings "I been in the valley / You ain't been up off that porch." Given the *Billboard* removal scandal—and our continuing discussion of white privilege—these lyrics now read as though Lil Nas X has worked for his place ("in the valley") while the country artist he presumes *to replace* has no real claim on the charts. He's been on his grind while the white artist has been sleeping ("ain't been up off that porch"). What's more, these (and other) lines invert the age-old stereotypes about "lazy blacks" and turn the American myth of meritocracy back against its would-be (white) beneficiaries.

The hook underscores the rapper's claim "can't nobody tell me nothing"—a swaggering line that echoes countless hip hop lines, from Melle Mel's signature message, "Don't push me, 'cause I'm close to the edge" (1982), to *Menace II Society*'s "America's nightmare: young, black, and didn't give a fuck" (1993), to Jay's "Nigga you broke, what the fuck you gon' tell me?" (1996), to Kanye's almost literal antecedent—the title lines to "Can't Tell Me Nothing" (2007). The common message: "we've paid our dues. Now we're going to take what's ours"—lines that simultaneously master the neoliberal order, undermine the myth of meritocracy, and threaten white supremacy. Indeed, on track 9 of *Watch the Throne*, Jay and Ye offer a swaggering take together. The track is titled, "Who Gon Stop Me?"

Just as the end of segregation would augur the African American takeover of American professional sports, the "Old Town Road" affair suggests that Black entertainers could easily *replace* white ones on the country charts were it not for the entertainment industry's enduring racialized structures.[66]

## CHAPTER OVERVIEW: *SUBHUMAN, HUMAN, SUPERHUMAN*

This book is organized around the unfolding narrative and conceptual terrain of the album itself. Indeed, *Watch the Throne* is a classic concept album, and my interest in it stems from its unified, if complicated and often vexing vision. By focusing on the first four tracks of the album in order, *Critical Excess* maps out this concept album's trajectory on its own terms, tracking performative moves from racial essence to transcendence, from subhuman to superhuman, from jungle to penthouse. The focus on the album's opening tracks also allows for the necessary depth of close reading while affording the possibility to examine how the rhetorical terrain of these hit singles spins out to the concept album as a whole. The book thus centers the opening of *Watch the Throne*, regularly referencing moments from the other seven tracks to highlight the album's conceptual unity and advance a better understanding of its ideas and production values without getting lost in the weeds.

Chapter 1, "'Welcome to the Jungle': Essence and the Western Inheritance" centers on the album's first track, "No Church in the Wild" (feat. Frank Ocean), while taking forays into related tracks such as "Welcome to the Jungle" (track 8). Through close sonic, lyrical, visual, and rhetorical analysis, the chapter establishes the themes of essence and transcendence that are central to both the album's radical constructivist critique of our house-of-cards political economy ("what's a god to a nonbeliever?") and to my larger argument about the bourgeois category of "the human." By unpacking Jay and Ye's litany of references to icons of Western civilization on this track, I ask us to confront Frantz Fanon's landmark study, *Black Skin, White Masks* (1967), wherein the psychoanalyst and decolonial activist remarks pointedly, "The Negro is in every sense of the word a victim of white civilization."[67] Here, I also perform a close reading of the album art, which ranges from Givenchy gilded flowers to Jay and Ye depicted as catlike beasts—images that underscore the category of the "subhuman" that undergirds bourgeois ideology and the capitalist logics that rationalize exploitations of labor.

The second chapter, "'Lift Off' to Sunday Service: Transcendence, Black Capitalism, Black Rapture," develops the argument with a focus on track 2, "Lift Off" (feat. Beyoncé). This analysis continues to engage close reading methodologies, examining, for example, the Afrofuturist discourses engaged on the space-travelling track that overcomes "scars" and takes it to the "stars." The chapter, however, augments these approaches with more historical and political analyses of the fraught place of capitalism and entrepreneurship in the African American community. In particular, the chapter pivots on "Lift Off" to launch into the terrain of Kanye's more recent Sunday Service—a series of outdoor Christian worship services that use the stylings of the Black church to reframe Kanye hits and otherwise offer a creative outlet for the newly right-leaning, Trump-loving West. Indeed, "Lift Off" was one of the first original tracks to be rearranged for use in the Sunday Services—a continuity that demands an analysis of Black transcendence from the Black gospel tradition of the Selah Singer's "I'll Fly Away" to the white "prosperity gospel" of Joel Osteen. In the chapter, I put these developments in dialogue with the end-times "rapture" theology of white evangelical Christianity legible on the "Not of this World" bumper stickers ubiquitous in Ye and Kim Kardashian's Southern California. The chapter thus further examines the idea of racial essence and the possibility of overcoming and transcending racial oppression via financial or spiritual means—or, as in this case, both. As Beyoncé puts it, "So many scars / 'Bout to take this whole thing to Mars."

The third and fourth chapters center the album's most controversial single—cut number 3, "Niggas in Paris"—moving from a textual analysis to a contextual one. Chapter 3 is titled "'After They've Seen Paree': The Mastery of Form" and examines the original luxury rap track itself—a posttranscendent escape scene featuring the two Black millionaires gallivanting around the city of light. Indeed, the Grammy-winning single that name-drops artifacts of European *haute couture* like they were "going on sale," is at the heart of the album and its strategy of critical excess. The chapter thus spends time digging into the racially fraught references and performed paradoxes linking, for instance, the luxury fashion house Maison Margiela to the 1960s-era Hanna Barbera cartoon, Magilla Gorilla. As one commentator put it in a piece for *Slate*, "'Niggas in Paris' is the most popular piece of Western culture to ever feature the word *nigga* so prominently" and "is so pungently evocative because with it, Jay and Kanye proudly place the barbarians ('niggas') not merely within the palace gates ('Paris'), but high up on the social ladder."[68]

Chapter 4, "'Niggas in Poorest' to 'That Shit Creil': NIP's Realpolitik in the US and France," puts this high-profile cultural text in its Black Atlantic contexts examining Yasiin Bey's (aka Mos Def) parody of the luxury rap track, fittingly titled "Niggas in Poorest," and then turns to Paris itself. Here, I examine the track in relation to my work with Parisian hip hop communities over the past decades with particular focus on the reception of François Hollande's use of the hit track as part of his (not unproblematic) minority outreach strategy in the Parisian *banlieues* during his 2012 campaign for French president—a campaign that proved successful. Through an analysis of an extended interview that I conducted with the video's producer, the French radio executive and hip hop activist, Bruno Laforestrie, I unearth some of the logics behind the video and its meanings in the majority nonwhite French *banlieues*. Together, the chapter thus situates the track in a history of Black American expat artists, develops the book's theory of "critical excess," and substantiates claims about hip hop's postcolonial politics with an analysis of its on-the-ground impact. The chapters thus examine the category of the human and move to the conceptual ground of anti-essentialism, examining Obama-era fantasies of a postracial society. As Jay puts it, "If you escaped what I escaped / You'd be in Paris gettin' fucked up too."

In chapter 5, "'Sophisticated Ignorance': The Deformation of Mastery" I argue that Jay and Ye's resignification of Otis Redding's "Try a Little Tenderness" on track 4, "Otis," is a form of sonic and social subversion that Houston Baker terms "the deformation of mastery"—a mastery so complete and aggressively forthright that it undermines, *exceeds,* and *redefines* the category of mastery.[69] In this analysis, I track the history of "Try a Little Tenderness" back to the original Great Depression–era versions by Bing Crosby and James Reese Europe, suggesting that Ye's resignification of the Redding version during the depths of the post-2008 Great Recession expertly indexed how much had changed—and how much hadn't. With this background, I suggest that this performed attitude of deformation exemplifies my theory of critical excess and move toward my final argument, that in exceeding conspicuous consumption, the album exceeds Europe and heralds the end of capitalism. In other words, that by mastering capitalism in the context of the (then) worst financial downturn since the Great Depression, Jay and Ye pour salt in the wound of a severely compromised white supremacy and primed the pump for Donald Trump (and condescending "Bernie Bros," it should be noted). The chapter is thus a case study in Baker's theory of the deformation of mastery, examining the übermaster category of superhuman and centering the concept of anti-anti-essence—a critique of postracial (white) fantasies. Indeed, Kanye's line, "I adopted these niggas / Phillip Drummoned 'em,"—a metaphor on "Otis" in which Ye takes on the role of a white millionaire adopting Black kids—functions as a perfect encapsulation of the double move of anti-anti-essentialism. Indeed, the line weaponizes anti-anti-essentialism through the lyrical image of a Black man playing a white man playing father figure to Black boys.

In the conclusion, "*Black Noise:* Re-composition in the Last Gilded Age," I reflect on the years since *Watch the Throne's* release in 2011, considering what has come to pass culturally, economically, and politically. Examining the deep ambivalences of our historical moment through the lenses of Black Lives Matter, Occupy, Me Too, Trumpism, and the politics of white resentment, I show how the album proved prescient; that long-promised freedoms for some—including the "human right to swagger"—have indeed been perceived as existential threats for others. To these telling developments, I relate Achille Mbembe's work on the long legacy of Afrodiasporic "repertoires of practices of survival" and the more recent "blueprint for social resistance and affirmation" that Tricia Rose finds in hip hop's *Black* noise. I project the luxury rap album's claims to the future against the deeply troubling present state of geopolitics to conclude that our racial capitalist patriarchy—and the current global alignment, writ large—is in its last throes, for better or for worse.

A final note on reading this book. As we get into it I encourage you to grab your copy of the album or launch Tidal (Jay-Z's very own streaming service)—or whatever streaming service is at hand—so that we can ride the coming wave of ideas with the sounds that perform them in our ears. For in hip hop ideas are not only textual, but performative; the rhetorics not only logical, but emotive. To best understand the performed ideas on *Watch the Throne* we need to hear the stories through the voices that deliver them—in all their sonic human swagger. As with most hip hop albums, it is the stories they tell that draw us in. Apropos of this point, I've gathered relevant sonic, video, and image links and compiled further resources at this book's companion website, www.criticalexcess.org.

As the *Game of Thrones* character Tyrion Lannister put it in his final monologue to this recent blockbuster consideration of human power, greed, and excess—of "thrones": "What unites people? Armies? Gold? Flags? Stories. There's nothing in the world more powerful than a good story. Nothing can stop it. No enemy can defeat it." The story of *Critical Excess*—and of *Watch the Throne*—is, then, a story we must read *and* hear to understand. As they put it on the album's ninth track, nothing beats a good story. "Who Gon Stop Me?"

CHAPTER 1

# "Welcome to the Jungle"

## *Essence and the Western Inheritance*

The idea of white supremacy rests simply on the fact that white men are the creators of civilization.

—JAMES BALDWIN, *NOTES OF A NATIVE SON* (1955)

*Watch the Throne* begins with an incessant four-on-the-floor bass drum and guitar loop. Built on a particularly buoyant Spookytooth drum sample and a spiraling, Escher-esque Phil Manzanera guitar ostinato, Kanye West's stripped-down opening reduces the bouncing drums to a death march and slows down the guitar line to sound a doomed, repetitive monotony.[1] Indeed, the track "No Church in the Wild" (feat. Frank Ocean), is itself something of a conceptual loop, playing in tautological arguments, ethical dilemmas, and narcissistic solipsisms. All the while, inhale and exhale gestures engrain the never-ending drudgery of the sonic loops.

After four repetitions of this musical backdrop, the unaffected voice of Frank Ocean enters with the lines:

Human beings in a mob
What's a mob to a king?
What's a king to a god?
What's a god to a non-believer . . .
Who don't believe in . . .
Anything?

Echoing the rhetorical up-spiraling of the Manzanera guitar loop, the play of hierarchies in this chorus rises level by level only to find itself back at the

Fig. 2. The social contract according to "No Church in the Wild"—"What's a god to a non-believer" schematic rendering of Frank Ocean's sung lyrics (schematic by the author and Alexander Khalil).

level of the individual, the human being, the "non-believer." The hierarchy of our social contract, it seems, is an illusion.

Indeed, the disorienting guitar sample that forms the basis of Ye's beat is cut from Manzanera's track "K-Scope"—a 1970s-era prog-rock tune, itself built from a swirl of *kaleidoscopic* sixteenth notes.[2]

Ex. 1. Sample of up-spiraling, "kaleidoscopic" Phil Manzanera guitar loop on "No Church in the Wild." The third through sixth sixteenth notes of the second half of the bar are an approximation as that section is layered with an overdub (transcription by the author and Mary J. King).

The lines spiral up and down without seeming to have a beginning or end—like the iconic sketches by Dutch graphic artist M. C. Escher.[3]

What's more—and this will be key to our analysis throughout this book—this opening performs in sound and lyric a rhetoric of contingency and constructedness. It offers up a worldview suggesting that we construct our own realities. As the above schematic suggests, the political economy of this power structure is centered on individual buy-in—whether that capitulation is to the inertial force of or in solidarity with "a mob," fealty to the monarchical political authority of "a king," or obedience to the moralizing religious power of "a god." If the individual buy-in fails, the house of cards tumbles.

While there are obvious caveats to this theory of a social contract (which we'll encounter along the way), the track's message is clear.[4] As the title implies, "No Church in the Wild" begins with the destabilization of religious and political authority, with the anarchic suggestion that such civilized structures are in no way natural, and with the repeated mantra that there is no essential truth. Frank Ocean concludes the chorus in the same uncharacteristically matter-of-fact deadpan:

> Will he make it out alive?
> Alright, alright . . .
> No church in the wild.

In a word, "No Church in the Wild" opens out onto a discourse of *nihilism.*

## THE WILD WILD WEST

Jay-Z's voice enters this musical texture and discursive space with an opening salvo steeped in Eurocentric imagery—ranging from the Colosseum to the Rolls Royce; from Socrates, to Jesus, to Roman Catholic priests. Yet by the end of just the second couplet, Jay has laid the groundwork for an iconoclastic takedown of the Western order via a brief, but cutting, catalog of typically Western hypocrisies.

> Tears on the mausoleum floor
> Blood stains the Colosseum doors
> Lies on the lips of a priest
> Thanksgiving disguised as a feast

The opening is a thumbnail sketch of Western civilization that simultaneously holds up the European inheritance and highlights its deep and enduring contradictions.

In the first couplet, Jay counterposes a sacred space for mourning death against an entertaining space for celebrating the vigor of life. In the context of a discourse on Western civilization and its discontents, the Roman mausoleum/colosseum juxtaposition reminds us that these monuments to death and life are united in human suffering—in "tears" and "blood." Indeed, the couplet gets to one of the album's first contradictions: its indictment of a society that claims to value human life, but finds utmost pleasure and entertainment value in suffering. While centered on 2000-year-old subjects, the critique rings true for a culture industry that commodifies violence and fetishizes human suffering more than ever.

The second couplet further elaborates these historical continuities, critiquing the Christian inheritance—from today's sexual abuse scandals in the Roman Catholic church back to the Protestant dawn of a centuries-long genocidal campaign against the "New World's" indigenous people. The active cover-up of this (unfinished) history in the United States, by way of a national mythology around "Pilgrims and Indians" sharing in God's bounty on that first Thanksgiving, seems, for Jay, a perfect encapsulation of our continued buy-in to lies about our histories, lies about ourselves and our common humanity.[5] As Aimé Césaire put it in his 1950 *Discours sur le colonialisme* (Discourse on Colonialism), "at the very time when it most often mouths the word, the West has never been further from being able to live a true humanism—a humanism made to the measure of the world." Thus begins *Watch the Throne*'s indictment of the West.

In the next lines, Jay rehearses his personal mythology as a local pusher turned global entertainment mogul while Ye builds tension with stuttering synth stab lines. It is here while "Rolling in a Rolls Royce Corniche" that Jay first gestures to whiteness. Fittingly, however, this whiteness flips the script on the "fair" purity of inherited Western codes. This is the whiteness of "Drug dealer chic"; of "Cocaine Seats / All white like I got the whole thing bleached"; the whiteness of coverups; of whitewashing. Indeed, with the lines "I'm hiding from police" and "I'm wondering if a thug's prayers reach," he connects his story and his politics not to the West's racial whiteness, but to its salient others: those classes throughout history that have been surveilled, contained, and punished—the mass underclasses and "mobs" from the Roman Empire's ethnically diverse slave classes, to the Victorian era's unwashed masses, to the Native American tribes that complicated America's "manifest destiny."[6]

As Ye adds another layer to the texture, and rising synth sustains begin to oversaturate the musical texture, Jay goes right to the (perceived) source, extending his discourse on the European inheritance.[7] Echoing Frank Ocean's nihilistic opening hook in his next line—"Is Pius pious 'cause God loves pious?"—Jay paraphrases a Socratic question from Plato's dialogues: "The point which I should first wish to understand is whether the pious or holy is beloved by the gods because it is holy, or holy because it is beloved of the gods."[8] The Socratic allusion thus stretches his European political history from the seventeenth-century Hobbesian social-contract language of Frank Ocean's "non-believer" chorus back to the Socratic method of Ancient Greece. Indeed, here, Jay's line refigures the "Euthyphro dilemma," which, like the chain of allegiance disrupted by Ocean's "non-believer," throws cold water on the otherwise elegant tautology—"That which is loved by God is pious and God loves that which is pious"—while simultaneously implicating the Catholic Church's Pope Pius (pick one: I–XII).

In short, by sampling Socrates's famous quip, Jay seeks nothing less than to disrupt and undermine the "naturalized" rational logic of the European intellectual tradition—the Western logos—with a bit of contrarian knowledge sampled from its own cultural DNA. Indeed, while Kanye disrupts Attali's code of repetition, by not engraining but *refiguring* the buoyant and fun drum and guitar samples with no small amount of gloom and doom, Jay-Z holds up the laudable icons of and monuments to The West, only to expose them as the products of centuries of unforgivable hypocrisy and injustice.

Like the track's chorus, Jay's nod to the Euthyphro dilemma disrupts the easy coexistence of democratic (mob) politics and Christian religion in Western civilization through a subversively nihilistic critique of hegemonic power. Indeed, Jay's interest in Socrates appears to go back at least to the MC's 2009 visit to one of Cornel West's university seminars on the European intellectual tradition. In an interview for *The Root* with Dayo Olopade, Professor West recounts the visit thus:

> [I]t was a brand new experience for him and he enjoyed it; he loved the dialogue. I had been talking about Plato and Socrates and how he said I am going to preserve the memory of my teacher for as long as I live, and I am in deep mourning for Socrates who died unfairly, and I will make sure that the world never forgets that there was once a man named Socrates. And that's when Jay-Z said: "I am Plato to Biggie's Socrates." Isn't that a beautiful thing?[9]

The anecdote clearly references the fall of—and order of succession from—hip hop's previous "King of New York," Biggie Smalls. It also makes it clear that this isn't the only comparison that Jay got out of Brother West's lecture.

Jay concludes his Platonic discourse on the track with the lines "Socrates asked: 'Whose bias do y'all seek?' / All for Plato, screech / I'm out here balling, I know y'all hear my sneaks." Drawing another internal continuity from the Roman Colosseum of the opening couplet to the "bias" of basketball fandom, Jay playfully declares himself "All for (Team) Plato." In short, this verse and the opening hook that precedes it perform for us the idea that despite all the European tradition's universalist scholarly posturing and ethical edifices, there is no objective truth. Every knowledge is positioned knowledge and all knowledge is a function of power. The West, it seems, is all about self-interest. Civilization is a ruse. Religion is a hustle. The social contract is simple mob rule. Welcome to the "Wild Wild West."[10]

## HIP HOP'S REFIGURATION OF EUROCENTRISM

In his "From Damocles to Socrates: The Classics in/of Hip Hop," the Princeton classicist Dan-El Padilla Peralta recalls his initiation into hip hop consciousness.[11] Hearing the powerful beats, seductive grooves, and gems of hip hop wisdom suffuse the streets of Harlem as a young man, he was hooked. In particular, hearing lines such as Wyclef Jean's "I haunt MCs like Mephistopheles, bringing swords of Damocles," on the Fugees's 1996 album, *The Score,* he was inspired to learn more. Indeed, Lauryn Hill's line "And even after all my logic and my theory / I add a 'Motherfucker' so you ignant niggas hear me," would become, for him, "an unofficial life motto" as a scholar.[12] As Padilla Peralta goes on to explain, "The Fugees were brainy, well read, sophisticated—exactly what the popular discourse of hip-hop as vulgar and disreputable, gaining in traction and vehemence throughout my teenage years, claimed rappers could *not* be."

In short, Padilla Peralta's recollections are revealing not just for how hip hop introduced the budding philosopher to the Western *classics* of the Greco-Roman inheritance, but for how Black and Brown Americans were self-consciously positioning themselves in relation to this esteemed—and *purportedly unique*—Western tradition of intellectual investigation. As Ms. Hill forcefully reminds us, hip hop *can* be—and usually *is*—rife with "logic and theory" but is most often casually dismissed, or worse, rendered invisible by America's age-old investments in white privilege and continuing commitments to structural racism.

In his 2010 annotated memoir, *Decoded*, Jay recalls debates about the pitfalls and promise of Barack Obama's candidacy in similar terms:

> And he was black. This was big. This was a chance to go from centuries of invisibility to the most visible position in the entire world. He could, through sheer symbolism, regardless of any of his actual policies, change the lives of millions of black kids who now saw something different to aspire to. That would happen on the day he was elected, regardless of anything else that happened in his term. No other candidate could promise so much.[13]

Of course, we now know that the promise of a Black president would, once realized, prove so repellent to a significant swath of white Americans (a "mob" would not be too strong a term) that the nation would elect a wholly unqualified, openly racist, and misogynistic bully whose platform was premised, first and foremost, on overturning Obama's legacy. Trump was gunning for Obama's throne (still is).

As Padilla Peralta stresses, the sword of Damocles—the threat of usurpers—emerged as a key theme in Kanye West's work during the Obama years, for instance on the track "Power" (released, like *Decoded*, in 2010). To be sure, Jay and Ye knew the stakes of Black power in America. Indeed, on track 10, "Murder to Excellence," Ye puts it thus: "It's time for us to stop and redefine black power." Knowing the heights of economic and artistic power—and the tightrope of Black excellence—Ye is searching for a new way.[14]

Just as *Watch the Throne* begins with a meditation on power structures, so too does it end with a meditation on the danger that comes with power. Indeed, we might think of this *threat to power* as the overarching theme of the album. On the last verse of the 2011 album from track 12, "Why I Love You"—Ye reveals the title line couched in the Damoclean imagery, political violence, and paranoia that give the powerful pause to "watch the throne." Jay begins: "Bussin' [shooting] at me, bub-buh-buh-bussin' at me / But I'm bulletproof, bitch you can't get nothin' past me." Jay continues: "Got body armor," to which Ye responds: "A nigga gotta watch the throne." Jay concludes: "And I'm bussin' back / So niggas in a glass house should not throw stones."

While the album title, *Watch the Throne*, ostensibly gestures to the album's gilded artwork and a society in thrall to wealth and power, here the two frame a more urgent meaning: those in power must fight to retain that power—even against those who were once friends. And, fittingly, the next lines include a warning that references perhaps the most iconic of all political violence in Western civilization: "Caesar didn't see it so he ceased to exist"—a succinct summary of the verse, and a nice bit of assonant wordplay that flips the script on the *ae* in the title "Caesar." If you don't "see it" you will be a deceased Caesar. You will be de-throned.

As Padilla Peralta explains, hip hop artists have thus carved out a space for enunciative critique on the back of the Western inheritance and its "classics"—a subject of inquiry "long constructed and promulgated as Eurocentric in focus and content." He shows how artists have alternately sampled and subverted the tropes of "escargot" (Biggie), "Shakespeare" (P. Diddy), "Faust" and "Damocles" (Wyclef), "Icarus" (Jay-Z), and the Egyptian "Horus" (Kanye), thus extending the Western tradition back to its own (carefully obscured) African inheritance, demonstrating their own cultural capital, and demanding their due.[15]

Indeed, this book picks up where Padilla Peralta leaves off. Before recounting the Cornel West story—and linking it to his analysis of the Euthyphro dilemma—the classicist summarizes Jay and Ye's project on *Watch the Throne* thus:

> First in [Kanye West's] "Power" and then in *WT*, classical allusion sweeps beyond the practice of naming to encompass a whole host of secondary claims about the rapper as kingly in his consumption of iconic symbols of white cultural power: not just the hard capital of flashy things but the soft capital of the classical past. Already with the Fugees but even more dramatically with Kanye and Jay-Z, Greco-Roman antiquity is integrated into a program of acquisition and (apotropaic) display—which program then becomes a subject for the rappers' own philosophizing.[16]

Having thrown down the gauntlet with these connections between "hard" economic and "soft" cultural power, I aim in this chapter not only to extend and elaborate Padilla Peralta's masterful reading of hip hop's entanglements and critical engagements with *the West*, but to theorize how *Watch the Throne* articulates the master trope of Western civilization—whiteness—to its uncivilized *other*—and, most specifically, to Blackness. Indeed, Padilla Peralta's gesture to Kanye's 2010 "Power" is also a gesture to that track's Nietzschean posture—that God is dead; that Rome must burn; that the West must fall. That track's hook begins, "No one man should have that much power / The clock's ticking, I just count the hours."[17]

In Padilla Peralta's conclusion, the scholar writes evocatively of how "For a dark-skinned child of the Dominican Diaspora who spent his formative years in Harlem, it was both captivating and empowering to detect the pulse of Greco-Roman antiquity in hip-hop. In the heat of that collision new worlds were born." In this chapter, I suggest that new worlds were indeed born in this collision; that, confronted with a history and a present reality that denied Afrodiasporic participation in these universalized tropes ("birtherism" comes to mind) via the denial of the humanity that provided their logic, the Black and Brown hip hop artists who Padilla Peralta heard on the streets of New York City had themselves seized an opportunity to refigure the West. In the space between *de jure* performances of Western humanism and *de facto* realities of nonwhite dehumanization, these hip hop artists saw a space for enunciative critique. This is the "collision" that Padilla Peralta describes—not a chance conflagration, but an opportunity seized on to "heat up the observational space," as Houston Baker would have it, that he and countless others recognized and took up for themselves.[18]

Indeed, Baker's entreaty for us to heat up the observational space is central to my aims and methods in the present volume. In working on this close reading I've come to think of my work as engaging in a sort of "speculative friction." That is, in my close reading practice I look to inform my understanding via historical, ethnographic, and other methodological approaches, not in the hope of getting at the essence of a cultural artifact—or the artist's "intention"—but to get as full a picture as possible of the impact it has had and continues to have in the world. I aim to do this by posing as many questions as possible, engaging cognitive dissonances that might "rub" the wrong way, and thus heating up the observational space. As Baker explains by analogy with the Heisenberg uncertainty principle, when we observe a cultural artifact, *we change it*. The more angles of observation we engage, the hotter the space becomes. And the more we change it, the more we escape the simplistic and depthless meanings that we've inherited or been encouraged to jump toward.[19]

Apropos of the West's dehumanizations and denials, in his foundational postcolonial critique, *The Location of Culture*, Homi Bhabha describes the "new worlds" born of this (transformative) combustive reaction. Citing Meiling Jin's "secret art of Invisible-Ness" and echoing Ralph Ellison's earlier descriptions of invisibility, Bhabha writes:

> The evil eye (the missing *person*), which seeks to outstare linear, continuist history and turn its progressive dream into nightmarish chaos, is exemplary once more. What Meiling Jin calls the "the secret art of Invisible-Ness" creates a crisis in the representation of personhood and, at the critical moment, initiates the possibility of political subversion.[20]

Bhabha's "evil eye/I" figure is foundational for our understanding of hip hop's asymmetric recognitions not only for its recognition that the ("evil," other) inhuman can *see* the ("good," white, Western) human subject (the "I"), but because the "evil eye/I" refigures Western subjectivities and provides a new template for a humanity. What "takes (the) place" is a new subjectivity.[21] It is a creation of "new worlds," of new codes. It is a replacement of the West.

## OF BEASTS AND KINGS

While I have endeavored to provide a sonic and lyrical snapshot of the opening to *Watch the Throne* above to establish some of the themes and rhetorics to come (we'll get back to it soon enough), it is worth taking a moment here to provide some visual context to the "luxury rap" album via an examination of the "ambiguous" "double game" of the album's cover art.

While the packaging has garnered much attention due to the luxurious Givenchy-branded "bling" of the gilded front cover (see fig. 1), considered as a whole, the full album insert accords remarkably well with Attali's "dangerous" duplicity, "simultaneously *excluded* (relegated to a place near the bottom of the social hierarchy) and *superhuman* (the genius, the adored and deified star)," "one of the first catalyzers of violence and myth."[22] In short, the album art pushes the poles of superhuman and subhuman into the realms of kings and beasts.

On opening the booklet, the first two inner folios tell a different story than the bright, gilded cover art; the expertly detailed gold leaf on the kingly throne.[23] At left, on the reverse of the cover, we see a full-page image of a detuned and fuzzy American flag—the stars and stripes dark and vaguely misaligned, like a bad print job from the textile factory.[24] At right, on the recto side of the first folio, we see the product of that vaguely misanthropic America: Jay-Z depicted as a catlike beast. Indeed, the image conjures up all the ugly, dehumanizing, threatening, and essentializing tropes of America's racializing history.

Turn the next page and, at left, we're presented with a full-page close-up image of the wood grain of dark and lustrous ebony (a texture that also appears on the disc itself). At right, on the recto side of the second folio, we see an even more badly deformed Kanye, also depicted as a beast. But here those deformities also include the compression artifacts of artfully glitched Photoshop work—like a digital mishap from the face-changing, race-changing video for Michael Jackson's "Black or White."[25] The effect is an aesthetically chilling one, moving effectively from the throne to the jungle, be it concrete and/or primeval.

Fittingly, after the track listings and credits pages in Gothic font (or perhaps it's Blackmoor LET), the last folio of the album art features a fractal-like, computer-assisted arrangement of flowers that give the gilded cover art many of its contours—as though it was this image that was dipped in gold leaf for the album's cover. The image reinforces the natural-to-civilized, jungle-to-throne duplicity, and, more, reinforces the glitched, pay-no-attention-to-the-man-behind-the-curtain constructedness of the artwork, both visually and—let's remember—musically. At bottom, the fractal-flower image bears a Givenchy branding banner: "Creative Direction by Riccardo Tisci. Artwork by courtesy of Givenchy by Riccardo Ticci © Givenchy All Rights Reserved," bordered like the nameplate on a painting hanging in a gallery. The verso side of the last folio features a final Photoshopped image of a translucent white-winged angel with a black star overlaid to obscure the face, and a forest background with smaller, even creepier, black angels.

Indeed, in close consideration of the gilded booklet that contains unbearable secrets and horrifying images, I am reminded of the Balzac quip, "behind every great fortune lies a great crime."[26] In my reading, though, the fortune is not that of Jay and Ye themselves, but of the West; the great crime is not their numerous personal affronts and offenses—legal and illegal—but our present reality of unprecedented inequality and ethnic and religious animus, on the brink of Malthusian crisis and environmental catastrophe. As much as we love hating West, says the album art, we'd do better hating the West.

In all, the album art is thus a fitting visual introduction to all of the overwhelmingly duplicitous simultaneities and wild vacillations between kingly and beastly, civilized and uncivilized, superhuman and subhuman—the *critical excess*—that we hear on the album.

## FROM NIHILISM TO NARCISSISM

Jay's verse on "No Church in the Wild" ends back on the subject of religion, here gesturing to the Christian inheritance and its concept of the Trinity. He concludes:

> Jesus was a carpenter
> Yeezy laid beats
> Hova flow the Holy Ghost
> Get the hell up out your seats
> Preach

On a number of levels, these last lines are a logical endpoint for Jay's conceptually unified and patiently ordered verse. First, they end on a bit of hip hop braggadocio that explicitly marks Ye's artisan mastery of beat joinery and Jay's demonstrated conceptual mastery and heavenly flow. Second, in his demand for his audience to "Get the hell up out your seats," they activate an audience response to his call—or better, inspire *his congregation* with the fiery power of the Holy Ghost. And, like a Pentecostal preacher, they exorcise the demons—that is, they "get the hell up out." Here, Ye's overwhelming synth chords finally subside and in the ensuing moment of respite Jay puts a period on his verse: "Preach."

Most importantly, in equating themselves with God, the Holy Spirit, and Jesus and embodying the Trinity—through their heretically deifying alter egos, (Jay) "Hova" (Jehovah) and "Yeezy" (Jesus)—these last lines bring the verse's apotheosis and studied nihilism to its logical conclusion. Indeed, through its disruption of European hierarchies and power logics, careful dismantling of Eurocentric values, and laying bare of the West's whitewashing lies about itself, the verse's nihilism clears the way for Jay and Ye to claim the throne.

Here, the subhuman becomes the superhuman, the Black man becomes god, and *nihilism becomes narcissism*—just in time for Ye to "get me some" in his remarkably self-centered verse about coke, threesomes, and the inevitable "sunglasses and Advil." Indeed, Ye is about to play hedonistic demon to Jay's enlightened angel; bad cop to Jay's good cop. And in a remarkably effective way, Ye is about to take us across the threshold from "good hip hop" to "bad hip hop." But first we need to "walk through the fire . . ."

After a reprise of Ocean's nihilistic critique of the God-King-Mob-Man order—now subtly overlaid with autotuned backing vocals—a second hook enters. In the space between the two hooks—buried in the texture so as to be nigh indiscernible—we hear barely audible monkey screeches followed quickly by a police siren.[27] The album's critique of dehumanizing racism and the "concrete jungle" is coming into focus.

The-Dream enters with a vocal bridge:

> I live by you: desire
> I stand by you: walk through the fire
> Your love is my scripture
> Let me into your encryption, yeah yeah

Recalling Kanye's 2004 hit, "To the Wire," the lines are a turning point in the track, using threshold and computational semaphore imagery to mark a move from Jay's thoughtful critique of the West—Padilla Peralta's "brainy" conscious hip hop—to a verse that gathers up all the negative stereotypes around hip hop and serves them up in a neat little dime bag.

However, The-Dream's bridge also marks an arrival at a new law: desire. Love is now scripture. Commitment to that love/desire is what matters. And, notably, the aesthetic here is wholly digital, almost post-human. Ironically, The-Dream's autotuned voice moving beautifully through floridly expressive melismatic passages out-humans Ocean's clinical, almost detached acoustic vocals. Indeed, the handoff from Ocean to The-Dream accomplishes both the shift from nihilism to narcissism and the shift in Attalian code; the shift from traditional R&B's sanctified, orthodox repetitions to a new world of our own composition. As Alexander Weheliye puts it in his "Feenin," R&B has always centered desire, but "contemporary R&B suggests a mechanized desire at the cusp of the human and posthuman"—a hyper-desire augmented through the digital circuitry of vocoders and autotune that he terms "feenin" (following the 1993 Jodeci title).[28]

Again, Attali is instructive about the relationships between music, technology, and new modes of social being and forms of value. Tracking the technologies that accompanied the emergence of previous codes, he sees new *instruments* as tied to the code of composition.

> Like representation and repetition, composition needs its own technology as a basis of support for the new form of value. While recording was intended as a reinforcement for representation, it created an economy of repetition. As with the preceding codes, the technology upon which composition is based was not conceived for that purpose. If representation is tied to printing (by which the score is produced), and repetition to recording (by which the record is produced), composition is tied to the instrument (by which music is produced). We may take this as a herald of considerable future progress, in the production and in the invention of new instruments.

Like autotune and vocoder technologies, hip hop is well known for its creation and popularization of new instruments. Indeed, we might say that hip hop culture was born of such new, usually repurposed instruments—from the turntable to the aerosol paint can.

Above all, it is the *subversive* repetition of DJ remix technologies and the art of turntablism that "turned a semiotically stable playback device (think code of repetition) into a creative instrument—an object into a subject."[29] Indeed, this technology was "not conceived for that purpose." Hip hop has made a habit of creating, repurposing, and popularizing new *live* instruments—creating "something out of nothing" as the adage goes—be it the turntable, mixer, vocoder, autotune, air horn, Roland 808, Akai MPC, Serato . . . or the mobile phone.[30]

## THE "SELF-DIRECTED GAZE"

Indeed, this shift from nihilism to narcissism and human to posthuman is a broadly important discourse for our current selfie-fascist political moment and a particularly salient feature of Attali's conclusion in *Noise: The Political Economy of Music.* Despite its focus on early hand-held video technologies of the 1970s, the critique rings remarkably prescient in the context of today's self-branding, social mediascape.

> But the essential usage of the image recorder seems to me to be elsewhere, in its private use for the manufacture of one's own gaze upon the world, and first and

> foremost upon oneself. Pleasure tied to the self-directed gaze: Narcissus after Echo. Eroticism as an appropriation of the body.
>
> The new instrument thus emerging will find its real usage only in the production, by the consumer himself, of the final object, the movie made from virgin film. The consumer, completing the mutation that began with the tape recorder and photography, will thus become a producer and will derive at least as much of his satisfaction from the manufacturing process itself as from the object he produces. He will institute the spectacle of himself as the supreme usage.[31]

The passage is notable for its prophesy of today's technology-driven image-centered narcissism. Notably, however, in its gesture to the myth of Echo and Narcissus, it also slyly gestures to the ways that Echo's *sound* presages Narcissus's *image*—"Narcissus *after* Echo." In brief, the myth from Ovid's *Metamorphoses* tells the story of the nymph, Echo, who is punished for her excessively beautiful voice—and who then passes this curse on to Narcissus, who becomes enchanted with his own image. Again, Attali privileges the disruptive, world-changing power of *noise.*

In the second half of "No Church in the Wild" Ye steps into this nihilistic freedom—this disruptive space—with all the self-satisfied swag of someone who has just decided the rules don't apply to him. The narcissistic verse, steeped in "I" and "me" language, begins:

> Coke on her black skin made a stripe like a zebra
> I call that jungle fever
> You will not control the threesome
> Just roll the weed up until I get me some

With its illicit references to cocaine, marijuana, and the deviant sexual excess of a *ménage à trois*, the verse is a remarkable turn from Jay's theoretical treatise on the Western inheritance. The lines pick up the racializing Africanity of "zebra" and "jungle" imagery, but personalize the nihilist critique, showing us how a critique of traditional moral structures and the social contract can logically materialize in something far less noble: pure narcissism and debauchery.

Importantly, however, the "black skin" of the line also inverts Fanon's infamous lines of the opening of chapter 3, "The Man of Color and the White Woman," from his landmark *Black Skin, White Masks*, "Out of the blackest part of my soul, across the zebra striping of my mind, surges this desire to be suddenly *white*. . . ." The evocative opening resonates not only with Kanye's refiguration of miscegenation, but with Jay's critical engagement with Western civilization. Fanon continues the first-person analysis: "When my restless hands caress those white breasts, they grasp white civilization and dignity and make them mine."[32] Indeed, lingering behind these lines is the psychoanalyst's core concept of a "dual narcissism" wrought of white supremacy, racial prejudice, and the compulsive mutual implication of those people who think themselves "white" and those people who think themselves "Black."[33]

The remainder of Ye's pointedly "bad hip hop" verse puts a point on this logic of narcissism, continuing:

> We formed a new religion
> No sins as long as there's permission
> And deception is the only felony
> So never fuck nobody without tellin' me

The lines undercut the freeing nihilist critique of the track's opening by suggesting that this is not a critique of religious submission to a god, but a new religion dedicated to pleasure and governed by jealousy. Indeed, this "new religion" re-institutes sin and has its own creed.

After recounting and reminiscing about his sexual conquests ("last night was mad real"), and the object of his desire, the nameless girl who had "Two tattoos, one read 'no apologies' / The other said 'love is cursed by monogamy,'" he concludes:

> That's somethin' that the pastor don't preach
> That's somethin' that a teacher can't teach
> When we die, the money we can't keep
> But we prolly spend it all 'cause the pain ain't cheap

Like the creed of his "new religion," the lines simultaneously critique the moral strictures of organized religion and traditional education while outlining a new law—the law of self-satisfaction. It is a law in which money compensates for and alleviates the pain of racial subordination. The final lines recall the moral authorities of the track's opening chorus and end just as Jay's verse: "Preach."

Ocean's God-King-Mob-Man chorus concludes the track with an overlay of The-Dream's wordless posthuman vocals. But now the monkey screeches and police sirens are centered in the musical texture as the final lines of the chorus, the title lines, are looped: "No Church in the Wild / No Church in the Wild / No Church in the Wild." And here a new "jungle" character is added to the mix, the rumbling growls of a big cat, a lion or tiger. The iconic *king* of the *jungle* has arrived, recalling the beastly humans of the album art and offering us one last memorable instance of Jay and Ye's "double game" of subhuman and superhuman. In the end, we hear a beast-king who "speaks of society and . . . speaks against it."[34] Welcome to the Jungle.

## OCCUPY THE CONCRETE JUNGLE: THE VIDEO CLIP

Set as a clash between Molotov-cocktail-wielding protestors and riot police in full paramilitary gear, the video for "No Church in the Wild" deepens the narrative of the music, lyrics, and album art and contextualizes the track in its 2011 Great Recession and Occupy Wall Street historical moment.[35] Through its gruelling slow-motion depiction of a violent clash set against the backdrop of a monument-rich cityscape with stately buildings and white marble statues, the 2012 video telegraphs the idea of the nascent Occupy Movement at ground zero for the global financial crisis: the New York Stock Exchange.[36] The video thus adds another layer of social upheaval and social transformation to the narrative.

Picking up on the grotesque sound of monkeys being policed, it also develops the concrete jungle imagery. Indeed, the video functions much like the track, beginning with serious images of confrontation filmed with human pathos and real narrative tension. We feel the human suffering of pepper spray, tear gas, and broken bones. We know that such police crackdowns do happen. They happen in Beijing and in Cairo, and they happen in Ferguson, Missouri, and Davis, California. Jay and Ye's cinematic work with director Romain Gavras is effective. But once the conflagration reaches full tilt and the video gets into Kanye's verse, the scene turns to night and, like a scene from Burning Man, seems less about class struggle and political ideology than a simulacrum of violence, as smoke machines, fireworks, and a green laser light show take the night. Though the shift is long and subtle, in brief, the video reads as a shift from nihilist critique of

Fig. 3. Class struggle to Burning Man. Stills from the beginning and end of the music video for "No Church in the Wild" (dir. Romain Gavras).

state power to narcissistic revelry in displays of macho violence—good hip hop to bad hip hop.

To complete the absurd transformation, at the end of the video we see a full-grown African elephant, chain around its neck, rearing up on its hind legs like the white-marble steeds with which the video began. Concrete jungle, indeed.

The question must be asked: Is the first half of the video a searing critique of the one percent and a humanization of the heroes of the Occupy Movement, while the second half is run-of-the-mill Hollywood drivel? Or is the video instead an indictment of our own insatiable appetite for representations and repetitions of people fighting the good fight? Does the second half of the video, in other words, go so far over the top that it forces us to ask what we mean when we root for the little guy in the impossible fight against the evil fascists, the greedy corporations, the repressive state, the hypocritical church (take your pick)? And further, is that what we hate about gratuitous violence? That it reminds us that violence is not a sustainable tool of social transformation (as seductive as David vs. Goliath scenes and narratives are)?

As a heuristic frame, *critical excess* asks us to consider these questions and reappraise our dislikes and dismissals of hip hop's most over-the-top statements—statements that, during the world-changing Black Lives Matter protests of summer 2020 seem to function as self-fulfilling prophesies. As we have seen, these critiques may be excessive, ugly, even seemingly incongruent, but most often their unfathomable details display fresh, sometimes world-changing cultural and economic logics that we'd do well to listen to.

A favorite lyric of mine in just this regard is the line from Birmingham (UK) MC Juice Aleem, who on his 2009 track "The Fallen" raps, "Those that think it's too harsh? They don't know the half." As I detail in the last chapter of *Flip the Script: European Hip Hop and the Politics of Postcoloniality,* the album that features the track is another systematic takedown of the Western order—indicting Europe's colonial history and neocolonial legacies, from oppressive regimes of logic and language to material details of daily life in the global postcolony.[37] The line here suggests that we don't listen; that the European inheritance has bulldozed other histories, other knowledges, other ways of knowing, to clear the way for a (white) universalism that presumes to speak for all. We thus find the arguments—about oppression, about inequality, about dehumanization, about reparation—"too harsh," indeed *excessive*, because we understand less than half of that reality. We haven't taken the time to learn even half of the facts.

Confronted with such a successfully silencing hegemony, one question remains: what is one to do in such a society? The tracks to come offer a range of answers.

## THE LAST GILDED AGE: THE NEOLIBERAL DEATH DRIVE

Before we move on we need to confront the other elephant in the room: the neoliberal machine to which the West has been reduced. The Jamaican novelist and scholar Sylvia Wynter offers searing insights into our present hegemony in her wide-ranging interview with David Scott, "The Re-

Enchantment of Humanism."[38] She explains the discursive shackles of the neoliberal order—and its vision of humanity—thus:

> This leads me to another point, a very slippery, difficult point to make. For what I'm going to suggest is that in the world in which we live today, it is not primarily the mode of production—capitalism—that controls us, although it controls us at the overtly empirical level through the institution of the free market system, and the everyday practices of its economic system. But you see, for these to function, the processes of their functioning must be *discursively* instituted, regulated *and* at the same time normalized, legitimated. So what I am going to suggest is that what institutes, regulates, normalizes, and legitimates what then controls us, is instead the *economic* conception of the human—*Man*—that is produced by the disciplinary discourses of our now planetary system.[39]

As Wynter suggests, in our present age the category of the human has been reduced to a purely economic conception—individual economic actors set against each other to dominate natural resources, like so many competing animals. This is the "transactionalism" we hear so much about in critiques of Donald J. Trump's worldview and *modus operandi*. But transactionalism was not his invention. It is the logical endgame of the neoliberal system in which we (and our labor) are all reduced to our monetary value. He has simply mastered the base economics of self-interest that our neoliberal age has prepared for us. He has raced to the bottom (line)—and he has won that zero-sum game.

Notably, Wynter's evocative language here echoes Attali's vision of the flow of history—how the seeds of each new age are planted in the soil of the preceding one; "whether in politics or epistemologies . . . discontinuities can erupt only out of seedbeds that have been empirically pre-prepared for them." Presaging Mitt Romney's reductively neoliberal construction of "makers and takers," Wynter continues:

> While this identity induces us all to behave as producers, traders or consumers, it unifies us as a species in *economically* rather than, as before, in *theologically* absolute terms. This means that in order to be unified in *economic* terms we have to first produce an *economic* conception of being human. Now, up until the end of the eighteenth century in the West, the conception was primarily *political*; up until the fifteenth century it was primarily *religious*. What I'm saying is that it is the bioeconomic conception of the human . . . that determines the hegemony

> of the *economic* system over the social and political systems—even more, that mandates the functioning of the capitalist mode of production as the everyday expression of that hegemony.[40]

Of course, it is this "bioeconomic conception of the human" that is at the core of neoliberalism. And it is this vision of the human that has facilitated the race to the bottom (line)—a race premised on the devaluing of human life and engineering of poverty. This is the ultimate logic of late capitalism. This is the neoliberal death drive.

As Marilynne Robinson writes in the midst of the Covid-19 global pandemic—a crisis that has exposed countless failures of our neoliberal order—at the very center of this bioeconomic conception is neoliberalism's Darwinian naturalization of "selfishness." "It comes down to the idea that the profit motive applies in literally every circumstance, inevitably, because it is genetic in its origins and its operations."[41] She explains:

> In recent decades, which have been marked by continuous, disruptive change and by technological innovation that has reached assertively into every area of life, a particular economics has become a Theory of Everything, subordinating all other considerations to some form of cost-benefit analysis that silently insinuates special definitions of both cost and benefit. If neither of these is precisely monetizable—calories might have to stand in for currency in primordial transactions—personal advantage, again subject to a highly special definition, is seen as the one thing at stake in human relations. The profit motive has been implanted in our deepest history as a species, in our very DNA.

Like Sylvia Wynters, in her sweeping historical analysis Robinson too offers the conclusion that late capitalism's neoliberal structure is undergirded by discursive practices and ideological commitments.

> Institutionalization may be less a factor here than inculcation. Long before the pandemic struck, the protections of the poor and marginalized that largely defined the modern Western state had been receding, sacrificed to the kind of policy that presents itself as necessity, discipline, even justice tendentiously defined. Wealth can be broadly shared prosperity, or it can be closely held, private, effectively underwritten by the cheapening of the labor of the nonrich, which reduces their demand for goods and services. When schools and hospitals close, the value of everything that is dependent on them falls. Austerity toward

> some is a tax cut for others, a privatization of social wealth. The economics of opportunism is obvious at every stage in this great shift. And yet Americans have reacted to the drove of presumptive, quasi, and faux billionaires as if preternatural wealth were a credential of some kind.

Robinson continues, noting how this "inculcation" and naturalization of the ideology of bioeconomic humanity has an in-built devaluating mechanism.

> All the talk of national wealth, which is presented as the meaning and vindication of America, has been simultaneous with a coercive atmosphere of scarcity. America is the most powerful economy in history and at the same time so threatened by global competition that it must dismantle its own institutions, the educational system, the post office. . . . This richest country has been overtaken with a deep and general conviction of scarcity, a conviction that has become an expectation, then a kind of discipline, even an ethic. The sense of scarcity instantiates itself. It reinforces an anxiety that makes scarcity feel real and encroaching, and generosity, even investment, an imprudent risk. . . .
>
> How is it that we can be told, and believe, that we are the richest country in history, and at the same time that we cannot share benefits our grandparents enjoyed? When did we become too poor to welcome immigrants? The psychology of scarcity encourages resentment, a zero-sum notion that all real wealth is private and is diminished by the claims of community.

The discourse of decline and dismantling resonates with David Harvey's theory of "creative destruction"—a theory of neoliberalism's much-lauded (and buzzwordy) "disruptive innovations." Through its focus on efficiency and totalizing maximization, claims Harvey, neoliberalism has worked tirelessly to reassert class dominance in the face of the communitarian gains that Robinson notes were, however incomplete, a signature of twentieth-century progress in the area of social welfare. Through the "destruction, not only of prior institutional frameworks and powers (such as the supposed prior state sovereignty over political-economic affairs) but also of divisions of labor, social relations, welfare provisions, technological mixes, ways of life, attachments to the land, habits of the heart, ways of thought, and the like," neoliberalism has, "in effect swept across the world like a vast tidal wave of institutional reform and discursive adjustment."[42]

This maximizing race to the bottom (line) is neoliberalism's death drive. It is the unsustainably compulsive and irrational commitment to the premise of scarcity in the face of astronomical wealth. It is the global race to colonize all remaining resources and the drive toward ever-higher inequality—a last gilded age. It is the economics of human devaluation—the bioeconomic ideology wherein "we need poverty in order to compete with countries for whom poverty is a major competitive asset." Revisiting Wynter's "bioeconomic conception of the human," it is a hegemonic dysfunction that sacrifices the "bio" on the altar of the "economic"—a death drive. It is a fitting description of those on the American Right who would sacrifice human life for the sake of "the economy."

For our purposes here, however, it is this "zero-sum" notion of pseudo-Darwinian bioeconomics and the "resentment" it foments that Jay and Ye are playing on. This is the bifurcated play of men and beasts on the album, of makers and takers, of subhumans and superhumans. These artistic visions are not so much novel ephemera as logical outcomes of our neoliberal bifurcations and inequalities—material products of our last gilded age.

And, notably, these visions are expressions of critical excess. By taking on the cultural features of this hegemony—by mastering its gilded bling ethos as well as its transactional systems—this critical excess accelerates the neoliberal endgame. But instead of using this "creative destruction" to restore and reinvigorate capitalism, this *critical excess* proceeds with a signal difference: race.

Recalling Wynter's "bioeconomic conception of the human," it bears repeating that at the heart of this figuration is a rupture that enables the asymmetrical fracturing of the ostensibly universal category of the "human." It is this *de facto* fracture of *de jure* humanism that Frank Wilderson, and others working on the critical terrain of Afropessimism, term the "Slave/Human paradigm." In the introduction to his interview with Wilderson about his book, Afropessimism, Aaron Robertson explains:

> Wilderson and I also make reference to a "Slave/Human paradigm." This is at the heart of Afropessimism, the theory and the book. It uses historian Orlando Patterson's idea of social death to make what is arguably *Afropessimism*'s most controversial claim: Black subjection is so unlike horrific experiences any other group of people face that one must think of Blackness as inseparable from slav-

> ery (or "slaveness"). The Human is a communal being that defines itself against the Slave, the Black person, the non-human.[43]

Detailing how the discursive categories of slave and human are mutually constituted—and premised on Blackness *per se*—Wilderson writes of the paradoxical "Slave/Human 'relation'" thus:

> Without Black people, Human existence would be unintelligible, in the same way that "cat" has no meaning without "dog." This is very different from Native American genocide. For Indians are, in fact, Humans. Wiping them out, empirically, does not threaten the stability of Humanity. Any more than the anti-Semitic violence of the Holocaust would have made "Humanity" unintelligible should the Holocaust have wiped out the Jews.[44]

While the racial differentiation may seem unnecessary—and is surely hard to read—Wilderson's aim here is to emphasize the foundational abasement of Blackness. He concludes: "if Blacks were completely genocided, Humanity would find itself in the same quandary that would occur if Black people were recognized and incorporated as Human beings. Humanity would cease to exist; because it would lose its conceptual coherence, having lost its baseline other."

Building on the work of Wynter and Wilderson, it is my contention that Jay and Ye understand these unfathomable equations. It is my contention that "No Church in the Wild" places this "Slave/Human paradigm"—this doubled (sub/super)humanity—at the center of its critique of the West, setting the stage for the coming tracks on *Watch the Throne*. In the pages that follow, I thus argue that Jay and Ye's critical excess, weaponizes the "Slave/Human paradigm" compounding the paradoxes of its asymmetrical valuations and accelerating us toward the neoliberal goal of a final accounting. I argue that they accomplish this feat by playing in the paradoxes of (sub/super)humanity—the "Slave/Human paradigm"—and exacerbating this "universalist" hegemony's in-built flaw—capitalism's racist foundations.

By stoking white resentment, *Watch the Throne* accelerates the neoliberal death drive and precipitates the fall of capitalism. This is how *Watch the Throne* functions prophetically as capitalism's death dance.

CHAPTER 2

# "Lift Off" to Sunday Service

## *Transcendence, Black Capitalism, Black Rapture*

However painful it may be for me to accept this conclusion, I am obliged to state it: For the black man there is only one destiny. And it is white.

—FRANTZ FANON, *PEAU NOIRE, MASQUES BLANCS* (*BLACK SKIN, WHITE MASKS*) (1952/1967)

On track 2 of *Watch the Throne*, "Lift Off" (feat. Beyoncé), we hear a bright, hopeful, and wholly different take on this history of oppression, hypocrisy, and denial—the *critical excess* of a track that will transcend these denials, transcend the West, and indeed, transcend the planet.

But before the second track begins—as the "Wild" sirens, monkeys, and lions of "No Church in the Wild" fade into the background—we are treated to twenty seconds of an off-kilter interlude featuring a small wind ensemble and acoustic guitar. The little acoustic cabaret ensemble plays a lilting oom-pah groove that evokes a Central or Eastern European café—and would offer a quaint respite from the previous track, if it were not also so oddly chromatic and menacing. First, a fingernail strums a haunting glissando on the strings inside a piano. Next, an eerie accordion chord sneaks in to interrupt the groove. Indeed, this creepy little ensemble is something of an *idée fixe* that is interspersed throughout the album, first here, then in "New Day" (track 6), "Welcome to the Jungle" (track 8), and then in the secret final track, "Illest Motherfucker Alive" (track 13), where it appears with additional sighing tones on accordion.

After some investigation (piecing together theories on Twitter and Reddit threads), the returning interlude appears to be inspired by the soundtrack to the Showtime serial *Dexter*. Indeed, this *idée fixe* on *Watch the Throne* seems to be a studio reperformance of the track that originally inspired that music from *Dexter*—an instrumental cut by the 1970s-era prog-rock outfit Orchestra Njervudarov.[1] While whosampled.com offers the too-simple answer that this unifying device is a "direct sample" from the track "Tristessa" (sadness), from Njervudarov's 1979 EMI album *Con le Orecchi di Eros* (With the Ears of Love), a close listen refutes this conclusion.[2] The Jay and Ye version is clearly reperformed, judging by the timbral difference between the classic synths on the original and the acoustic timbres of the 2011 version (the double-reed sonic profile of a bassoon on the Ye beat is the obvious giveaway).

Further, judging from online chatter looking to crack open this seeming Easter egg, the inspiration for the track is likely to have been the creepy ethos of the show *Dexter* itself—a program with a serial murderer as the protagonist. Since the Dexter track "Courting the Night," by television and film composer Daniel Licht, is in the same key (A minor) as both the Italian prog-rock original and Kanye's hip hop reworking, it seems most likely that Kanye wanted to model the creepy ethos of the Dexter soundtrack and found that the Licht version was, itself, modeled on the Italian prog-rock tune. The interludes offer an uncanny and repeated rejoinder to the album's emancipatory trajectory—especially the "Lift Off" ethos of the coming track. The *idée fixe* thus seems to sound the album's dark underside, challenging us to hear the murderous and monstrous rot that lies just behind its gilded beauty. As such, it is a fitting pivot from "No Church in the Wild" to "Lift Off."

### THREE, TWO, ONE . . . "LIFT OFF" (FEAT. BEYONCÉ)

Right on cue, the second track of *Watch the Throne* begins with the shimmering synth fanfare of a motivational and uplifting sort of *Magnificent-Seven*-meets-*Chariots-of-Fire* riff. That is, the driving riff that runs throughout "Lift Off" borrows the motivic shape and basic rhythmic patterning of the musical theme from the classic western film *The Magnificent Seven*—here transformed into 6/8. Again, Ye's riff happens to use the same pitches (F-A-G) as the source material: the second, more rhythmically driving iteration of Elmer Bernstein's 1960 *Magnificent Seven* theme in its recorded arrangement.[3] Similarly, the track's timbral profile of fat, oversaturated synth chords seems to be modeled on Vangelis's main theme to *Chariots of*

Ex. 2. Rhythmically driving theme from *Magnificent Seven* (top) compared with the opening hook of "Lift Off" (bottom) (transcription by the author and Mary J. King).

*Fire*. That Academy Award–winning theme is, of course, a driving, motivational arrangement that perfectly matches the ethos of "Lift Off." For our purposes here, it's also worth noting that the *Chariots* theme sets the tone for a film that is essentially meritocracy porn about outsiders competing for acceptance at Cambridge University, and then the Olympics.

While almost certainly unintended, the collapse of these sonic signifiers of "the West"—the cowboy film and the elite university—underscores the album's studied Eurocentrism. Read in conjunction with the interlude's Euro-centered ethos, this early moment of transition on the album is a blindingly white one. Allusions to the television serial killer and the creepy prog-rock groove paint an unsettling portrait of whiteness, just as the motivational gestures to the galloping western film and the transcendent university sports film work in the service of a sonically uplifting whiteness. The transition is, we might say, white on both sides.[4]

It is this latter musical whiteness that establishes the tone of "Lift Off"—driving and motivational. For four bars the galloping synth hits push ahead, supported by a low synth-brass line. Just as we hear that this opening cycle is about to complete, a (weird, white) voice informs us, "all engine running." For the next four bars, the texture is thickened with high brass and swirling synth sequences in the upper lines and percussive bass hits that build the energy. Against this backdrop, Beyoncé's track-stealing hook enters:

Now we gon' take it to the moon, take it to the stars
How many people you know can take it this far?
I'm supercharged
I'm 'bout to take this whole thing to Mars

Now we gon' take it to the moon, take it to the stars
You don't know what we been through to make it this far
So many scars
'Bout to take this whole thing to Mars

Beyoncé's full-throated yet perfectly controlled vocals exude confidence and, together with the driving synth line, establish the "supercharged" ethos of the track, setting in motion the upward trajectory of the album's narrative. Indeed, Beyoncé seems singularly well equipped to exercise her agency in this context.[5] From the first notes, this African American superstar is in her element galloping astride this white steed—clearly shaping her own history, "but not under circumstances of [her] own choosing," as Kelley, per Marx, might put it.[6] "Lift Off" is a track about Black Americans mastering white structures . . . and transcending them.

On Beyoncé's hook, we have a lyrical commentary that references the dehumanizing hierarchies of "No Church in the Wild" but catapults beyond that oppressive hegemony. As we can hear even without the victorious lyrics, her voice transports us into an aesthetic and lyrical realm that we might characterize as a *transcendent superhumanism*. Between the third and fourth syllables of the line "I'm super-*charged*," in particular, Beyoncé juices that important structural moment, ever-so-slightly delaying the entrance of the last syllable, scooping into it, and thus charging that word—"*charged*"—with extra power. When the melodic line comes around again on the word "scars," the approach is repeated to even greater effect—now with a slight upward cry at the back of the voice.

With this demonstrated performative excellence—and in response to the big questions posed on "No Church in the Wild"—"Lift Off" develops a contradictory theme that is at the heart of the album. That theme is central to this book's analysis of this (Black) capitalist album—a quandary we might describe as a vexingly simultaneous escape/escapism. The track's performed figuration of "escape/escapism" as the *sine qua non* of Black capitalism recognizes a double bind that we might call "individual success and/as selling out." While we rightly revel in Beyoncé's mastery and the transcendent power of her voice, the question demands resolution: what of us mere mortals? You're right, I don't know any people who can "take it this far." After you take it to the stars, will you come back for us? Is that what you mean by taking "this *whole thing*" to Mars? Given its "luxury rap" ethos and recurrent theme of escape/escapism, this album thus centers the vexed question of Black capitalism unlike any other artifact.

We'll return to the subject of Black capitalism later in this chapter, but for now it's important to understand that, with her star-centered hook, Beyoncé has just invoked the artistic and critical field of inquiry known as Afrofuturism. Premised on the very real Afrodiasporic histories of abduction and alienation, Beyoncé's invocation of Black "scars" in rhetorical and performed (rhymed) connection to "stars" and "Mars" activates a well-established and now critically legible history of Afrofuturist cultural production.[7] Together, the "Lift Off" title and opening space-travel discourse clearly signal this track's performative relationship to the previous track, "No Church in the Wild": if the Western (racist) universalist inheritance is nothing more than a house of cards, it's time to "Lift Off" for greener pastures—Martian ones.

Indeed, the weird white voice that we hear in the track's intro is that of Jack King, a mission-control officer known as "the voice of Apollo 11"—a fitting sonic artifact from the bygone heights of white civilization. Whether by design or not, this invocation of the Apollo program's messenger mission to other civilizations on "Lift Off" neatly collapses white civilization's rise and fall—from Troy to Khe Sanh, from Socrates and Plato to Nixon and Trump.[8]

As we will see, the connections between an impending climate crisis, threatening Malthusian pandemics, and worldwide resurgent nationalisms have created a cottage industry of privatized space travel. Indeed, the endgame seems to be in sight. This track thus offers us a chance to connect the transformative histories of Afrofuturism that we can hear on this track to those clear and present dangers—of which Donald Trump is merely a symptom. More immediately, it offers a chance to examine the connections between the (white) futurist and private space-travel projects of Elon Musk, Richard Branson, and Jeff Bezos and the transcendent (?) Black capitalism of Bey, Jay, and Ye.

Importantly, in examining these contemporary discourses, we'll also need to visit Kanye and Kim Kardashian's evangelical Christianity, the recent "Sunday Services," and the transcendence that they offer—a transcendence that recalls both the white transcendence of the "Not of this World" movement's evangelical "rapture" and the cultism of Jim Jones and his People's Temple Agricultural Project. In short, in light of the recent development of a more forthrightly religious, even *born again* Kanye, we might call this Black capitalist escape/escapism *Black rapture*.

## "I'M SUCH A SHOW OFF"

Immediately after Beyoncé's inspiring opening chorus, Kanye's verse begins in "bad hip hop" mode. He begins: "Lift off . . . takin' my coat off / Show all my tattoos, I'm such a show off," punctuating the line with his signature, self-satisfied nasal gesture, "heh!" The drums drop out just in time to let us hear the entitled disdain in his voice as he issues the ugly, conceited lines. Despite the shadiness of the preceding interlude, the verse is something of a surprise, cutting directly against the moral authority and transcendent cultural capital of Beyoncé's "So many scars / 'Bout to take this whole thing to Mars." Instead, Kanye revels in the self-aggrandizing exceptionalism of "How many people you know can take it this far?"

Yet the next lines pick up on the unresolved "stars/scars" tension of Beyoncé's Afrofuturist hook, continuing "I fill/feel the pen/pain and then roll off / I got the whole city they about to go off!" Notably, the first half of the couplet sets up a pair of homophones around "fill/feel" and "pen/pain." If we hear it in the first vein, the line comes off as a simple boast about a tossed-off lyric—"I fill the pen and then [simply let the lyrics] roll off"—seemingly confirming his self-avowed mastery of form and communicating his personal ease of excellence. Yet, in the other hearing we get a sense of Black excellence as a form of overcoming adversity, overcoming "scars"—as in "I feel the pain and then [despite that pain, let it] roll off." The lyric is as remarkable for its inscrutability as it is for its nonchalance.[9]

The next half of the couplet revels in his well-established bona fides and mastery of form to suggest that regardless of our interpretation—and despite how weak and artless his flow is here (it is)—the "whole city" is, nonetheless, "about to go off" and erupt with excitement. The next lines proceed:

> How many niggas with me up and in the aisle?
> How many people want to roll on me now?

Like you know, na-ni-na, you know me by now
Know me, know me by now

Despite the lines' vagueness, the message is clear: Kanye has fans. Kanye has lots of fans. Kanye has a tried and true posse that is with him through thick and thin. To borrow a line from A Tribe Called Quest's late, great MC, Phife, Ye seems to say, "If you don't know me by now, you'll never know."[10] Because of his past body of work—because of his cultural and political capital, because he had three Grammy-nominated albums before hip hop albums were really kosher with white industry elites, because he said "George Bush doesn't care about black people" on live television—Kanye can walk onto a track with no flow and drop a couple of barely interesting lyrics and still score a chart-topping hit and have books written about him.[11]

Performatively, the point of this boast is crystal clear: Kanye could stand in the middle of ~~Fifth Avenue~~ South Shore Drive and shoot somebody and he wouldn't lose any ~~voters~~ fans.[12]

Here, the Beyoncé hook re-enters—"We gon' take it to the moon, take it to the stars"—now with a new rising countermelody on "take me to the stars." In the immediate aftermath of Kanye's blatantly self-important verse, however, Bey's chorus is somewhat drained of its counterhegemonic, transcendent power. As the hook ends, Kanye picks up where he left off—as if rubbing it in—"Lift off, agh! / Like you know, na-ni-na, you know me by now / Know me, know me by now." Strangely, however, here he switches almost imperceptibly to a more gentle, even vulnerable affect, extending the melody up a minor third and taking on a distinctly melancholic frame. He concludes his lines on the track "You know, know me by now, know me, know me by now," fading out on a descending, sighing line. The line, with its autotune ethos—and now with searching melodic lines—immediately recalls Kanye's emo classic *808's and Heartbreak* from three years earlier (2008)—an album that launched a whole array of "emo" hip hop subgenres marked by emotional availability and vulnerability.

By veering wildly between emotional highs and lows, Kanye thus further develops the track's—and the album's—duplicitous terrain, adding an emotional complexity to the sometimes maddening political complexity of a track that is, on the surface, something of a stereotypically motivational arena anthem. In any case, by the end of Ye's lines on the track, the gauntlet is laid. You're a fan or you're not. You're a *loyal* fan or you're not.

As Patty Labelle put it way back in 1985, "If you don't know me by now, you will never, never, never know me . . ." If you're with me, then you're in it through thick and thin. If you're not with me, then this is not for you.

## "IF YOU FIND EARTH BORING"

After Ye's sudden melancholic turn, Jay's verse enters, returning to the solid ground of self-confident hip hop braggadocio. But here we also hear Jay engaging more directly with the classic Afrofuturist theme of transcendence that lurks just beneath the surface of Beyoncé's hook. While still in the profane language of capitalist escap*ism*, Jay's verse also gestures more forthrightly to escape.

> Lift off, rappers hear *Watch the Throne*
> They gon' be pissed off
> Earth is boring to 'em
> Shit is making my dick soft
> When you Earnhardt/earn hard as me eventually you hit a big wall
> Five, four, three, two we need fuel
> Lift off!

The "Earnhardt/earn hard" line in particular plays on the scars-to-stars message of African American success and Black excellence. The wordplay puns on the famed NASCAR driver, Dale Earnhardt, who was killed on the final lap of the 2001 Daytona 500, crashing into a wall and fracturing his skull. The transformation from star to scar—and to death—inverts the track's uplifting direction, while suggesting that escape is the only way to not end up like Earnhardt—a figure who, like Jay and Ye, was also at the top of his game.[13] And, while I don't wish to overstate the obvious, there are few things whiter than NASCAR. (Maybe figure skating . . . we'll get to that.)

Most importantly, the verse suggests an Afrofuturist reading through its implication that the "big wall" is not just a financial limit, but a glass ceiling—for in his line "Earth is boring to 'em," Jay references the Sun Ra classic, "Outer Spaceways Incorporated" (1971).[14] The hook to that track proceeds:

If you find Earth boring
Just the same old, same thing
C'mon sign up
With Outer Spaceways Incorporated

Given the track's scars-to-stars Afrofuturist hook and the resurgence in interest in Ra's work over the last decades, the quotation is surely a purposeful one.

In one scene from the narrativized version of Ra's Afrofuturist vision, the 1974 feature film *Space Is the Place*, intertwining futuristic Moog lines accompany a long camera shot as it walks the streets of inner-city Oakland.[15] Finally, we hear the film's version of "Outer Spaceways Incorporated," as long-time collaborator June Tyson sings the repeated hook accompanied by Ra on organ and the camera turns to inspect a red door emblazoned with a golden pyramid. Above the door, we see on the storefront the name of the business: "Outer Space Employment Agency." On the right side of the sign, it reads "Accepting Applications & Interviews NOW!"

Through a series of comic encounters with ill-suited applicants—a laid-off (bigoted, white, male) NASA engineer, a jive-talking Black man (looking to score his next bottle), a white woman also looking to score (drugs and sex)—we learn that the agency is an African American–owned-and-operated business that promises to take Black people to the stars, where they will no longer face the limiting capitalist structures of an anti-Black racist Earth. The scene ends with a shot of Ra at his desk, explaining "Everything you desire from this planet and never have received will be yours in outer space."

As both the intertextual reference and Jay's usage make clear, "Earth is boring" thus signals far more than "boring" might suggest. The phrase opens out onto a long and frustrating history of unfulfilled promises for Black people—both in the falsely meritocratic US context and around the world. Indeed, as Ra put it in his foundational critique of the (white) liberal democratic ideal of humanity, "I don't expect to be a citizen of this planet. It takes too long."[16]

The doubleness, indeed duplicity, of this most paradoxical of hip hop albums—this "luxury rap" celebration of "black excellence, opulence, decadence"—demands that we look more closely at "black capitalism," an idea that Sun Ra broaches in this scene and his film's broader FUBU (For

Us By Us) ethos. Indeed, Black capitalism is a deeply fraught cultural and political field that is at the very center of this book's argument about the destabilizing effects of Black success on the (white) capitalist system—how "the spell" of white nobility "is suddenly broken."

## "THE CONTINUING MYTH OF BLACK CAPITALISM"

In his 2000 article for *Black Music Research Journal*, "Celebration or Pathology? Commodity or Art? The Dilemma of African-American Expressive Culture," Berndt Ostendorf recounts the story of Ralph Ellison signifying on a white historian's reductive analysis of Black performance in its white-supremacist, capitalist, entertainment-industry context.[17] Summarizing the scene, Ostendorf explains, "The historian analyzed in agonizing detail the demeaning role that Hollywood had assigned to Bill 'Bojangles' Robinson in a Shirley Temple movie and attacked the representation as pure and simple racism. Clearly, this film confirmed Stanley Elkins's pathology thesis, popularly known as 'Samboism.' When Ellison's turn came to judge the film's merits, he merely asked, 'Did you notice how Mr. Robinson danced?' The African Americans in the audience instantly got his point and chuckled."[18]

As Ellison suggests, what is most noteworthy is Mr. Bojangles's agency within this white supremacist structure—this performance of Black excellence that is all the more impressive because of its oppressive context. Indeed, the anecdote is a fitting example for us to train our analysis on the complex, doubly-bound dilemma of Black performance. As Ostendorf explains, in the language of Du Bois's double consciousness,

> African-American historical memory is torn between the dual and alternating heritages of pathological ascription and celebratory achievement, between outside habits of racist ascription and the appreciative inside view, and between past significance and present meaning. Both poles are inscribed, as overlayered palimpsests, in the representational logic of black cultural productions. They have settled in historically grown patterns of commodification that are in turn controlled by an ever-changing tyranny of expectations. To complicate things further, the social playing field in which these representations are made public is marked by the binary push and pull of the color line, a racialized killer opposition that controls and choreographs the conceptual frameworks and discursive traditions.[19]

In this context, our dilemma of "escape/escapism" can be read not as particularly unique, but as part of a long experience of a double bind that would always threaten to mark Black success as selling out. As De La Soul put it in their 1993 "Patti Dooke"—via a sample from the Robert Townsend film, *The Five Heartbeats*—"Crossin' over ain't nothin' but a double cross."[20]

The dilemma is not a simple one for communities that are constantly judged by competing sets of expectations and values. This, again, recalls Kelley's paraphrase of Marx wherein hip hop artists must constantly work both within and against the systems in which they find themselves—industrial, creative, economic, social, or political. In the original rendering Marx writes, "Men make their own history, but not of their own free will; not under circumstances they themselves have chosen but under the given and inherited circumstances with which they are directly confronted."[21] Yet in the doubly conscious reality of Black artists, this already vexed praxis is further complicated by a totalizing system in which success is always already marked as white and reserved only for agents who accept that destiny.

The dilemma of Black success is simply and comically depicted in the cover art for Swamp Dogg's 1981 album, *I'm Not Selling Out / I'm Buying In!*.[22] On the cover, the country funk artist is outfitted in *all-white everything*—white tuxedo tails, shoes, top hat, and cane—an image somewhere between Mr. Bojangles and a disco-era pimp. He stands atop a boardroom table, arms spread in offering, presenting himself to a room full of (mostly white) businessmen. Indeed, on the album's third track, "It's Just a Little Time Left," we hear the details of Swamp Dogg's regressive, market-based solutions to America's problems. Misappropriating leftist language from the Black Power movement, he begins: "We gotta take the chains / From the black man's brain," continuing with some victim blaming, "We gotta make some jobs / We gotta make 'em fast / That's the only way to get the poor folks / Off their ass," and concluding, Reagan-style, with "Then we can axe the welfare."

Importantly, the staging of the album's image and discourse recalls another famed funk artist—none other than James Brown—and his own perception of having "sold out" to Richard Nixon in the name of Black economic advancement. An October 1972 *New York Times* article offers a fitting summary of the discourse around Black capitalism and its "Uncle Tom" stigma, replete with notable characters from the Black elite of that era.

> Sammy Davis Jr. was repeatedly booed two weeks ago at the annual Black Expo in Chicago, and a record shop owner here in Washington has stopped selling the entertainer's recordings.
>
> Howard University's radio station, WHUR, broadcast here yesterday a scathing attack on James Brown, the soul singer, and picketers protested his appearance last night in Baltimore.
>
> Blacks in Baltimore have also announced that they will picket future films of Jim Brown, the former football star turned movie actor.
>
> These were reactions to the endorsements of President Nixon for re-election by the prominent blacks. The incidents are indicative of the bitter political battle for black votes this election year.[23]

Stressing the systematic focus on "black capitalism" by Nixon's re-election campaign, the article continues, "The historical difficulty that Republicans have had making inroads in the black community is compounded this year by the strong belief, right or wrong, that the President is buying Black support through the Administration's black capitalism programs."

Notably, this fifty-year-old reportage on Black capitalism is framed by the same sense of betrayal and comments on the same transactional mechanisms surrounding Kanye's MAGA turn—his currying of favor with Donald Trump.

> Most of Mr. Nixon's new black support is from holders of Federal contracts and grants, employees of the Federal Government or persons working in federally funded programs and projects.
>
> Included are some former civil rights activists—for example, Floyd McKissick, former director of the Congress of Racial Equality, and the Rev. Albert Sampson, former aide to the Rev. Dr. Ralph David Abernathy, president of the Southern Christian Leadership Conference.
>
> "The President has bought them, and they have sold out," said Representative Louis Stokes, Ohio Democrat who is chairman of the Congressional Black Caucus.

Charges of "Uncle Tom" and "political prostitutes" have kept black Republicans on the defensive and under intense pressure.

Paving the way for Swamp Dogg (and Kanye), the 1972 article continues, "When James Brown announced his support of the President at the White House Friday, he told reporters, 'I'm not a sellout artist. I never got no Government grant, I never asked for one, don't want one. *I'm not selling out, I'm selling in.*'"[24]

Indeed, for JB and Ye the discourses of betrayal—from "Uncle Tom" to "sellout"—are rooted in a cognitive dissonance between the former's "Say It Loud, I'm Black and I'm Proud" militancy, just as in the latter's "George Bush doesn't care about black people." Both had immense cultural capital in Black communities—and both complicated those relationships with their seeming betrayals. Indeed, Swamp Dogg's entreaty to "Take the chains from the black man's brain" recalls Kanye's own take on "freedom of thought" contra Black political orthodoxy: his TMZ comments that "slavery was a choice"—a (pseudo-)insight that was foreshadowed on the 2013 *Yeezus* track "New Slaves." In short, Black capitalism is always already freighted with white appeasement and thus, betrayal. Black capitalism is always already associated with white assimilation, because capitalism was—and is—premised on racial exploitation.

As Earl Ofari Hutchinson writes in "The Continuing Myth of Black Capitalism," "Self-help and 'black capitalism' alone must not be regarded as THE economic rescue plan for African Americans. The problems of crime, drugs, poverty, and institutional racism piled high on the doorsteps of African American communities, demand both economic AND political solutions. African Americans cannot afford to forget that."[25] Underscoring, the Black escape/escapism of Jay, Ye, and Bey—of James Brown, of Sammy Davis Jr.—he describes the structural reality belying this "myth" thus: "While some black firms have prospered, most prospective black entrepreneurs still find the door shut when they seek credit and capital from lending agencies or managerial and technical training from corporations. The result is that black capitalism is still largely a myth."[26]

## MASTERING WHITENESS, DEFORMING MASTERY

In his landmark *Black Skin, White Masks* Frantz Fanon writes, "However painful it may be for me to accept this conclusion, I am obliged to state it: For the black man there is only one destiny. And it is white."[27] In the current structure—the "inherited circumstances," "the social playing field"—there is only this future. All other/nonwhite futures are foreclosed, out of bounds.

This is, of course, the whiteness that I have presented throughout the chapter thus far—a whiteness that is engineered into these opening tracks of *Watch the Throne* on every level. From *Magnificent Seven* and *Chariots of Fire* to NASCAR and the voice of Apollo 11, to Dexter and prog rock, and—looking back at "No Church in the Wild"—to Socrates and Caesar and Hobbes and Pilgrims and priests and Phil Manzanera and Spookytooth and Benzes and bleach, this album is built on the Euro-American (white) inheritance. Indeed, on the album these African American artists have, again and again, employed the masters' tools to construct a monument to whiteness and lay claim to its edifying and enriching power.[28] It is my contention, however, that Bey, Jay, and Ye, knowing the dilemma of escape/escapism all too well, have marked out a strategy that engages the contradictions of race—of whiteness and Blackness—so masterfully, that they far exceed the threshold of victory. It is a strategy wherein the only victory is to dominate the game, claim their whiteness, claim their nobility, and watch the world's head explode in the process. Judging by the responses to Ye's white evangelical turn and Bey and Jay's widely criticized NFL work (for typically disparate reasons), it seems to have worked.[29]

In the same study, Fanon writes, "I believe that the fact of the juxtaposition of the white and black races has created a massive psychoexistential complex. I hope by analyzing it to destroy it."[30] I contend that on *Watch the Throne* Bey, Jay, and Ye similarly hope that by performing this massive psychoexistential complex they might end it. That by bringing it to fruition they might destroy it. That by playing the meritocracy game and so utterly crushing their competition that they might break the system. This is critical excess.

Notably, this fraught strategy seems successful in large part because it unmistakably evades the political orthodoxies that have defined Black advancement projects as running in the same ruts—the ever-evolving "tyranny of expectations"—that characterize Ostendorf's "Celebration or Pathology? Commodity or Art?" frame and the "victim vs. problem" analytic that animates his analysis. As recent scholarship has clearly established, these frames find their most enduring templates in the stock characters of blackface minstrelsy: Jim Crow's subhuman (bumbling) appeasement vs. Zip Coon's inhuman (violent) threat.[31] And notwithstanding the fiction of these tropes, their dualized habits of thought make their intrepid way into the political discourses that plague discussions of Black liberation: the long game of civil rights organizing and legislating equality *or* the immediate action of revolution—armed if necessary.

Digging down beneath Ellison and Elkins, we see the "overlayered palimpsest" of this "binary push and pull" in the debates about (and between) Du Bois and Booker T. Washington—a central if not foundational discursive opposition that would come to echo down the decades as a sort of "changing same" in debates about (and between) Alain and Langston, about (and between) Martin and Malcolm, about (and between) Cornel and Ta-Nehisi.[32] As an analysis of the recent debate between Cornel and Ta-Nehisi concludes, "Historically speaking, as black intellectuals gain any degree of institutional credibility or popular acceptance, they face criticism from more radical thinkers of traitorous capitulation. The same type of charges were once levied by WEB DuBois at Booker T. Washington, and by Marcus Garvey at DuBois. A generation later, Martin Luther King and Malcolm X were famously caught up in a similar dynamic."[33] I suggest that *Watch the Throne*'s critical excess explodes these debates, questioning the very premises of their overengineered binaries and evading their racialized ruts. Instead it takes up Fanon's "painful" but singular conclusion: "For the black man there is only one destiny. And it is white."[34] In this way, critical excess plots a course to Black emancipation through whiteness, by bringing whiteness to its conclusion. But as we will see, it is a *deformed* whiteness.

In his 1986 *Modernism and the Harlem Renaissance*, Houston Baker advanced his widely influential theory linking Black excellence and its concomitant "mastery of form" (artistic, literary, oratorical, etc.) to a next-level transformation of that excellence—a subversive "deformation of mastery." Focusing on the famed Black business leader who is often diminished or dismissed as a white collaborator and appeaser, Baker's revisionist theory suggests that Washington's famed "Atlanta compromise" advocating for slow Black economic advancement instead of immediate political upheaval was won through a sort of performative whiteface. As Baker argues, the minstrel mask was the key to effective communication with white society. While "the Tuskegee orator" wore that stereotyping Black mask to appease his white audience of industrialists and politicians throughout his career, in so doing he also demonstrated a mastery of white expectations, of white ideas about entrepreneurship and uplift, of white conditions of possibility.[35]

Washington performed to the expectations of his late-nineteenth-century crowd using the blackface stereotypes of language, sound, and gesture he knew inside and out. But that dazzling performance of blackface, in Baker's reading, obscured the fact that Washington had also mastered white codes and expectations. It is in his masterful use of Black stereotypes coupled with the mastery of white modes of capitalist thinking, argues Baker, that Washington birthed a Black modernism. And it is in his toying with white ideas spoken through the performative contours of Black performance that Washington *masters* his audience of white planters and industrialists. This is the deformation of mastery—inhabiting stereotypes in order to subvert them. Or more to the point: employing racist stereotypes to undermine the very racist structures that created them, and the white supremacist economics that perpetuate them.

This is where we can see Kanye and Jay-Z's critical excess as an extension of Baker's deformation of mastery. Just like Washington over a century before them, Ye and Jay are playing to (and with) the "ever-changing tyranny" of racial expectations. And just like Washington's context of blackface minstrelsy—his era's most popular musical form—it is still the contours of "Black" musical performance that power those stereotypes most effectively. The difference is that Zip Coon—the comic image of a well-dressed "Black urban dandy" (with a shiv up his sleeve)—is, today, covered in real bling. The difference is that these ever-lucrative Black stereotypes are today predominantly performed by Black people. The difference is that these stereotypes sit increasingly uneasily next to the reality of Black millionaires.

The difference is that in 2011, a Black man was in the White House.

## "WE GONNA NEED A MILLION MORE"

Such images of Black wealth no longer generate such cognitive dissonance in America's racial imagination. They are no longer straightforwardly comedic and freighted with irony. While the stigma of Black poverty remains—and while poverty is still regularly engineered and reinforced in African American communities—Black wealth is now a reality that white people see daily, parading across all media platforms in music videos, sports news, entertainment programs, and reality shows.

In his book *From Jim Crow to Jay-Z: Race, Rap, and the Performance of Masculinity,* Miles White elaborates the connections between age-old blackface stereotypes about urban hustlers and today's entertainment industry. In a section titled, fittingly, "Roc Nation: Jay-Z and the Takeover of the American Dream," he writes:

> The apotheosis of the contemporary hardcore "crack rap" performer is unquestionably the Brooklyn-born lyrical genius Jay-Z, a former New York City drug figure turned multimillionaire entertainment mogul whose repertoire is filled with songs and lyrics that boast of his rise from "bricks to billboards" and "grams to Grammys," and who has built an empire from slinging crack in the 'hood one rock at a time. The double entendre implied in Jay-Z's Roc-A-Fella Records seems almost obscene in its celebration of capitalist excess enjoyed by the few made possible by the many. . . . It is complex. It is contradictory.[36]

White's analysis interrogates hip hop's nightmarish Black masculinities and tracks gangsta tropes of thugs and pimps back to blackface minstrelsy. In making his case in this section, he lays a central piece of my argument in this book—that the "Started from the Bottom" narrative of Black wealth accumulation is, for many, a "Takeover of the American Dream." Black capitalism is always already nefarious (such stories of drug dealers and pimps being taken at face value), and further, it takes over the meritocratic narrative that is the birthright of white men—it *replaces* white masculinity.

Importantly, the double entendre that White is speaking of here connects the crack "rock" of the drug trade to the famed industrialist John D. Rockefeller, founder of Standard Oil. By linking the street hustle of "slinging rocks" to the famed business magnate, Jay-Z links his own self-made story to Rockefeller's. In so doing, he echoes Booker T. Washington's dealings with the businessmen of his era, but Jay doesn't just use them to achieve his own ends—he becomes them. He is no longer satisfied to play the long game of appeasement and subversion, "his attitude toward charity is sullen anger rather than humble jollity." Now "he insists on his human right to swagger and swear and waste." Now "the spell is suddenly broken."[37] This critical excess has it both ways, collapsing Washington's Black capitalism upon Du Bois's Black militancy.

As such, his refiguration of Rockefeller as "Roc-a-Fella" is a perfect deformation of mastery for the twenty-first century. Indeed, it is a takeover reflected in the 2014 remake of *Annie* wherein Jamie Foxx plays the Daddy Warbucks character—a swaggering and unapologetic Black tycoon *replacing* a white one for today's mediascape. Of course, Jay saw that coming too. On his "Hard Knock Life (Ghetto Anthem)" (1998), he raps in "bricks to billboards" fashion: "From standin' on the corners boppin' / To drivin' some of the hottest cars New York has ever seen" over a sample from the 1977 original Broadway cast recording to the stage musical *Annie*.

*Watch the Throne*'s performance of Black excellence thus epitomizes Baker's theory of "deformation of mastery." However, it also exceeds that theory insofar as Jay and Ye are not so much seeking to take their place among equals—to leverage Black performance in service to economic access like Washington—as to replace those white capitalists. As we have seen, the very fact of Jay and Ye's Black excellence on its own would be hateful to conservative whites. But they go a bridge too far, exceeding that truth and taking on the mantel of replacers forthrightly. Indeed, this swaggering excess is an affront on two levels: as if the economic replacement weren't enough, this Black excellence even robs the narrative of meritocracy that is the white man's birthright. In this sense it is also a cultural replacement—it robs the privilege of making oneself as one wishes: the core of whiteness itself. What is whiteness if not the privilege of being an unmarked *tabula rasa*—a blank slate—ready to become a "self-made" man?

Despite his popular maligning, it often seems that Washington's project of patient (quietly subversive?) economic advancement proved more successful than Du Bois's more overtly political projects and ever-increasing militancy. To be sure, little has changed for the millions of Black men, women, and children suffering at the labor end of the capitalist exploitation machine as the political gains of the 1960s are rolled back and gerrymandered out of existence. But at the top the heights are staggering. As Jay raps on "Murder to Excellence" (track 10):

> Now please: domino, domino
> Only spot a few blacks the higher I go
> What's up Will? Shout out to O
> That ain't enough we gonna need a million more

Beginning with the subhuman/superhuman binary of murderer/millionaire, the verse plays on the bifurcated Black and white imagery of the domino—and riffs on their "spot(s)." The "few Blacks" at the top are none other than those media superstars and moguls, Will Smith and Oprah Winfrey. Jay argues that these exceptional figures are just that—exceptions to the rule. For any real and lasting change there need to be "a million more" such as them.

Yet the lines demand the question: what then? What happens when you have "enough"—a million Black millionaires? The answer seems to also be embedded in the lyric: if you have a million Black millionaires, the house of cards will tumble. As Donald Byrd put it in 1975, "We'll stand our problems all in a row / Watch them fall like dominoes."[38] Dominoes—like houses of cards—are meant to fall. What's more, the lyrical reference to dominoes connects to the ethos of high-stakes gambling threaded throughout the album, serving as a reminder that capitalism is always a game of winner take all.

Recalling Ostendorf's frame of "Celebration or Pathology?" around the dilemma of Black performance and Fanon's psychiatric evaluation of the racial capitalism that forecloses all futures except white ones, it is worth returning to Ellison. In his 1944 review of Gunnar Myrdal's *An American Dilemma*, Ellison also brings Freud and Marx together to describe the seemingly intractable "dilemma" of American racial dysfunction—of white supremacist capitalism. He writes, "For in our culture the problem of the irrational, that blind spot in our knowledge of society where Marx cries out for Freud and Freud for Marx, but where approaching, both grow wary and shout insults lest they actually meet, has taken the form of the Negro problem."[39] While he finds much admirable in the Swedish economist's study (funded by the profits of another American industrialist, Andrew Carnegie), he, too, pushes the agency side of Kelley's dialectical formulation that "young urban black men make their own history but not under circumstances of their own choosing."[40]

Ellison's masterful analysis in the review is worth citing at length:

> Some of the insights are brilliant, especially those through which he demonstrates how many Negro personality traits, said to be "innate," are socially conditioned, even to types of Negro laughter and vocal intonation. But with all this he can only conclude that "the Negro's entire life and, consequently, also his opinions on the Negro problem are, in the main, to be considered as secondary reactions to more primary pressures from the side of the dominant white majority."

> But can a people (its faith in an idealized American Creed not-withstanding) live and develop for over three hundred years simply by reacting? Are American Negroes simply the creation of white men, or have they at least helped to create themselves out of what they found around them? Men have made a way of life in caves and upon cliffs; why cannot Negroes have made a life upon the horns of the white man's dilemma? . . .
>
> It does not occur to Myrdal that many of the Negro cultural manifestations which he considers merely reflective might also embody a rejection of what he considers "higher values." There is a dualism at work here. It is only partially true that Negroes turn away from white patterns because they are refused participation. . . .

To summarize—and return to "No Church in the Wild"—it is also true that Black people "turn away from white patterns" because they know that these "higher values" are a lie. They are a house of cards, wrought through centuries of violence and oppression.

Yes, Black people are denied access to white civilization. But Black people are also *done* with white civilization. As another great critic of Western humanism, Sun Ra, once put it, "I myself am rising up above what *they* call liberty and what *they* call equality—and whatever man thinks is the greatest thing."[41]

## BLACK TRANSCENDENCE, BLACK RAPTURE: FROM "NO CHURCH IN THE WILD" TO "SUNDAY SERVICE"

Perhaps the most remarkable whitening that has taken place in the fallout from *Watch the Throne* and its critical excess is Kanye's conversion to born-again Christian—an identity wholly in keeping with his conversion to Trump sycophant. In a string of albums since 2011's *Watch the Throne*, Ye has turned on a trajectory toward overtly religious themes, starting with *Yeezus* (2013), continuing with *The Life of Pablo* (2016), and culminating in the gospel album, *Jesus Is King* (2019). The first of this, what we might call "Christian trilogy," continues West's penchant for the narcissistic God-play that began on *My Beautiful Dark Twisted Fantasy* (2010) and *Watch the Throne*. The second steps back from that heresy to take on the role of the Apostle Paul (the "Pablo" of the title)—the Roman citizen who we should note underwent his own conversion "on the road to Damascus." The third is something of a culmination of this unorthodox conversion story from God to ordinary believer—and is, notably, the fruit of the live worship services that the newly evangelical Christian started leading in 2019.

Indeed, on March 10 2019, Kanye West performed a version of "Lift Off" with a live band, horn section, and full gospel choir in the hills of the 300-acre property around his Southern California home. The performance was week ten of Ye's new series of "Sunday Services" rooted in the gospel traditions of the Black church that Ye had been organizing since early January. His partner, Kim Kardashian West, had started posting short clips from the invite-only worship services, many of them featuring such gospel arrangements of Kanye hits set against the backdrop of rolling hills and oak forests.[42] There is, it seems, church in the wild after all.

In the short clip of the "Lift Off" arrangement—which has now been compiled as part of a Sunday Service medley on YouTube—we see that Kanye has outfitted the fifty-member choir and band members in simple all-white two-piece uniforms. The group sways and bounces with the music in a manner not unlike a standard Black gospel choir as they riff on the chorus to the original track: "We gon' take it to the moon / Take it to the stars / How many people you know can take it this far?" Kanye, apparently the only one deviating from the all-white uniform, directs from the midst of the circled instrumentalists and singers as we hear shouts of "hey" in call and response. The groove drops out suddenly, allowing space for a single trumpet to reset with the *Magnificent Seven* hook. The rest of the horn section joins in a sort of fanfare before the full band enters, turning the beat around (in an admittedly hip arrangement) and cuing the choir's re-entrance. A young girl gets down in the foreground—probably one of Kardashian and West's children.

While the music for Kanye's Sunday Services is rooted in the Black gospel tradition, Kanye and Kim are attendees of—and sometimes collaborators with—the Los Angeles branch of Hillsong, an evangelical megachurch founded by the white Australian evangelical pastors, Brian and Bobbie Houston.[43] Surely, the braggadocio of "Showing my tattoos" and "shit is making my dick soft" from the original would not fit in the hugely successful catalog of Hillsong's Christian Contemporary Music (CCM) praise songs.[44] Further, set against the rolling hills of SoCal, the unadorned all-white outfits do give the distinct impression that this gathering is that of neither a Black church nor a white church, but of a cult. But in this evangelical, born-again context, the exceptionalist message of "How many people you know can take it this far?" does make a certain sense.

In his, "The Racial Ideology of Rapture," Nathaniel P. Grimes tracks the Reconstruction-era emergence of an evangelical theology commonly known as "rapture." Developed and disseminated by nineteenth-century Christian pastors such as Cyrus Scofield and Dwight Moody, this theology proved to be profoundly comforting to a generation of white men and women who had very recently lost their privilege and status. Grimes explains:

> The rise of rapture theology in America occurred after the Civil War and can be understood as resulting from major cultural crises related to the war itself. The first crisis involved the way in which American notions of racial identity were disrupted. Slavery had provided definition to ideas of whiteness and blackness, placing them within a defined power structure. In 1857 the Supreme Court decision *Dred Scott* v. *Sanford* summed up the prevailing view: to be black was to be a non-citizen and even to "justly and lawfully be reduced to slavery" for the benefit of whites. The collapse of slavery, and the adoption of the Reconstruction Amendments, called previous hierarchies into question. Black Americans responded by making tremendous strides in business, politics, and education.[45]

As we know, this Reconstruction would not stand in the minds of most whites. These gains were rolled back over the course of the ensuing decades as Jim Crow laws were passed in the South, and redlining and myriad other structural oppressions were instituted nationwide.

But in the midst of these political regressions, (white) American religion was already redrawing its tenets of faith to address the crisis, recover white privilege, and reassert white supremacy. Central to these theological developments was the development of "premillenialism"—the idea that the world was on the brink of a new "dispensation" wherein the individual piety of whites and scriptural prophesy about the "curse of Ham" (read as Black people) would pave the way forward to "reforge the white republic."[46]

Today, this highly individualist and eschatological idea is better known as "the rapture" and imagines a time when the lucky few will be plucked from the Earth and ferried off to heaven while the rest of the world perishes in flames.[47] As Grimes concludes, the premillenial theology of these hugely influential revivalists prophesied that "When the whole earth had fallen to the level of ancient cities like Babylon, Nineveh, and Athens, rapture was the catalyst to set the world right and provide an escape to a heaven 'Where pollution cannot enter.' Rapture portrays God's answer to the destruction of the sins wrought in the nineteenth century by war, greed, and white supremacy as a move to create a state of cosmic segregation."[48] If you're not able to have your white supremacy here on Earth, then at least you can have it for eternity.

Surely, most evangelicals driving the highways of Southern California with "Warning: In case of Rapture this car will be unmanned" or "NOTW" (Not Of This World) plastered across their bumpers aren't likely to be thinking of these terrifying histories. Indeed, the Afrofuturist imagery of "Lift Off" has a history in Black gospel that draws on abolition and emancipation imagery from the Fisk Jubilee Singers' rendition of "Swing Low, Sweet Chariot" up to the Selah Singers' "I'll Fly Away"—a track Ye references in the line "I'll be fly when Easter's over" from "Why I Love You" (track 12). Yet coupled with the political power of white evangelicals, the implicit racism of rapture ideology lives on, "serving a sociological and political purpose and legitimating American evangelicalism's abandonment of society's marginalized—a disaster from which neither America nor the church has recovered."[49] Today, rapture's racist legacy of individual(ist) salvation echoes through megachurches like Hillsong and preys on the mental and financial well-being of countless millions through the "prosperity gospel" of Joel Osteen and others. In this regard, the Sunday Service version of "Lift Off"—and Kanye's evangelical turn writ large—takes on an unimaginable whiteness. How many people you know can take it that far?

### THE CULT OF CELEBRITY, PARADOX OF THE POPULAR

The Sunday Services have been widely perceived as a form of rehabilitation for Ye, whose appeasement of Donald Trump, his statement that slavery was "a choice," and his seemingly unhinged, sometimes unexplainable behavior (this list of offenses, of course, goes on) has confused and enraged fans and critics alike. Much ink has been spilled questioning whether this rehabilitation was a PR stunt to burnish his image and win back his fans or an honest effort to find a modicum of peace, create a mental health space, and atone for his sins.[50] Indeed, Ben Roazen framed the rehabilitation question in a recent article as "Kanye West's Sunday Service—a Religious Experience or a Cult?"[51]

Yet, set against the backdrop of *Watch the Throne,* the question matters little. Indeed, what exactly separates a "religious experience" from a "cult"? Is there a legal test of the gray area, or is it more a matter of morality and cultural background? The cult of Donald Trump has an air of religious devotion. So too does the cult of celebrity around Ye and his made-for-TV family. The question returns us to "No Church in the Wild": "What's a god to a non-believer?" While we all feel that we know one when we see one, we might also consider that "cult" is just a judgy word for the cultures that don't pass our own tests of right and wrong, be they moral, ethical, or legal. A "cult" is—like that house of cards that is our social hierarchy—also a social construction, a culture.

In a way, then, it makes perfect sense that Ye would go directly from nihilist to preacher. He has worked out this constructedness and chosen to believe. That his belief is in both the power of celebrity and the power of Jesus Christ is a fitting cult(ure) of his own making. Indeed, all the way back in 2004, on the release of his "trinity" of videos for "Jesus Walks" (the good old days for many fans), Ye went on record about his faith in an interview with the *New York Times*'s Lola Ogunnaike. Ogunnaike reports, "Mr. West refused to describe himself as religious. 'Religion just means that you do something over and over,' he said. 'I will say that I'm spiritual. I have accepted Jesus as my Savior. And I will say that I fall short every day.'" The sentiment is a common one among American Protestants, and fully in keeping with the messaging and theology of the Sunday Services (from what we can tell at present). Such believers are encouraged to cultivate personal relationships with Jesus and create their own brands of "spirituality"—often eschewing the structures of organized religion. Therefore, just one question remains: will Ye settle in to the well-worn paths and cultural inheritances of the West, accept not just Christ but the churchgoing legacies of Christendom, and become "religious" by doing the Sunday Services "over and over"? Time will tell.

We will return to the matter of celebrity throughout this book, but for now, suffice it to say that one of the greatest tricks of popular culture in the age of social media is how the industry has helped us to mistake the art for the artist. For better or for worse, today's popular musicians are synonymous with their music—especially in the realm of hip hop, where authenticity is king and the idea of a cover version is a nonstarter. For ease of marketing and niche targeting, popular musicians are collapsed into a single, simple, and easily legible unity—an authentic "brand" that listeners can identify with. In this streamlined relationship, listeners (consumers) can follow artists on social media, make (or at least perceive) direct connections, and establish a sense of intimacy with their favorite figures. The tastemakers, influencers, and other media personalities (like those at the Sunday Services) have done a thorough job of cultivating the authenticity of today's celebrity artists—with our help.

At the center of this nearly complete process of celebrity branding is a vexing paradox: why in the world would we look to celebrities for authenticity? We know about the constructedness of selfie culture, about Instagram filters, about CGI films, and we bemoan the slickness of studio tricks and autotune, and yet it is in the very place where the cultivation of image is most obvious—popular culture—that we seek out authenticity most fervently. It is here that we look to satisfy our ever-more-intense cravings for realness. (The paradox calls to mind the witnesses to natural disasters or mass shootings, who remark, "*It was like I was watching a movie!*"). Why search for authenticity in popular culture? This may be an unanswerable question, but it puts in focus the paradox of popular music as simultaneously "mass music" and "the people's music."

As we continue with this analysis of *Watch the Throne*, it will be useful to think of the two sides of this paradox as akin to the paradox of this album—the paradox of "luxury rap." Where the idea of "mass music" stands for all of the ills of capitalism, crass commercialism, one-percenter luxury, and our Trumpist reality-TV reality, "the people's music" is rooted in our ideals of authentic community, real striving and struggle, and unmediated expressions of the soul—an ideal that has purchase in Black music more than anywhere else. Indeed, it is my assertion that this paradox is what powers the album—the paradox of the popular. Further, it is in pushing this paradox to its logical conclusion—luxury rap—that *Watch the Throne* helps accelerate the life cycle of our neoliberal order, bring down the house of cards, and draw our current era to a close.

* * *

## ENDGAME: "THE SPACE PROGRAM"

On November 17, 2016—nine days after the election of Donald J. Trump to the US presidency—the classic politically conscious crew A Tribe Called Quest released their final album, *We Got It from Here . . . Thank You 4 Your Service*, a compelling and deeply disturbing critique of a dystopian future that suddenly seemed upon us. Today, a mere five years later, the album is something of a time capsule of that era of Obama and #BlackLivesMatter—and their impending #MAGA backlash. With rhetorical constructions such as "Leave us where we are / So they can play among the stars" on the opening track, "The Space Program," the group critiques the white-supremacist project of private space travel, prophesying the colonization of outer space.

Indeed, on the track—and in its Afrofuturist video—Tribe plays on the continuities between this privatization of outer space and the anti-Black redlining in gentrifying urban space. The track imagines a dystopic reality wherein the neoliberal order has become total, completing its mission of total evisceration of the earth's resources and looking for new planets to destroy, new markets to saturate. As if responding directly to "Lift Off," the hook reminds us of the reality: "There ain't a space program for niggas / No, you stuck here, nigga." Just as neoliberalism's (white) recolonization of America's urban centers—aka gentrification—doesn't have space for people of color, this lift-off will also displace and bypass Black people.

The track recalls Gil Scott-Heron's 1970 spoken word piece, "Whitey on the Moon," wherein the proto–hip hop poet concludes his broadside against the (white) space program—and the Apollo 11 moon landing in July 1969:

> How come there ain't no money here?
> (Hmm! Whitey's on the moon)
> Y'know I just about had my fill
> (of Whitey on the moon)
> I think I'll send these doctor bills,
> Airmail special
> (to Whitey on the moon)[52]

As Scott-Heron's performative critique makes clear, the US Space Program and its "one small step for man, one giant leap for mankind" moon landing was perceived by many (if certainly not all) African Americans as a white universalist project.[53] The millions of dollars that it spent to realize this scientific vision—and its Cold War projection of American supremacy—could easily have been spent taking care of its poor Black citizens and their quotidian needs. As both Tribe and Scott-Heron suggest, the US space program is a typical instance of a nation whose priorities are badly out of line—priorities wherein the official future excludes people of color. The skepticism is well founded.

Recalling our discussion of neoliberal privatization and recolonization, from the depths of the Covid-19 global pandemic, on 26 May 2020, NASA officially announced plans to hand over mission control to "serial entrepreneur" Elon Musk.

> Instead of building its own replacement for the shuttle, NASA is handing over responsibility for carrying astronauts to a private company, SpaceX, one of the obsessions of the serial entrepreneur Elon Musk. If Mr. Musk's engineers succeed on Wednesday in sending Douglas G. Hurley and Robert L. Behnken to orbit, it will forever change how the world thinks about getting people to space.[54]

Utilizing NASA's launchpad and facilities, the privately owned and operated craft will lay the groundwork for the privatization of space travel.

> Those missions might fly as soon as a year from now. One would take space tourists on a visit to the International Space Station; the other would be a trip on an elliptical orbit around Earth that might view the planet from an altitude two to three times as high as the space station's orbit. Tom Cruise has even expressed interest in using the space station for a film.

White billionaires Jeff Bezos and Richard Branson are hot on the heels of Musk in this new space race, with their own branded space competitors, Blue Origin and Virgin Galactic.

While scholars have tracked the cultural field of Afrofuturism from the mid-century work of Ralph Ellison and Sun Ra through Parliament's funky 1970s and Janelle Monae's cybernetic present, Tribe's uncanny artifact includes a signal change: the future is now.[55] The endgame is clear. From our impending environmental crisis to close-minded and belligerent nationalisms to Malthusian global pandemics—we now have quantifiable data that "the end is nigh." Fittingly, rich white one-percenters are making arrangements.

The video for "The Space Program" makes the writing on the wall clear as Q-Tip teleports out of his space pod to play chess with Death—a reference to Ingmar Bergman's *The Seventh Seal* (1957) and its filmic vision of the end times. Even though Tip wins the game, Tribe's front man succumbs to an oxygen leak. A small onboard screen in the spacecraft connects our present Black Lives Matter moment to the newly (?) bleak future: "I can't breathe"—a chilling reference to the final words of police brutality victim Eric Garner. The message puts these fantastic end-time scenarios in dialogue with the interminable, real, and present history of end-time realities of 400 years (and counting) of African American oppression.

Notably, a central hypertext in the nexus of meaning of Tribe's landmark recording is the main sample of the track's hook: a repeated line and core message of Andrew Hill's 1970 cut for Blue Note Records, "Lift Every Voice." The line that Tribe samples from that angularly futuristic, yet funky experimental jazz piece, is an Afrofuturist one: "Move on to the stars." Indeed, with lines like "Our spiritual life has laid the foundation to evolve," the Hill track lays out a vision wholly in keeping with Sun Ra's episteme of Black transcendence. Read against "Lift Off," the Hill sample vibes with this track's "scars"-to-"stars" ethos, even if Tribe's "you stuck here" hook takes a decidedly skeptical view of Black transcendence on the wings of (white, privatizing) neoliberalism.

But most remarkably in this hypertextual nexus, just as Tribe's DJ Ali Shaheed Muhammad uses this sample to bridge the ghetto and the stars—transcending both gentrification and SpaceX—so too does Andrew Hill in 1970. For the title of that high-modernist Blue Note recording about the spiritual inheritance and continuing mission of African Americans is "Lift Every Voice," a titular excerpt from—and clear reference to—"Lift Every Voice and Sing," the 1905 "black national anthem" penned by James Weldon and John Rosamond Johnson, which tracks the path of transcendence "Out from the gloomy past / 'Til now we stand at last / Where the white gleam of our bright star is cast."

"The Space Program" is thus a rich offering in the tradition of Black songs of transcendence. Updating the old adage, it keeps "our feet on the ground and our head in the ~~clouds~~ stars." If Tribe's "The Space Program" fails to fully endorse the Black transcendence of "Lift Off"—and Jay, Ye, and Bey's critical excess—it does, nonetheless, give us something of a confirmation of their prophetic work on *Watch the Throne*. The endgame *is* upon us. We must escape or evolve.

Or we can party like it's 1999 . . . in Paris!

CHAPTER 3

# "After They've Seen Paree"

## *The Mastery of Form*

When my restless hands caress those white breasts, they grasp white civilization and dignity and make them mine.

—FRANTZ FANON, *PEAU NOIRE, MASQUES BLANCS (BLACK SKIN, WHITE MASKS)* (1952/1967)

The third track of *Watch the Throne*, the Grammy-winning single, "Niggas in Paris," gets to the heart of Jay and Ye's project of excess and critique on the album. As "Lift Off" ends, Beyoncé's voice echoes through the heavens on the reverberating and remixed lines "We gon' take it to the moon, take it to the stars / How many people you know can take it this far?" The track is empowering, transcendent, and uplifting—excessive and transformative in all the right ways. But as the first lines of "Niggas in Paris" crossfade in, we begin to hear very different valences of excess. In what seems to be a direct response to Queen Bey's rhetorical question—"How many people you know can take it this far?"—Will Ferrell posits the unlikely answer: "We're gonna skate to one song, one song only."

The line, of course, is from the 2007 film *Les Rois du Patin* (The Skate Kings)—a comedy better known by its US release title: *Blades of Glory*.[1] The absurd Ferrell sample is an odd rejoinder to the story of African American transcendence that we've just left. Yet it is also a formal device common to Kanye's production style, which regularly includes such unlikely cameos and breakneck changes of pace and feel. Indeed, the film sample sets the tone for the track as a whole, pivoting—or, better, pirouetting—from the life-and-death, heaven-or-hell moralizing of the first two cuts to the swaggering and pointedly offensive spectacle of "Niggas in Paris."

The sample comes from a moment in the film's narrative where the self-styled bad boy of competitive figure skating is himself *taking it too far* by demanding that he and his partner skate to "My Humps," a singularly cringey track from the Black Eyed Peas 2005 album, *Monkey Business*.[2] Continuing the string of signification here, Jay enters with the menacingly pitch-shifted and slowed down line "Ball so hard motherfuckers wanna fine me." Here, his Black excellence has also taken it *too far.*

In the space of five seconds, the album's heady considerations of Eurocentric hegemony spiral downward from Beyoncé's celebratory excess to Ferrell's sophomoric excess and Jay's Black excellence as excess—a troubling change in tenor that recalls the 180-degree turn from Jay's good cop to Ye's bad cop on "No Church in the Wild." For "ball so hard motherfuckers wanna fine me" is Jay's "human right to swagger and swear"—the right to excel and the right to boast of that excellence. Most importantly, here in these opening lines we get the first clear instance of a paradoxical theme that runs throughout the track, and the album more broadly: the idea that Black success must be punished. It is a theme central to Jay and Ye's strategy of critical excess and is one for which we've been prepared in the previous lyrical and musical rhetorics. The incessantly repeated line, "ball so hard motherfuckers wanna fine me," entrenches the track's central critical message: Black excellence makes a mockery of established (white) norms and must be stopped at all costs.

The theme is well established in US history and a common one in the African American experience of racial oppression. Black people who rose above their pre-ordained station by excelling in their fields of expertise were subject to deep hatred and structural disqualification from the powers that be—in the US and Europe alike. From Jack Johnson, Jesse Owens, and Jackie Robinson to Shaquille O'Neal and Serena Williams; from Marian Anderson, Paul Robeson, Louis Armstrong, and Nina Simone to Kendrick Lamar, Nicki Minaj, Young Thug, and Lil Nas X; from W. E. B. Du Bois and James Baldwin to Angela Davis and Ta-Nehisi Coates—to name just a very few—Black excellence was *and is* routinely constructed as alternately impolite and cutthroat, excessive and deviant. What's more, excessive ability in fields ranging from sports and music to arts and letters and beyond is essentialized, naturalized, diminished, and systematically disqualified from participation or otherwise given an asterisk to explain away their place in history; to racialize their personal gifts, hard work, and dedication, to dethrone them from their rightful places.[3]

*Watch the Throne*'s performance of excellence is, by virtue of its very

Blackness, excessive. It is an excess that is, by virtue of its very Blackness, an immanent critique. And in its 2011 Obama-Era context, *Watch the Throne*'s swaggering celebration of "Black excellence, opulence, decadence" appears to have come at an inflection point—a point when Black excellence exceeded the limits of white tolerance. This is a time when "*the obligation*" of Du Bois's "lordly and generous whites" has run out and, instead, requires a new level of policing and punishing. Indeed, the album appears to have come at a time in America's socioeconomic life when Black excellence had reached a *critical mass.*

## "LIABLE TO GO MICHAEL": CRITICAL EXCESS AND STRATEGIC ESSENTIALISM

Jay begins the first verse of "Niggas in Paris" riffing on the opening "Ball so hard" line and further developing the theme of punishing Black excellence. After issuing swag-filled lines about his entrepreneurial vision and ownership role with what would soon be the NBA's Brooklyn Nets ("Movin' the Nets to BK"), Jay continues:

> (Ball so hard) This shit weird
> We ain't even 'posed to be here
> (Ball so hard) But since we here
> It's only right that we be fair
> Psycho: I'm liable to go Michael, take your pick:
> Jackson, Tyson, Jordan, Game 6

That Black excellence is *always already* constructed as deviantly "psycho" seems all too apparent to Jay. Black advancement is policed (by "fine," prison, gerrymandering, or worse) and maintained as "weird" and out of place—whether that felt lack of belonging is of the rapper-at-the-Met-Gala variety or the displacement of the Middle Passage. And despite this weirdness, Jay seems to argue, what's fair is that we give our best effort—even if playing "fair" in this way is liable to elicit cries of "foul!"

Importantly, with his opening list of three Michaels, "Jackson, Tyson, Jordan," Jay gives a nod to his mentor and predecessor on the throne, the "King of New York," Biggie Smalls. On, "Victory" (1997), the last recorded verse before his untimely demise, Biggie raps:

Excellence is my presence, never tense
Never hesitant, leave a nigga bent real quick
Real sick, brawl nights, I perform like Mike
Any one: Tyson, Jordan, Jackson

From his "excellence" to his "never hesitant" internal-rhyming flow, Biggie's swaggering verse equates his own "sick," "psycho," out-of-his-head performative excellence with the Black excellence of the forthcoming "Mikes." Each a generational talent in their field—Mike Tyson (boxing's "Iron Mike"), Michael Jordan (basketball's "GOAT"), Michael Jackson (music's "King of Pop")—what these three Mikes also have in common is that they were all so transformatively *good* that they became (with our help, I will argue) dangerously *bad*. That is, what they all had in common was that their excellence was defined as freakish—and this definition eventually came to define them. Indeed, this is a social discourse and material dialectic that we will investigate later in this chapter—and in chapter 4 as we investigate the construction of Black deviance and/as madness from Frantz Fanon to Nina Simone and MAGA Kanye.

In a 2015 *Rolling Stone* feature on the late, great soul singer Bill Withers—an article that made the rounds after the artist's 2020 death—the Roots' Questlove offers the following tribute: "He's the last African-American Everyman," says Questlove. "Jordan's vertical jump has to be higher than everyone. Michael Jackson has to defy gravity. On the other side of the coin, we're often viewed as primitive animals. We rarely land in the middle. Bill Withers is the closest thing Black people have to a Bruce Springsteen."[4] Questlove's characterization of Withers as the "last African-American Everyman" cuts right to the heart of this book's frame of subhuman and superhuman—and the obscured category of human, the obscured, nigh-impossible "African-American Everyman." And notably, this celebrated hip hop knowledge bearer also uses two of the Michaels (Jordan and Jackson) to make his point: the Black everyman is dead. There is no Black Springsteen. American racism only allows two categories of Black people: the best and the worst, the exceptional and the beastly.

Returning to "Niggas in Paris," in his line "Psycho: I'm liable to go Michael, take your pick: / Jackson, Tyson, Jordan, Game 6," Jay transforms Biggie's "Mikes" to "Michaels," but now with a signal difference: a heightened critical excess. Indeed, the changed order seems important. From a pop-culture perspective, we might take Jay's "psycho" frame, and thus my reading, at face value for the first two: Jackson and Tyson. We might agree that Michael Jackson and Mike Tyson exhibited "deviant," most likely dangerous, tendencies, but why include Michael Jordan in this list? The answer seems to come in the "game 6" specificity of *this particular Michael*. For the phrase "game 6" signifies, for any serious NBA fan, not only Jordan's last game, but Jordan's last shot. (Even though it wasn't.)

While that "last shot" secured Jordan's sixth NBA title—and his legacy—the mythology around Michael Jordan obscures the reality of his complicated career, and like Michael Jackson, splits devotees into love-him and hate-him camps. Take your pick: hero or villain. There's no middle ground. While the former camp sees the Greatest of All Time (in pretty much anything), the latter group sees a player who *took it too far*; a victim of his own excellence; a star who betrayed his fans at the height of that excellence to pursue a childhood pipe dream (professional baseball); a player who returned unceremoniously to reclaim his throne after that seemingly self-centered and unmitigated disaster; a player who spent a forgettable final two years playing for a different team—*after his last shot.*

Indeed, as the award-winning sports journalist Michael Lee writes in his exploration of that "last shot," this, Jordan's crowning achievement, was more likely a foul on the man who was guarding him, Byron Russell of the Utah Jazz. This is the other Jordan that Jay sees. As Lee writes, "Shoving aside Russell added a few layers of intrigue, because there will always be a debate over whether the shot should've been allowed and it only added to Jordan's mystique of having mind control over officials."[5] Further complicated by allegations of a long-running gambling problem, it is this "mind control" Jordan—this superhuman performer—that Jay has in mind. But Jay does not eschew this tension. He embraces it. Jay seems to say: if you want me to be *that* Michael, the "game six" "psycho" figure, I'm happy to oblige. Indeed, since Black excellence is always already policed and constructed as "psycho," I'd rather own that shit and tune this discourse to my advantage.

For our purposes here, this "liable to go Michael" disclaimer is a form of *strategic essentialism* that allows Jay to parlay America's nightmare of Black excellence into sociocultural power—be it *Menace II Society*'s "young, black, and didn't give a fuck" or Du Bois's "human right to swagger and swear and waste." What's more, this cultural jiujitsu—this flipping the script—is central to an understanding of the cultural mechanics of critical excess. Indeed, this is the same strategic reversal that transforms

Biggie Smalls into "the *Notorious* B.I.G."—an alter ego that is the same but better. And worse.

This paradoxical discourse with no middle ground—this racial mechanics that demonizes Black success just as it endemicizes Black failure—is key in understanding the intersectional nature of race and racism.[6] Recalling the beastly discourse of the catlike humans in the *Throne* album art, Ronald Radano writes of the "beastly" gendered, sexualized, disabled, and dehumanized valences of racial excess in his article "Hot Fantasies: American Modernism and the Idea of Black Rhythm." Describing the emergence of the Black cultural forms that would power the nascent popular music industry at the dawn of the twentieth century, Radano's analysis of these mechanics is worth considering at length:

> Black music's propulsive and seductive "hot" rhythm—a term linked etymologically to forms of *excess*—seemed at once undetermined and saturated with context-specific meaning. As a conflation of musical and racial discourses, it brought together two primary realms of otherness: those "unspeakable things unspoken" that consumed as they were denied by modern white America. . . . The primitivist orthodoxy of "natural rhythm" afforded a new sense of racial pride that was ironically reinforced by white supremacist assumptions of a bestial Negro instinct.[7]

In a footnote elaborating those etymological links between "hotness" and "forms of excess," Radano explains: "By the 1890s, the term [hot] had also identified positive attributes ('hot art'), together with extremes of physical display and self-indulgence: hotness evoked images of violence, suffering, danger, and intoxication."[8]

Notably, this dehumanizing musical/racial excess is discursively linked to Black masculinity through "[t]he vast repetition of references to black music as a fever, drug, disease, and intoxicant," indicating that "the threat of black music related above all to fears of miscegenation, through which hot rhythm becomes a metonym of the black male body and, specifically, Negro semen or blood."[9] In short, the same hypermasculine, infectious, and "bestial" stereotypes that were cast on Black men at the dawn of the mass culture industry became the bedrock on which popular music's driving and "seductive" rhythms would gain form. Indeed, these excessive stereotypes of the Jazz Age grew directly out of America's first popular music and its animalized master tropes: the swaggering, hypermasculine Zip

Coon (and his foil, the bumbling but witty Jim Crow).[10] Gifted with that much power, it's no wonder these same performative stereotypes would be taken up, honed, and deployed, "providing a means of affirming positive identities in an egregiously racist, national environment."[11] This is strategic essentialism; this is critical excess.

## "HOW YA GONNA KEEP 'EM DOWN ON THE FARM?"

After the Will Ferrell sample ends and the detuned "ball so hard" line comes to a close, the track begins in earnest with a high-pitched beeping hook emerging from the background and gaining direction with a deep swinging bass line against sharp quarter-note snare hits, evocative of Southern trap music. Lingering in the background of the loop is what seems to be a call and response between a higher-pitched questioning "yeah?" and a lower-pitched affirming "yeah!" that, almost imperceptibly, adds propulsive syncopation by anticipating each downbeat on the "and" of the fourth beat of each respective bar.

Notably, the beeping hook is drawn from a trap sample library called *Dirty South Bangaz*, while the call and response is sampled from the opening of an Alan Lomax field recording, released on *Sounds of the South* (Southern Folk Heritage Series). Together with the trap snare patterns and a trunk-rattling bass pedal point, the samples thus elaborate a theme of "the South" despite the temporal and stylistic distance between the two. Where the beeping hook sample is titled "072.5 Fm," the Lomax recording is titled "Baptizing Scene (1959)—Reverend W. A. Donaldson & Congregation."[12] The two samples could not be more different; one, the posthuman synth tones of the Big Fish Audio licensing group (which *seems* to be somewhere in California) and the other, the hyperlocal and immediately human cries of the African American congregation at St. James Baptist Church in Huntsville, Alabama, in 1959—a recording that goes on to feature the whooping of the African American pastor and the ecstatic cries of a newly saved believer.[13]

The sonic rhetoric of southernness that Kanye deploys on "Niggas in Paris" paves the way for a heightened and transcendent swagger that casts Jay and Ye's luxe Parisian escapades in stark relief against Du Bois's "humble black folks." Indeed, those Du Bois lines from his *Darkwater* (1920), which are central to my framing of critical excess's "human right to swagger and swear and waste," are preceded by an opening chapter that personalizes the economic trajectory of the Du Bois family, from South Carolinian slavery to subsistence farming in the Berkshire Hills of Western Massachusetts—freedom, of a sort, in the North. "At about the time of my birth economic pressure was transmuting the family generally from farmers to 'hired' help. Some revolted and migrated westward, others went cityward as cooks and barbers."[14] The chapter, "The Shadow of Years," recounts the postslavery Reconstruction Era's retrenchment of racial oppression, both South and North, and frames the great majority of Black Americans trapped in sharecropping poverty as "revolting" from that exploitative form of farm labor. This cycle of poverty may be freedom of a kind, but it is freedom without reparation. Freedom without a leg to stand on. "Freedom to hunger" as Dr. King put it.[15]

Importantly, Du Bois describes those "revolting" from farm labor in the 1860s and '70s in terms that echo one of the biggest popular hits of his own postwar period—a tune that appears to have been ringing in Du Bois's ears in 1920: "How Ya Gonna Keep 'em Down on the Farm (After They've Seen Paree?)." The 1919 tune was popularized for the vaudeville stage by Sophie Tucker and recorded for Pathé in March of the same year by James Reese Europe and his 369th US Infantry "Hell Fighters" Band. The lyrics tell a fitting story for the famed African American military band freshly returned to Harlem from Paris and their deployment in World War I.[16] While ostensibly about any enlisted man returning from Europe to the family farm, in the Hell Fighters' up-tempo and syncopated interpretation, African American histories of slave plantation labor and the lingering question of racial equality loom large.

To highlight this elephant-in-the-room subtext of the tens of thousands of *Black* soldiers returning from the war, Europe's arrangement of the song interpolates a fragment of the famed blackface minstrel tune "Zip Coon" (aka "Turkey in the Straw") just before Noble Sissle's voice enters, with the lyrics:

> How ya gonna keep 'em down on the farm
> After they've seen Paree?
> How ya gonna keep them away from Broadway,
> Jazzin' around and paintin' the town
> How ya gonna keep 'em away from harm?
> That's the mystery

They'll never want to see a rake or plow
And who the deuce can parlez-vous a cow?
How ya gonna keep 'em down on the farm
After they've seen Paree?

With sharp diction, elegant phrasing, and rolled Rs that ooze European class, Sissle lays it on thick. The performative rhetoric is perfectly tuned to add insult to (white) injury, twisting the knife in the hegemonic structures that had kept African Americans in servitude for (then) 300 years. How can you continue to oppress us now that we've served our country; now that we're more cultured than you? The swag is palpable.

Indeed, just the year before, Du Bois had argued in no uncertain terms for African Americans to take up the cause of "equality, freedom, and democracy" by joining their white compatriots in supporting the war effort and enlisting as soldiers. In that July 1918 article for the NAACP journal *The Crisis,* titled "Close Ranks," Du Bois urged his African American readership "Let us, while this war lasts, forget our special grievances and close our ranks shoulder to shoulder with our white fellow citizens and the allied nations that are fighting for democracy."[17] Du Bois's strategic position was clear: by taking up the cause of freedom and earning their stripes, African Americans could simultaneously demonstrate their patriotism and highlight the unfinished project of "equality, freedom, and democracy" at home. Surely, this greatest sacrifice would earn Black people equality and respect at home.

In a follow-up article for *The Crisis* after the war, Du Bois passionately detailed the irony of Black soldiers who fought for freedom abroad returning to their own county that is not yet free. Du Bois cautioned "This is the country to which we Soldiers of Democracy return. . . . But by the God of Heaven, we are cowards and jackasses if now that the war is over, we do not marshal every ounce of our brain and brawn to fight a sterner, longer, more unbending battle against the forces of hell in our own land."[18] In that May 1919 article, "Returning Soldiers," Du Bois was arguing for what Houston Baker would come to term the "Mastery of Form" in his *Modernism and the Harlem Renaissance.* Baker's argument held that in mastering the forms of white discourse and artistry, African Americans could gain voice and powers of representation. While focused on the literary realm, Baker's theory clearly applies to Du Bois's strategic effort to play by the rules of white civic engagement and patriotic discourse in arguing for African American citizens to "Close Ranks" and join white Americans in support of the US war effort. The endgame, of course, was to prove their fitness for citizenship—to prove their Americanness—by mastering the forms of white civic engagement. Such a strategic approach was central to the Harlem Renaissance program of cultural and economic uplift—a wide-ranging program elaborated and debated in landmark works of the postwar years, from Alain Locke's *New Negro* (1925) to Langston Hughes's "The Negro Artist and the Racial Mountain" (1926) and beyond.[19]

Du Bois systematically, rationally, and eloquently builds his case for equality by mastering the form of (white) American patriotism in "Returning Soldiers," his prose dripping with the studied nationalist pride of "Make way for Democracy!" and "This is the Fatherland for which we fought!" Yet, just as he writes of "we soldiers of Democracy" he pivots to more critical territory, formally enumerating the enduring hypocrisies of structural racism in this land of freedom through sections on lynching, disenfranchisement, theft, and insult against its Black citizens. Indeed, his prose anticipates the same fire of "swagger and swear and waste" he would conjure in *Darkwater* a year later.

In a section that begins "It [the US] encourages *ignorance*," Du Bois picks apart the dehumanizing hypocrisy of white American double-dealing in (withheld) education.

> It has never really tried to educate the Negro. A dominant minority does not want Negroes educated. It wants servants, dogs, whores, and monkeys. And when this land allows a reactionary group by its stolen political power to force as many black folk into these categories as it possibly can, it cries contemptible hypocrisy: "They threaten us with degeneracy; they cannot be educated."[20]

The language is a perfect accounting of structural racism's dehumanizing tautological mechanics. How does one miseducate a whole demographic? Why, simply say "they cannot be educated" to begin with, of course! Through a combination of oratorical passion and logical rhetoric—scattered with strategically dehumanizing images—the passage does its work. It details the blatant hypocrisies and double binds of US racial structures.

More importantly for our purposes here, the passage illuminates the roots of this double bind thus laying bare the logic of strategic essentialism: *if society is going to systematically deny us access to our rights, lynch us, disenfranchise us, miseducate us, steal from us, and insult us—if that's how they're gonna keep us down on the farm—then we're going to systematically become its nightmare. We can master the forms of American civic engagement and take our place among equals if given a level playing field. But if you want whores and monkeys, we can give you whores and monkeys.*

So, what happens when those systematically dehumanized people game the system? What happens when that "ignorance" becomes "sophisticated?" What happens when, 100 years on from "How Ya Gonna Keep 'em Down on the Farm (After They've Seen Paree)," those people not only master the forms of white (capitalist) hegemony but learn to deform and remake those same rules to suit themselves. "Niggas in Paris" offers us a chance to examine these questions and examine this movement from the "Mastery of Form" to the "Deformation of Mastery," offering up a snapshot of the continuing salience of Du Bois's critique of white universalist hypocrisy and the continuing relevance of Baker's strategic nomenclature from the Harlem Renaissance to today's #BlackLivesMatter movement—and the racist "dominant minority" that still holds power over a century later.

## FROM "THE TALENTED TENTH" TO ONE-PERCENTERS

The balance of Jay's verse moves from the MC's "we ain't even 'posed to be here" sense of displacement in upper-class *soirées* to the "shock" of not only having escaped the US, but having escaped his own drug-dealing past and a prison-industrial complex that should have successfully policed and disciplined him.[21] After the "this shit weird" and "Michael" lines, the track continues:

> (Ball so hard) Got a broke clock
> Rollies that don't tick tock
> Audemars that's losing time
> Hidden behind all these big rocks
>
> (B-Ball so hard) I'm shocked too
> I'm supposed to be locked up too
> You escaped what I escaped
> You'd be in Paris getting fucked up too

Of course, Paris is not only the preferred destination for Jay and Ye, but has been the gold standard for such escapes since Josephine Baker and Sidney Bechet first reported back about that city's cosmopolitan promise of equality—of humanity. Of course, that promise was never perfect and belied the colonialist realities and racial fantasies of the "City of Light"—what Fred Moten calls, "that capital of national cosmopolitanism-in-primitivism."[22] As we'll see, on "Niggas in Paris" Jay and Ye take that twinned opulence and decadence, remaking the city in their own image—and taking the idea of Europe to its postcolonial conclusion.

Nonetheless, Jay and Ye's escape fantasy is grounded in the reality of the unparalleled racial disparity in US incarceration rates. Despite comprising around 12 percent of the US population in 2011, "African Americans constituted 2.3 million, or 34 percent, of the total 6.8 million correctional population," a rate more than five times that of European Americans.[23] The track thus continues the liberating "escape" narrative trajectory of "Lift Off," and its question "how many people you know can take it this far?" But now the "escape" leads not to the rarefied and transcendent space of "Lift Off," but to a degraded, belligerent, and "fucked up" space centered on a wholly different valence of excess—material wealth. Notably, this "fucked up" space is Europe.

"Niggas in Paris" is the first track on the album that prominently features the "luxe lives," champagne parties, and *haute couture* brands that garnered such attention in the popular press. Here, Jay-Z boasts how his high-end watches are so loaded with diamonds that they cease to function—a form of excess that nicely mirrors his boastful earlier line "The Nets could go 0 for 82 and I look at you like: this shit gravy." In other words, like high-end watches that don't work, this is a team that increases Jay's cachet despite the possibility that they may never win a game.[24] Interestingly, while the so-good-I'm-bad constructions of "Ball so hard motherfuckers wanna fine me" and the monstrous excellence of the three Michaels gesture to Jay's hypermacho potency, the bling of these first "luxury rap" lines seems to ring hollow. Jay has assembled a collection of expensive sportsmen and a collection of expensive watches that are merely for show.[25]

As we continue to position Jay and Ye's album in a longer historical view of Black music, it is of foundational importance to understand their work in relation to the Harlem Renaissance's race leaders of 100 years earlier: "the talented tenth" in Du Bois's construction—the top 10 percent of Black race leaders. As we have seen, from Du Bois's erudite prose and

James Reese Europe's seductive rhythms to Alain Locke's uplifting philosophical project and Zora Neal Hurston's empowering folkloric research, this work in arts and letters was drafted into service to pull up the community on the strength of such Black excellence, intellect, and artistry. Indeed, Langston Hughes's "The Negro Artist and the Racial Mountain" is a searing critique and revision of this "ideology of uplift"—a recognition that the mastery of (white) form is a Sisyphean task; that Black people will never be judged equal on white terms; that African American artists must trust in their own excellence and "stand on top of the mountain, free within ourselves."[26]

Indeed, this is the subtle critique of "Rollies that don't tick tock" and "Nets could go 0-for-82 and I look at you like this shit gravy." Just as Jay rises from talented tenth to one-percenter and masters that whitest of forms—capitalism—so too does his hyper-masculine Black excellence seem strangely impotent. Famously coupled with "opulence" and "decadence" on the album's tenth track, "Murder to Excellence," the symbols of wealth and luxury here evoke the lazy aristocracy of "the one percent." This is a very different excess than the work and suffering that are rewarded in "Lift Off." It is, instead, the gilded excess of "Lifestyles of the Rich and Famous"—the excess of Donald Trump; of silver spoons; of luxury materials and leisure time; excess as escapism; of "getting fucked up." The track seems to recognize the pitfalls of being in thrall to wealth. But it also seems to revel in it. It is, after all, a pop song—a unit and a signet of capitalist exchange value.

One of the best examples of this flattening of the Racial (capitalist) Mountain comes in the secret final track "Illest Motherfucker Alive." As Jay escapes the thrall of this most elevated form of white supremacy, Jay and Ye also nod to Langston Hughes's infamous peak. As Jay puts it on the track:

> When I say it then you see it, it ain't only in the music
> Basquiats, Warhols serving as my muses
> My house like a museum so I see 'em when I'm peein'
> Usually you have this much taste, you European
> That's the end of that way of thinking, nigga never again.

Just as he seems to accede to the museumized logic of Western ideologies of high art, Jay exceeds the logic thereof by placing these icons—works by Basquiat and Warhol—in his bathroom. In just a few lines of verse—and a few bars of urgent sonic swagger—he undermines the ideology of museumized art, nobility by birth, and Europe's *sine qua non*, whiteness. With critical excess typical of the album, here Jay simultaneously claims his non-European capacity for "taste" and goes on to offer the idea that he has so much taste that his muses accompany him on a trip to the bathroom. With poignant irony, however, he does so both artfully and passionately—as he and Ye do with countless other conceptual and performative gems throughout the album.

Indeed, the final track is something of a reprise of "Niggas in Paris," from its "big face Rollies" to the black-tie imagery of Jay and his family taking over for previous generations of (white) pop royalty—Elvis and the Beatles—"front row at the Grammys." Most of all, Jay's first lines reprise his "ball so hard" mantra and perform a detailed accounting of his "Michael Jordan swag":

> King Hov, I'm exactly what the fuck you think
> Eleven in a row, Bill Russell rings, Michael Jordan swag
> Y'all think Michael Jordan bad
> Nigga, I got five more rings than Michael Jordan had

Here Jay—the one-percenter—puts his accomplishments in historical context. If you think Michael Jordan is bad (excessively good) with his six championships, don't forget that Jay's got "five more rings" (in this case, number-one albums), totaling eleven, just like Bill Russell.

But just as "Niggas in Paris" sets the bar impossibly high, so too does "Illest Motherfucker Alive" remind us of the dangers that come with Black excellence. In the hook's title lyrics for this final track, Jay and Ye reprise the sword of Damocles imagery from "No Church in the Wild."

> JAY: Whole world aiming at a nigga head
> YE: Because I'm the illest motherfucker alive

Just as "bad" is good, so too is "illest" here, best. And, as ever, Black excellence must be policed and targeted.

## "DOCTORS SAY I'M THE ILLEST"

At the end of Jay's verse on "Niggas in Paris" a menacing rising synth line builds tension and marks the transition to the hook: Jay's "ball so hard" call and Kanye's repeated "That shit cray[zy]" response. Ye's verse on the track picks up where Jay left off—"You'd be in Paris getting fucked up too." Notably, Ye's verse is something of a master class in offensiveness, rattling off sexist, classist, and racist tropes in ever-more-inventively excessive forms. Over the beeping hook and a now-prominent hollow-toned bass drum, the track begins with a humiliating scene that reduces the institution of marriage to a transactional sexual test in a public toilet. To let the scene do its work, Ye mutes the final three notes of the *Dirty South Bangaz* hook and the accompanying bass and drum lines. The exposed setting highlights Ye's crass, drawn-out "Ah" sounds.

> She said "Ye can we get married at the maaall?"
> I said "look you need to crawl fore you baaall
> Come and meet me in the bathroom staaall
> And show me why you deserve to have it aaall"

Both lyrically and sonically, the effect is simply ugly.

From here, Kanye (convincingly) develops his asshole one-percenter character. He belittles a woman for ordering the "fish fillet" and humblebrags "oh, this old thing" about his luxury car—while laughing at his own jokes throughout. Yet, more than simply acting the fool, on "Niggas in Paris" Kanye lays bare and further elaborates the ways that class and language work to uphold the fallacy of race and its entanglement with received ideas about Europe and/as nobility. It is here that his irredeemably ugly setup pays off.

After the rising synth line reprises, further heightening the tension, he spits the infamous lines:

> Bougie girl, grab my hand
> Fuck that bitch (if) she don't wanna dance
> Excuse my French, but I'm in France,
> I'm just sayin'
> Prince Williams ain't do it right if you ask me
> 'Cause (if) I was him I woulda married/Mary Kate and Ashley

In the first two couplets, Ye plays on the idiom "excuse my French," misdirecting the listener toward the ear-catching, misogynistic red flag, "Fuck that bitch," while slyly playing on the only French word in the lyric: *bougie*.

The wordplay is a subversive bit of artistry for listeners patient enough to abide the apparent sexism. For here, Ye is showing us what happens to signifiers of European superiority when confronted by "Niggas in Paris"—what happens to European modes of deference at a grand ball, when that (white) authority is questioned. In short, "the spell . . ." (of anyone giving a shit) "is broken."

Continuing his dismantling of the institution of marriage and the fragile white femininity (that *always already* masks fragile white masculinity), he trolls the British royal, Prince William—getting his name wrong in the process. Here, he drags the Duke of Cambridge down to the gutter level of pop culture by proposing a polygamist arrangement with TV's "Olson twins." Punning on the word/name "married"/"Mary," Ye uses a slowed-down sample to reference the child stars of the 1990s sitcom *Full House.* Here, he's probably referencing an eerily slowed-down 2010 internet meme created from a 1995 Mary-Kate and Ashley "rap" video called "Gimme Pizza."[27] Indeed, the child stars also did a series of direct-to-video feature films about the trouble-making Americans travelling abroad, the first of which was 1999's *Passport to Paris.* Ye seems to be collapsing the pizza meme onto the film series, with the well-established trope of irreverent-young-Americans in too-fancy-old-Europe. Importantly, in bringing together these seemingly disparate worlds—"real" royals and wannabe movie stars—he also reminds the listener that both the royal and the B-list celebs exist in their truest form in *the tabloid press*—a fact that, today, is manifestly obvious in Brexit-era England. And as Donald John Trump's election has shown us, the tabloid press now wags the dog globally—a new shared reality across the Atlantic.

Just as Jay flattens the "Racial Mountain" and the idea of European superiority with his artistic critique, so too does Ye systematically deface and destabilize the received idea of Europe. And just as Jay raps about his luxury European watches that don't work, so too does Ye transform luxury European brands "Gucci" and "Louis" (Vuitton) into ghetto greetings, rapping "What's Gucci my nigga? / What's Louis my killa?" As Jonah Wiener writes in his 2012 article for *Slate,* "The case is significant because 'Niggas in Paris' is the most popular piece of Western culture to ever feature the word *nigga* so prominently. . . . The song itself touches, crucially, on themes of racial transgression and racial progress. Its title is so pungently evocative because with it, Jay and Kanye proudly place the barbarians ('niggas') not merely within the palace gates ('Paris'), but high up on the social ladder."[28] As we will see in the next chapter, these transformational transgressions are deformations of white mastery. By collapsing rarefied European *haute couture* and aristocratic comportment on to street-level ghetto culture and vacuous American media culture, Jay and Ye are not just revisiting age-old gags about uncultured Americans in Europe, they are reframing what is possible. They are ending "Europe." "That's the end of that way of thinking, nigga never again."

In the penultimate couplet of the verse, Ye turns the mirror back on himself. He situates all of the studied offensiveness over his previous lines with the couplet "Doctors say I'm the illest / 'Cause I'm suffering from realness," offering a bit of self-reflexivity and giving us a sense that he can see himself, his own ugly reflection. The moment is an important one, as it gives us a modicum of assurance that Ye is not "off the rails" (as he's so often accused of being) and also offers us further insight into his critique. Just as the "Whole world (is) aiming at a nigga head / Because (he's) the illest motherfucker alive," Kanye is here flipping the script on this causality, suggesting that he is "the illest" not because he is losing his grip on reality, but because his reality is one that polices and punishes Black excellence. This is a reality that mobs and lynches; a reality that polices and murders Black and Brown people with impunity.

Importantly, in its reference to mental illness vis-à-vis societal norms, Ye's line recall's Frantz Fanon's diagnosis of Western racial/colonial oppression. Asked to treat the mentally ill in colonial Algeria, the famed psychiatrist and anticolonial activist concluded that mental illness was, in a way, not an illness at all, but a logical outcome of and a healthy response to an illogical and unhealthy environment. This is Fanon's truism that you cannot cure a sick patient without first curing the society that is causing the illness, the realization that treating mental illness such as this is merely tending to the symptoms and will never cure the disease. Writing to the Resident Minister of Algeria's colonial government in 1956, Fanon explains.

> If psychiatry is the medical technique that aims to enable man no longer to be a stranger to his environment, I owe it to myself to affirm that the Arab, permanently an alien in his own country, lives in a state of absolute depersonalization. . . . The social structure existing in Algeria was hostile to any attempt to put the individual back where he belonged.[29]

Fanon's argument in *Toward the African Revolution* will be of central import as we consider the discourse around Kanye's own "madness"—his unconscionable "gaffes" and mind-blowing conciliations to white power in the Trump era. For now, suffice it to say that Ye's ugliness is clearly not off the cuff. Ye has earned his "human right to swagger and swear and waste"—and he wants you to know it.

### "APESHIT": OF GORILLAS AND GUERRILLAS

Where Jay ends his verse with the lines "If you escaped what I escaped / You'd be in Paris gettin' fucked up too," Ye ends his verse with the title lines "Got my niggas in Paris / And they goin' gorillas (huh?!)." Here, the track's second offering from *Blades of Glory*—an ensuing argument about "My Humps" between the two figure skaters—is cut into the track as a direct response to Ye's ear-catching and provocative "gorillas" line.

HEDER: I don't even know what that means
FERRELL: No one knows what it means, but it's provocative!
HEDER: No it's not, it's gross
FERRELL: Gets the people *going*!

Of course, the difference is that Ye does know "what it means." The "provocative" "goin' gorillas" line resonates with a long line of strategically essentialist "gorilla" imagery in hip hop—and the much longer history of dehumanizing animal imagery in blackface minstrelsy that hip hop engages and deforms.

Ye's "niggas . . . goin' gorillas" here invokes Ice Cube and Da Lench Mob's 1992 *Guerillas in tha Mist* and countless other script-flipping deformations of the racist trope of Black-man-as-gorilla in the hip hop pantheon. Notably, it also prefigures Ye's own 2013 work on *Yeezus*, an album that follows up on *Watch the Throne* by further developing the connections between royalty, whiteness, Black excellence, and policing. In particular, the track "Black Skinhead" opens with a meditation on these connections:

Enter the kingdom (Black)
But watch who you bring home
They see a Black man with a white woman
At the top floor they gone come to kill King Kong

The royal "Black beast" on the top floor, King Kong, seems perfect proof of concept for Jay and Ye's work on the policing of Black excellence via the dehumanization of Black people—the subhumanization of superhumans.

Notably, Beyoncé's 2018 work with Jay on "Apeshit" from their duo album, *Everything Is Love*, also develops this gorilla discourse along with the main themes of *Watch the Throne*—now with a much-needed Black feminist update. The track's widely discussed music video was shot in the Louvre and embraces the positive, "Black excellence" valences of the primitivizing phrase "goin' Apeshit" (going wild for).[30] After asking her listeners, "Have you ever seen the crowd goin' apeshit?" while posing and dancing among the Louvre's countless icons of the Western tradition (the *Mona Lisa, Winged Victory of Samothrace, The Coronation of Napoleon,* etc.), Beyoncé gets down to the bottom line:

> Gimme my check, put some respect on my check
> Or pay me in equity, watch me reverse out of debt
> He got a bad bitch, we livin' lavish
> I get expensive fabrics, I got expensive habits

This is a not just a Black takeover, but a Black *feminist* takeover of the Louvre.

Indeed, Beyoncé and Jay's video for "Apeshit" is nothing less than a realization of Jay's verse from the seventh track of *Watch the Throne,* "That's My Bitch," where Jay raps, "Put some colored girls in the MoMA" and concludes of his partner, Beyoncé, "you belong in museums." Where that track mentions New York's Museum of Modern Art by name, it also references the Louvre through a mention of its most famous painting: the *Mona Lisa.*

> Picasso was alive he woulda made her
> That's right, nigga, Mona Lisa can't fade her
> I mean, Marilyn Monroe, she is quite nice
> But why all the pretty icons always all white?

Further, through his reference to Marilyn Monroe, Jay recalls Andy Warhol's prints of the actress and pop icon and suggests that Beyoncé is of equal or surpassing beauty and fame but is systematically overlooked because of her race.

Thus, 2018's "Apeshit" answers *Watch the Throne*'s critique and makes good on its promise, as we see Beyoncé and Jay preside over a Black feminist takeover of the West's most prestigious museum. It is a performance of Black excellence, as Black and Brown women dance through the museum, highlighting the whiteness of the Louvre and becoming iconic artworks in and of themselves.

The "Apeshit" video begins in pitch black, yet the sounds of church bells and the descending major thirds of European police sirens locate us in Paris. Next, we see a shirtless and dreadlocked young Black angel in torn jeans squatting on the steps outside the museum's façade, warming her/his hands. From this setup, the video moves inside the Louvre, alternating between wide shots of the gilded and frescoed ceilings and tight shots of details from the collection—close-ups of the brushstrokes of the West's canonized artistic geniuses. A bell tolls for us ominously, with the hollow sounds of synth chords filling the empty, darkened galleries. Now, footsteps echo down the corridors and a suspenseful sweep of white noise heightens the tension, spilling out into the opening sounds of the track—a sparse trap beat of metallic attacks alternating around pitches a menacing minor sixth apart. Voices moan and interject "yi, yi, yi, yi, yi" as the camera slowly tightens in on a Black couple in front of a small painting at the far end of a long gallery space. They are standing, as you will by now have guessed, in front of the *Mona Lisa*. And for anyone who's ever been to the Louvre, the scene is utterly impossible. Not only are they not competing with 500 other tourists for a glimpse of the tiny painting, but they have their backs turned to da Vinci's masterpiece. As the scene turns to the two in all white atop a grand staircase, now with their backs to the *Winged Victory of Samothrace*—aka Nike, goddess of victory—we hear the wild screech of monkeys. The stage is thus set for the Carters' Black takeover of this singular monument to white civilization.

Beyoncé enters this rhetorical space with bling lyrics that could be drawn directly from *Watch the Throne*—lines about stacking money and sports cars, "expensive fabrics" and *haute couture*. Indeed, in one line from the last verse Bey *replaces* white wealth, flipping the script on equality discourses with the superhuman Afrofuturist inflections of "Lift Off":

> Look at my jewelry, I'm lethal
> These diamonds on me, they see-through
> I'm a Martian, they wishin' they equal
> I got Ms like the back of Evisu

Indeed, in addition to her excessively "lethal" riches and superhuman "Martian" characterization here, in an earlier line she proposes to "Call my girls and put 'em all on a spaceship." Echoing the "How many people you know can take it this far" of "Lift Off," Bey ends the "lavish" chorus with "I can't believe we made it / Have you ever seen the crowd goin' apeshit? Rah!"

Jay's verse offers an extended play on the racialized gorilla/guerrilla theme, beginning "I'm a gorilla in the fucking coupe / Finna pull up in the zoo," and continuing to riff on "monkey business" and "Gorilla Glue." Jay's verse also reprises the replacement theme with a nod to the Fab Four in the line "Ran through Liverpool like a fuckin' Beatle"—he is now at the top. After claiming his entitlement that he "Said 'no' to the Super Bowl / 'You need me, I don't need you,'" he ends the line by spurning the same (racist) culture industry that missed a chance to "put some colored girls in the MoMA," rapping: "Tell the Grammys: 'fuck that 0 for 8 shit / Have you ever seen a crowd goin' apeshit?' / Rah!"

## INTERSECTIONALITY IN A RACIAL CAPITALIST PATRIARCHY

What separates "Apeshit" from its precursors on *Watch the Throne*—and "Niggas in Paris" more specifically—is that Beyoncé has injected into this racial critique a more robustly intersectional Black feminist critique. Indeed, an important precedent for the critical excess on *Watch the Throne*—and my examination thereof—is the flurry of controversies surrounding 2 Live Crew's swaggeringly offensive 1989 album *As Nasty as They Wanna Be.*[31] It was the deep ambivalences between 2 Live Crew's (First Amendment) right to "swagger and swear and waste" and the demeaningly misogynistic form that that "freedom of expression" took, that launched the work of legal scholar Kimberlé Williams Crenshaw into the public imagination, highlighting her world-changing toolbox of theory and practice known today under the umbrella of "intersectionality."

In an article first published in the *Boston Review*, Crenshaw frames this ambivalence with the help of two high-profile views of the 2 Live Crew affair—a heavily mediatized binary opposition between political columnist George Will and professor Henry Louis Gates Jr.—notably, two men: one white, one Black.[32] Crenshaw writes:

> The most prominent defense of 2 Live Crew was advanced by Professor Henry Louis Gates, Jr., an expert on African-American literature. In a *New York Times* Op-Ed piece, and in testimony at the criminal trial, Gates portrayed 2 Live Crew as brilliant artists who were inventively elaborating distinctively African-American forms of cultural expression. Furthermore, Gates argued, the characteristic exaggeration featured in their lyrics served a political end: to explode popular racist stereotypes about Black sexuality precisely by presenting those stereotypes in a comically extreme form. Where Will saw a misogynistic assault on Black women by social degenerates, Gates found a form of "sexual carnivalesque" freighted with the promise to free us from the pathologies of racism.[33]

Where Will's argument toed the line of a mainstream (white) view of Black male deviance in which the well-being of Black women is all-too-often a secondary concern, Gates's cultural argument suggested that 2 Live Crew's music was being decontextualized from its African American traditions.[34]

Of course, this debate—and Crenshaw's place in it—is important for our considerations of critical excess because Gates doesn't stop with this cultural defense, but puts forth a political defense, suggesting that 2 Live Crew's otherwise indefensible misogyny and objectification of women holds the promise of exploding racist stereotypes. The argument is admittedly close to my own in this study. Crenshaw continues:

> As a Black feminist, I felt the pull of each of these poles, but not the compelling attractions of either. My immediate response to the criminal charges against 2 Live Crew was ambivalence: I wanted to stand together with the brothers against a racist attack, but I wanted to stand *against* a frightening explosion of violent imagery directed at women like me. My sharp internal division—my dissatisfaction with the idea that the "real issue" is race or that the "real issue" is gender—is characteristic of my experience as a Black woman living at the intersection of racial and sexual subordination. To that experience Black feminism offers an intellectual and political response: aiming to bring together the different aspects of an otherwise divided sensibility, it argues that Black women are commonly marginalized by a politics of race alone or gender alone, and that a political response to either form of subordination must be a political response to both. When the controversy over 2 Live Crew is approached in light of such Black feminist sensibilities, an alternative to the dominant poles of the public debate emerges.[35]

While the Black feminist toolbox of my own intersectional scholarship is still in development, I seek here to undermine the polarization that says—following Crenshaw's lead—that the "real issue" is race or that the "real issue" is *class*. Indeed, what's different with Jay and Ye's objectification and still-too-typical use of sexist language and imagery—besides the obvious *degree* of pornographic-level misogyny (like that in *As Nasty as They Wanna Be*)—is that their critical excess is not only focused on racism, but also well-attuned to the very binaries that undergird our habits of thought, our Enlightenment hegemony. It is my contention that on *Watch the Throne* Jay and Ye target the binaries and contradictions themselves. Like me, they are less proficient at targeting the contradictions of patriarchy, but make no mistake: to that Western hegemony that I describe in this book as "racial capitalism" we might easily add "patriarchal."

Ultimately, Crenshaw's intersectional Black feminism is "a political identity for Black women that will facilitate a simultaneous struggle against racism and patriarchy." Thus on Bey and Jay's "Apeshit" we should consider this intersectionality to be at once antiracist, antipatriarchal, *and anticapitalist*. In this way the critical excess of "Apeshit" holds an even stronger capacity for deformation of our racial capitalist patriarchy—the West—than *Watch the Throne*.[36] Indeed, despite the ostensibly materialistic ethos on "Apeshit," through her line "pay me in equity / watch me reverse out of debt," Beyoncé instead calls attention to the material concerns of poverty—concerns that are reflected through the vulnerabilities of Black women presented in scenes at the margins of the video's action.

Those vulnerable—and humanizing—margins begin with the lonely Black angel and the Black and Brown backup dancers, who appear throughout the video in various hues of flesh-colored body suits. The choreography of the video has the women exploring the rarefied spaces of the Louvre even more than Bey and Jay, moving in sync as embellishments to the two superstars, laying exposed on the grand staircase and voguing on statuary pedestals, but also posing as the artworks themselves, gathering in hallways, and dancing freely and joyously. In another shot, we see a collection of young men kneeling—Colin Kaepernick style—outside the Louvre at the mention of the NFL in Jay's verse. Also notable for the video's critique are the brief shots of the few Black bodies represented in the Louvre's collection intercut with shots of the living Black women and men—shots of rope, shots of servant girls and boys intercut with shots of

Fig. 4. Still from the music video for "Apeshit" (dir. Ricky Saiz). Beyoncé and Jay-Z stand atop the Louvre's grand staircase with the *Winged Victory of Samothrace* at their backs and dancers lying supine on the steps.

Black men and women embracing and doing each other's hair—shots that open up slippages into the real.

In one of the more authentically human sequences from the last minute of the video, we see the gathered dancers—male and female—dancing to the celebratory "can't believe we made it" chorus in front of the Great Sphinx of Tanis. Through its juxtaposition to those images of Blackness—centuries-old (white) renderings and contemporary filmed intimacies—the scene comments on the pillaging of African art from Europe's former colonies.[37] The collected dancers dance, unchoreographed, with Bey and Jay in the presence of the Sphinx as if reclaiming the art for their own darkened after-hours party. It is here that the images of a Black woman picking out a Black man's hair—with *their* backs to the *Mona Lisa*—stand out as human slippages. The shot of Beyoncé dressed in African "expensive fabrics" and Jay dressed in a hip hop gold medallion sharing an intimate moment has a similar effect. At the end the two slowly turn, hesitantly, to finally look at the *Mona Lisa*.

* * *

But despite the cultural critique of "Apeshit," despite Bey and Jay's Black colonization of this most rarefied European space, despite *Watch the Throne*'s critical excess and reframing of Black excellence for the Obama era and beyond, does the album merely reinforce capitalist hegemony by celebrating Black one-percenters? Does capitalism merely diversify its portfolio by allowing for such images of excellence and artistry—of a Black feminist takeover of the Louvre? These are the questions raised in a critical parody and response track by Jay and Ye's peer, Yasiin Bey—aka the acclaimed MC, Mos Def—the first subject of the next chapter on this central track from the "luxury rap" album. Indeed, we now pivot to Yasiin Bey's insightful response to "Niggas in Paris" and traverse the Black Atlantic to take a deeper look into another response to the album's Grammy-winning hit—a Parisian one.

CHAPTER 4

# "Niggas in Poorest" to "That Shit Creil"

## *NIP's Realpolitik in the US and France*

In January 2012, four months after Jay and Ye dropped "Niggas in Paris," Yasiin Bey (formerly Mos Def) released "Niggas in Poorest," an anticapitalist critique of *Watch the Throne's* swaggering "luxury rap."[1] The critical parody was part of Bey's short-lived "Top 40 Underdog" series of freestyle remakes and saw the politically conscious artist issuing a corrective to his long-time friends and collaborators, Jay and Ye. But as fellow Brooklyn MC Sharief Easterling explained in his HuffPost article, "Despite the angle taken by Yasiin on 'Niggas in Poorest' it isn't a 'diss record'" per se, but an answer track that went about correcting, clarifying, and otherwise repoliticizing many of the original's most—shall we say—"provocative" ideas.[2]

> Mos Def had a long history of collaborations with Kanye West, and was never really a confrontational MC to begin with. He simply allowed his art to reflect real life, which in this fake it til you make it industry is a rarity. It's great for Jay and Kanye to celebrate their unprecedented wealth and success, but the average fan just can't relate. . . .
>
> "Niggas in Paris" was undoubtedly the single of the year, but did the genre an even greater justice by creating the opportunity for such a contrasting remix. "Niggas in Poorest" is rap in its purest form. Truthful words, over a borrowed beat, spit by an exceptional lyricist.

While there is no direct condemnation of Jay and Ye on Bey's remake, the critique found on "Niggas in Poorest" is in keeping with the Occupy Wall Street ethos of the time and Mos Def's long catalog of politically engaged music.[3] The track examines how it is poor Black and Brown people who are the greatest victims of capitalist greed and the unrivaled inequality of our "new gilded age."[4]

The track anticipates the rise of the Black Lives Matter movement in its attention to the hostile environment that the US creates for its working-class people of color. Transforming Jay's transcendent "ball so hard" lines into the everyday nightmare of Black dehumanization, Bey details the racist police state:

> Poor so hard, this shit crazy, walk outside the whole world hate me
> Nervous stares at the thoroughfare, surveillance cameras, police tracing

The track continues, turning Jay and Ye's "Michaels" (Jackson, Tyson, Jordan) into "Myers, Myers, Myers, same shit"—a reference to the supernatural serial killer of the *Halloween* horror films that also draws inspiration from the "psycho" line of the original. Bey, it seems, is not interested in the Black capitalist fantasies that Jay and Ye are selling. He is interested in the realpolitik of quotidian American racism.

The first verse concludes with the lines "Poor so hard, who getting faded [killed]?: little Maurice in the sixth grade" over a remake of the original track's Dirty South beat. Given that Trayvon Martin would be shot mere days after the release of "Niggas in Poorest," the track seems prophetic. Yet for Black and Brown people—especially those in the poorest conditions—the devaluing and loss of young life is an everyday reality and has been for decades—no, centuries. It is a reality that Bey is all too aware of. Indeed, thanks to #BlackLivesMatter it is a reality that mainstream (white) society is just now finally beginning to open its eyes to.

Given the somber tone and serious tenor of Bey's critical parody, it is worth pointing out that Jay and Ye's frustratingly joyful album is, nonetheless, also prophetic of the type of socially sanctioned anti-Black violence that would continue unchecked after Trayvon's murder. Track 8, "Welcome to the Jungle," begins with Ye's chilling lines: "I asked her where she wanna be when she twenty-five / She turned around and looked at me and she said 'alive.'" While the ethos and aesthetics of the original and the parody are miles apart, I'd like to suggest that the cultural work they do is of a piece; they meet different audiences where they are, but lead them to the same place. There has long been a "reach people or teach people" quandary in hip hop—and popular music in general. Yet my analysis holds that this is a false dichotomy, that hip hop can reach people *and* teach people. Indeed, the verdict is still out on whether hip hop engineered to be wildly popular needs to be intellectually or ethically corrupt—and, on the other hand, whether the "cultural spinach" of conscious hip hop really does make one more conceptually and morally woke. In short, this is why it is useful to think of Bey's critique of "Niggas in Paris" as more elaborative than condemnatory. We need to remember that *Watch the Throne* is much more than that "luxury rap" moniker would lead us to believe. Indeed, that epithet and the album's gilded packaging seem to give the lie to a set of songs that is, in many ways, dead serious—and "politically conscious" in its own fresh, innovative, and, yes, often joyful ways.

The second verse of Bey's parody includes a sendup of Ye's "bougie" lines—bringing the Black one-percenter back to reality: "Bougie girl, grab your hand, show you how to do this ghetto dance / Fuck your French, we ain't in France." To this image of Black poverty in and against white wealth Bey continues the mixture with an image of miscegenation: "Prince Williams ain't do it right if you ask me / If I was him I'd put some black up in my family"—another prescient image given Prince Harry's 2018 marriage to African American actress Meghan Markle. Indeed, at this point, the "Niggas in Poorest" video clip of Bey rapping in his home studio includes a cutaway shot that is one of the highlights of the clip—a visibly darkened Queen Elizabeth.[5]

Perhaps most importantly, Bey elaborates the political valences of Ye's "Goin' Gorillas" line in both lyric and the album art. The line, "It's them niggas in poorest [that] be them rebel guerrillas," best evinces Easterly's claim that Bey's parody is not a "diss" of the Jay and Ye original. The line suggests that Bey not only understands the historical critique of Ye's racializing "apeshit" line, but that the MC is interested in furthering the anticolonial "guerrilla" message hidden behind the surface of the luxury rap original. The cover art for Bey's release of the parody furthers this freedom-fighter reading with an evocative photographic image that portrays a mid-twentieth-century dispute between what seems to be a white, uniformed, and rifle-wielding colonial gendarme and a Polynesian man.

In the photograph, the shirtless, dark-skinned man is in a strong fighting posture with dozens of fellow workers standing by as witness as he grabs the barrel of the rifle. Yet the colonial soldier/overseer looks to be in complete control, staring steely-eyed at the would-be insurgent, his hands firmly in control of the weapon—and its trigger. The image is an important one for framing "Niggas in Poorest" as not only an anticapitalist, but an anticolonial reframing of the Jay and Ye original. But again, we need only think back to the previous two tracks to see that the anticolonial frame is already there on the original. From "No Church in the Wild" and its "Thanksgiving disguised as a feast" line to the Afrofuturist critique of Black alienation on "Lift Off," *Watch the Throne* is awash in anticolonial rhetorics. While I, like Easterly, read Bey's parody as an elaboration rather than a diss, the track does further complicate "Niggas in Paris," and, in fact, extends the larger project of critical excess on *Watch the Throne.*

## MARGIELA-GORILLA

Furthermore, in my close reading of the original "Niggas in Paris," one moment sticks out as particularly Janus-faced: the line "What's that jacket, Margiela?" Where Bey turns the line into "who the fuck is Margiela?"—echoing most of Jay and Ye's fans and much of the popular and journalistic discourse around the album—it seems to me that Ye is doing something more than simply lording his knowledge of *haute couture* brands over all of us. Importantly, in the poetic structure of the last eight bars of his verse, it is the word "Margiela" that provides the rhyme scheme's pivot to "Gorilla"—a structural relationship that links the two "huh?!" words vis-à-vis Ferrell's "no one knows what it means, but it's provocative" punch line.

Collapsing the luxury goods business with the drug business, the first four bars proceed:

> What's Gucci my nigga?
> What's Louie my killa?
> What's drugs my deala?
> What's that jacket, Margiela?

To which, the second four bars respond—connecting the illicit drug trade to the legal drug trade of prescription treatments for mental illness:

> Doctors say I'm the illest
> 'Cause I'm suffering from realness
> Got my niggas in Paris
> And they goin' gorillas, huh!?

As such, it is important to consider that the "no one knows what it means" line refers not just to the provocatively racialized "niggas . . . goin' gorillas" lyric, but to the line that references the little-known (to the unwashed masses) luxury brand Maison Margiela.

My point in raising this implicit connection is that once again, Ye is collapsing the subhuman and the superhuman—and having it both ways. Although most reportage on the track draws a line directly from the "gross" Ferrell and Heder sample back to the ugly and provocative "gorilla" line that immediately precedes it, the line that best fits the "no one knows what it means" sample is the high-end name drop of "Margiela." Like the "excuse my French" ("bougie . . . bitch") gambit, Ye again uses a red herring to subtly double and further complicate the web of signification. Surely, Ye knew that no one was going to know who or what Martin Margiela is—the whole album is about Jay and Ye alternately bragging of their exceptional knowledge and trying to teach "soldiers" to be "kings"—so the phrase "no one knows what it means but it's provocative" is the perfect encapsulation of the collapsed binary of ultracivilized culture and uncivilized primate, of Margiela and Gorilla.

Indeed, this Margiela-Gorilla structural linkage (yes, it also conjures up Magilla Gorilla—as the rhyme seems to have done for Kanye) also pulls the curtain back on all of the linguistic slippages that Jay and Ye use to their advantage on the album. Here, the incessant wordplay and wildly divergent meanings should serve to remind us that just as there is never a direct line between signifier and signified—between *langue* and *parole*—neither are there ever easy answers for intention. We can try to scour Kanye's beats, lyrics, and voice for evidence of truth—of essence—but we will *always* fail. Indeed, it is this slippage—not just in language, but in our understanding of meaning itself—that provides the space for the "deformation of mastery," the game-changing space for agency in our seemingly inflexible and ruthlessly commonsensical regime of meaning-making.

As we saw in chapter 2, it behooves us to try and reimagine Kanye as neither snake-oil salesman nor authentic religious visionary, neither pathological cult leader nor inspired revolutionary, neither "just in it for the money" nor "actually born again." These binaries—multiply inflected with our own racial, class, and religious stereotypes—misunderstand Kanye's agency as a *human* being (i.e., thoroughly flawed and inconsistent) and reinscribe the *dehumanizing* "problem or victim" stereotype that has dogged Black people for four centuries.[6] Where Enlightenment regimes of meaning-making encourage us to choose between the binaries of *stereo*typed truths, the deformation of mastery enlists the common-sense (i.e., unquestioned) power of these binaries to subvert the dominant order. Masters of deformation play on our reality in order to unmake—and remake—reality through sleight of hand. This magic is usually musical.

The collapse of superhuman and subhuman in the Margiela-Gorilla construction thus recalls Attali's argument that the musician's "double game" plays with speech and meaning to simultaneously occupy the roles of "deified star" and "outcast."

> He plays a double game. He is simultaneously *musicus* and *cantor,* reproducer and prophet. If an outcast, he sees society in a political light. If accepted, he is its historian, the reflection of its deepest values. He speaks of society and he speaks against it. This duality was already present before capital arrived to impose its own rules and prohibitions. . . . simultaneously *excluded* (relegated to a place near the bottom of the social hierarchy) and *superhuman* (the genius, the adored and deified star). Simultaneously a separator and an integrator.
>
> In the civilizations of antiquity, the musician was often a slave, sometimes an untouchable. But at the same time, the ancient religions produced a caste of musician-priests attached to the service of the temple, and mythology endowed musicians with super-natural and civilizing powers.[7]

Recalling Justin Burton's summary of the album as embodying a "double life of fun, sophomoric tracks juxtaposed with biting social critique" with "a salient critical hidden agenda hidden inside a collection of catchy tunes built from the debris of greatest hits past," it becomes clear that the civilized-uncivilized binary is only a detail of more important cultural work that the album performs. This work is the destabilization of meaning—an increasingly central reality of our contemporary "fake news" reality-TV reality era.[8] Indeed, casting this superhuman—this Nietzschean *Übermensch*—as simultaneously subhuman destabilizes the inherited (white) evolution narrative of transcendence that the album tracks and returns us to the "god is dead" ethos of "No Church in the Wild."

As part of an artistic and critical legacy that stretches back to the Harlem Renaissance's hegemonic critique, to the double entendre of the blues, and further back to the first African American expressions of critique and subversion encoded in the slave spirituals, hip hop's decades-long destabilization of hegemonic regimes of meaning-making should be a good thing.[9] Indeed, what Fred Moten calls the "improvisation of singularity"—an *un*fixing of normativity, of (white) logocentric power—is at the heart of much contemporary work on the liberatory potential of the Black radical aesthetic, as it is with critical race, queer, and feminist studies more broadly.[10] Yet as we have seen in recent years, the primary beneficiaries of this destabilization seem to be the dog-whistling racists, their narrowcasting alt-right media, and its well-honed use of gaslighting, plausible deniability, and "alternative facts."

As such, regardless of whether Yasiin Bey was clarifying or correcting Kanye when he spit "Who the fuck is Margiela?!" on "Niggas in Poorest," the track does important work in elaborating the Black radical tradition and the critical work of the original track, making explicit the implicit and game-changing "double game" critique of *Watch the Throne*. "Niggas in Poorest" concludes with the lines "don't get caught up in no throne" as we see images of infamous men who did just that—lusted for power, for the throne—and leaned heavily on legalized regimes of white privilege and plausible deniability when their insatiable thirst for power got them in trouble.

The "Niggas in Poorest" video moves from shots of Occupy Wall Street protesters counterposed against NASDAQ chairman and convicted fraud artist Bernie Madoff, to shots of US-supported dictators, Saddam Hussein and Augusto Pinochet, and Enron CEO and convicted fraud artist Ken Lay, before turning to images of more historical villains such as Richard Nixon and Adolf Hitler. The sequence ends with close-ups of George Bush. The string of images paints a clear picture of corruption at the highest levels, indicting capitalist collusion between governments and business. In the historical context of the Occupy Wall Street movement—and from the depths of the global recession—the anticapitalist critique is a clear and big-picture one: Bey is illuminating the interdependence of colonialism and capitalism and showing us how those entanglements are reproduced in today's neocolonial networks of global finance.

With the benefit of hindsight, we can also see that it is the frustrating entrenchment of this antidemocratic collusion between global capital and world governments that has led us to our current political realignment. It is a frustration that summons a need, in the words of the Brexit campaign, to "take back control"—and notably, it has also led to a point where anti-establishment movements on the right and left have more in common than they might care to admit. Indeed, in the US context Bernie Madoff and most of the big corporations and financial services companies were Democratic Party donors—as was Donald Trump, we should remember. The major difference in view of this realignment, of course, is race. Where one side looks to one-percenters, corporations, and their offshore accounts as the culprits, the other looks to the poor, to migrants, and to people of color.

With its twin slogans of regression—"Take Back Control" (UK) and "Make America Great Again" (US)—today's Right frames the need to recreate a colonialist golden age wherein white privilege is once again underwritten by capital. In contrast, the Left targets capitalist exploitation and holds up social equality, while too often sidelining the issues of racial justice and the dreaded "identity politics" that so many Democratic constituencies rely on for collective voice. In the 2016 US presidential elections that ultimately pitted a violently disruptive change candidate on the Right against a neoliberal centrist and status-quo candidate on the Left, frustration took the day.[11]

Standing in the eye of this political hurricane are the Black one-percenters, Jay and Ye, two Black men who have long stoked the politics of white resentment on the political Right and increasingly provoked ire as sellouts on the political Left. In many ways, these Black one-percenters who gamed the system are at the center of gravity of today's political realignment and can tell us much about the nature of our current predicaments with regard to race and capitalism. As we have seen, race and capitalism—those twin colonial-era inventions—are also the twin features of *Watch the Throne*. In short, this is why we can see the seeds of this global political realignment in the musical and rhetorical contours of *Watch the Throne*—as well as in the cultural discourse it generated on tracks such as "Niggas In Poorest."

## "THAT SHIT CREIL": 48H AVEC FRANÇOIS HOLLANDE

One of the most shocking (and telling) global cultural artifacts powered by "Niggas in Paris" was a campaign video for the 2012 French presidential candidate, François Hollande, that featured the Jay and Ye track. The track, which would go on to win the Grammy for best rap song, had by the spring of 2012 become an international mega-hit, including in France—the second largest global market for hip hop.

The campaign video, 48H AVEC FH (48 hours with François Hollande), was the feature piece of a guerrilla marketing campaign documenting the famously vanilla candidate interacting with the postcolonial Black and Brown citizens of Paris's low-income *banlieues* (suburbs). The video was shot over two days in the spring of 2012, just as the campaign was heading into its final weeks—and posted to YouTube on 10 April by the "2H12 Crew."[12] The most shocking (and telling) feature of the video was, of course, that these images of the lily-white candidate campaigning in the poor "black, blanc, et beur" (Black, white, and Arab) *banlieues* was set to the soundtrack of . . . "Niggas in Paris." Ouch.

This seemingly tone-deaf use of the hit track for his "unofficial" 2012 campaign video as part of his minority outreach strategy in the Parisian *banlieues* attracted immediate and global attention across the Twitterverse, ending up on CNN and garnering over one million views on YouTube (before being taken down under pressure from Universal Music Group). At the core of the ensuing discussion was the question of whether the video misappropriated the "N-word" and misapplied it to the French context. Isn't this an offensive mistranslation? Why not use a French hip hop artist as the soundtrack to the *banlieue* video? As the French-language Swiss news site, 20min.ch, put it, "*Pas sûr que ce soit de cette façon là que François Hollande souhaite devenir célèbre aux Etats-Unis*" (Not sure that this is how François Hollande wants to become famous in the United States).[13]

Yet a closer look at the clip and its genesis reveals a more nuanced—and potentially empowering—story behind the ostensibly cringeworthy political marketing ploy. Like the album *Watch the Throne* itself, and the track it borrows from, the campaign video, 48H AVEC FH, is carefully calibrated to push our buttons—"No one knows what it means, but it's provocative . . . Gets the people going!," as the sample heedlessly (and pointedly) declares. In the end, the video did seem to get the people going, and on 6 May 2012, François Hollande was elected to the French presidency in a close contest with 51.6 percent of the vote.

The campaign video begins with the phrase "Le Changement C'est Maintenent" [Change is Now] in block letters, clearly riffing on Barack Obama's successful 2008 "Change" campaign theme across the Atlantic in both substance and style. The appropriated messaging was deployed to appeal to France's sizeable postcolonial communities of color and foment anti-incumbent sentiment against his rival, the law-and-order rightist, Nicholas Sarkozy—a favorite natural enemy of French hip hop.[14] As the campaign video gets underway and we hear the Will Ferrell opening to "Niggas in Paris," the guerrilla marketing crew's name appears as a social media hashtag #2H12CREW. Next, the meme's title appears as "48H AVEC FH" followed by the names of low-income Parisian suburbs flashing across the screen: "Creil," "Les Ulis," "Clichy Sous Bois," "Aubervilliers," "Aulnay Sous Bois."

Here, the first shot of the campaign video establishes the main visual trope: a waist-up shot of François Hollande with the candidate extending his arm to show his instrument of change as a French citizen: his *Carte Électorale*, his voting credentials—the very currency of French democracy. In the three-minute clip filled with the quick cuts of a music video, our next images are of French women: one headscarved, one Black, one East Asian, all extending their arms—and their *Cartes Électorales*—in the same fashion. The message is clear and powerful: *one person, one vote*. Despite their religious or racial backgrounds their voices count as much as any (white, male) French person's.

Most importantly to our analysis here, the gestures—and there are countless more to come in the video—are tantamount to flipping the bird to the white gaze of the camera. *We're citizens too! We have rights! And we're gonna vote, motherfucker!* In short, the video's use of the track confirms my reading of "Niggas in Paris"—and of *Watch the Throne* more broadly—as a kind of longform "fuck you" to white fragility. And the message seems to translate well to the *banlieue* context.

Indeed, in my 2007 interview with the Parisian hip hop duo Blackara, the two MCs, Xiao Venom and Mani Peterson, demonstrated a clear commitment to African American modes of self-representation and self-empowerment. As signified in their name, Blackara—a portmanteau of the English "black" and the French "karat"—their espoused ideology was one fully in keeping with the classic FUBU (For Us By Us) economic self-improvement ideology of the African American brand and that of more recent hip hop artists such as Nipsey Hussle and Killer Mike—to whom we'll return in the conclusion.[15] While I talked with other MCs who held fast to the more traditional French ideology of *laïcite*—a fully secularized eschewal of identity politics—Blackara saw such silencing of difference as a tacit whitening of the public sphere. As Mani reflected on the upcoming election that would see Sarkozy put in power, "Sarko is gonna do things for

Fig. 5. Still from the musical campaign video *48H AVEC FH* (dir. Leïla Sy and Bruno Laforestrie). French voter "gesturing" to the camera with his *Carte Électorale*.

his friends and Ségolène for her friends . . . but it's not for us really.[16] But remember, they are all friends." Indeed, for the purposes of our discussion of the 48H AVEC FH video and the 2012 election, it is worth noting that, indeed, the 2007 Socialist candidate Royal was and is the spouse of the 2012 Socialist candidate Hollande.

In short, returning to the question of whether Hollande's marketing team misappropriated the "N-word" and misapplied it to the French context—it is clear to me that Xiao and Mani would have approved of the visibility that the clip afforded. While I was unable to reconnect with Blackara to ask them their thoughts on the 2012 viral campaign video, they were clear about the unprecedented visibility that the 2005 antiracist and anti–police brutality rebellions brought to their communities in the *banlieues*. The ugliness of France burning on TV was a necessary evil to finally focus the nation's attention on the structural underdevelopment and particular needs of the working-class postcolonial communities living at the margins of French society.

Over the course of the guerrilla campaign video, 48H AVEC FH, we see countless men and women—many of them young, and most of them nonwhite—at Hollande rallies or caught up in the bustle of the whistle-stop tour and repeating the signature gesture of holding out their voting cards to the camera. Most of them are surprised and energized to see a candidate for president of France in their too-often-forgotten neighborhoods on the peripheries. In one close shot on the Paris Metro, we see a young Black woman on her phone, expressing surprise that Hollande is on her train, ". . . dans le train, il est dans le train . . . à Gare du Nord!" (. . . on the train, he's on the train . . . to Gare du Nord station!). In another scene we hear a couple of North African teenaged boys smile and say: "Big up François Hollande!" In yet another, we hear, then see, a middle-aged Black woman chanting "François, President" before a quick cut to her adding "insha'Allah, insha'Allah" (God willing, God willing). The clip paints a diverse and energized citizenry at the literal margins of the city who have long been marginalized from French political life. *This time*, says the video with its one-person, one-vote message, *we will be heard*.

On the same day as the viral video's release, the center-left daily, *Libération*, reported the following under the headline "François Hollande, en clip sauce rap americaine" (François Hollande, remixed in American-style rap video). In a section devoted to the day-to-day developments of France's first true internet election, titled "Net-Campagne," the editors wrote, with a mixture of snark and begrudging admiration,

> It's possible for François Hollande to mix with American rap. A video featuring the song "Niggas in Paris" by the American rapper Kanye West [*sic*] was shot during the socialist candidate's 48-hour visit to the Paris suburbs. François Hollande went to Vaulx-en-Velin, Creil, Clichy sous Bois, Aubervilliers . . . with a camera over his shoulder. The video, posted Tuesday, April 10 by the "2H12 CREW," was made by two rap video directors. At the origin of this project, we find Bruno Laforestrie, founder of hip-hop Radio Générations and advisor to François Hollande. He works with him on issues of youth and culture. "The idea of this clip was born during a meal I had organized so that François Hollande could meet people from the world of urban culture," explained Bruno Laforestrie. "He agreed for me to follow him, without having the right to watch the video, the idea was also to work on his image with a different approach."[17]

While the clip's launch was widely reported in the Francophone press, little else on record expands on this explanation, which is surprising given that the video was designed and received as a controversial and high-profile media event.[18] Thanks to an introduction from global hip hop and media studies scholar Murray Forman, I was able to connect with the mastermind of the guerrilla marketing campaign—the French hip hop radio impresario and sometimes political operative, Bruno Laforestrie—who elaborated on the genesis of and thinking behind the clip with me in a June 2019 interview.[19]

Of the beginnings of his political involvement, he explained to me that in 2012, as he was leaving the helm of Radio Générations (88.2 FM in the Île-de-France), a position he'd been in since 1996, he was turning his attention to other projects—and looking to actualize the power of "young people in the suburbs." He explained in fairly clear English (clearer than my French, in any case):

> I was quite involved in the matter of young people in France, because I was the editor of Radio Générations, and Générations was one of the first rap stations in Paris twenty years ago. So, as the owner and editor of this hip hop radio in Paris we were really involved in urban culture and political matters about young people in the suburbs. So, I knew and worked with all the artists and know the ecosystem of hip hop in Paris, because everyone was starting and going through the radio, you know?

He continued, explaining his first forays into politics—an engagement that was prompted by then Minister of the Interior, Nicholas Sarkozy, who went on record referring to the antiracist rioters involved in the infamous 2005 riots as *racaille* (rabble). "So, I've never been a politician," he explained. "I'm not a politician professionally, but I was involved in some fights for supporting young people in the suburbs. And one of the fights was to fight against, you know, some years ago, Sarkozy, which was quite a feud with young people from the suburbs.[20] And so in that fight, I met a lot of politicians and I met François Hollande before the campaign [for president]."

Laforestrie went on to elaborate the story first reported in *Libération,* describing in detail how it was the candidate's son, Thomas Hollande, who brought the idea of a dinner meeting to the campaign's attention.

> I met his son, Thomas—Thomas Hollande—and I said to Thomas if you want I can organize a dinner with fifteen, twenty people from hip hop culture to discover that different universe. So, we organized that two months before the election and it was a really nice time and Hollande was quite a good man, and at the dinner I invited Leïla Sy, the realisatrice [director] of all the clips of [MC] Kery James—and she made the new film *Banlieusards.* And so, I said, we will do a clip for you and so that was the beginning of the discussion.

As Laforestrie explained, "I knew François Hollande was going to make a tour of the suburbs to finish his campaign," and knowing that the candidate had already signaled his intentions of focusing on the *banlieue*, he looked to further the candidate's understanding of the suburbs by adding detail and nuance to his understanding of hip hop. "And so, I said, okay, I can make the movie of this campaign. And I proposed to Leïla to realize the movie. And I said it won't be you [Hollande], it will be the product of me and Leïla—indirectly. You cannot check it, you give us all access, and we're gonna do something that will be an 'unofficial clip.' Because it will be a kind of energy with the image we can give to the end of this campaign, with young people, diversity, the new French people from the suburbs."

Laforestrie's narrative of the video's genesis is revealing, not only for how he was looking to sharpen an already-chosen campaign focus on diversity by putting Hollande in contact with artists and tastemakers from "urban culture," but for his narrative focus on those "fifteen, twenty people from hip hop culture" that he brought to the meeting with Hollande. Indeed, the fact that he invited Leïla Sy to the dinner and then put her in charge of the video casts the project—and its "Niggas in Paris" soundtrack—in a new light. As Laforestrie name-dropped for me, his American interviewer, Sy was indeed the director of the acclaimed French MC, Kery James's, videos and is the director of the new Netflix film *Banlieusards*. The self-described "française, noire, métisse" (French, Black, mixed) film director's involvement in the project went unreported in most media accounts of the guerrilla clip, but is an important point in considering the ethos and ethics of the project.[21] Indeed, it is important to consider that the director was a woman of color not only for the "optics" of the campaign video and our impressions of its support of a white, establishment candidate. It is also important to know this fact as we think about the camera that was moving about the *banlieues*, that the creative eye behind that gazing camera was "française, noire, métisse"—Leïla Sy.[22]

Getting a sense of Laforestrie's message and his narrative of the diverse, *Black, blanc, beur* brain trust behind it, I asked him about the challenges—"the pros and cons"—of framing the video footage with what would be a controversial soundtrack: "Niggas in Paris." "What happened," began Laforestrie, "was the first concept of the movie was the *Carte Électorale*, you know? So, Leïla's first idea was we give the power to people. So, we decided," he continued, "François Hollande gives the cards to people, [indicating] they have the right and the power to vote. So, that was the first idea: you have the power to vote for him or not. . . . It's important. So, all of the movie was in different train stations of the suburbs and we finished in Creil, which is a small city in the suburbs, very far from Paris. *Creil*."

As we'll see, by repeating and emphasizing the name of the community on the far outskirts of Paris, he was foreshadowing what Slate.com has called "one of the best examples of wordplay ever used in a political advert" and setting the record straight on the genesis of the controversial campaign video. He explained:

> And so, we did the whole movie without thinking about the music before. *You have to think about that*. We did that movie *without music*. And after, when we worked with Leïla Sy and the guy working on the image [the film editor], we made the first montage and we talked about what kind of music we should put on that. And after thinking and thinking it was the ménage [edited video] that fit the tune, and "Niggas in Paris" was really "us in Paris." I was playing this song on my radio and I said to Leïla, we should try it with "Niggas in Paris" because the music is really adapted to the image—because it was a movie with a lot of cuts and we need a really fast rhythm, da-da, da-da. Really coarse, you know?[23]

Here, on the "da-da, da-da," Laforestrie's voice rose stepwise in pitch space to approximate the rising tension and rhythmic energy they were looking for in the video.

He continued, using the word "coarse" again—which, it now became clear, was intended as a synonym for crass, gritty, vulgar, or—as he goes on to put it—"crazy."

> And so, I said to Leïla, why not try that? Because it's kind of coarse. It's kind of crazy. It's kind of "Niggas in Paris." In the movie François Hollande is with niggas in Paris now, you know. It was a kind of creative thing, you know. And we talked about that. It's crazy! Why not? And when we put the music on the movie we realized that it was exactly this music. Because, it's kind of "cray"—the expression. Like, he's in Creil with cray, you know?! And so, it was a creative thing. And after, Leïla and I worked together to put the music right on the image.

Here, while speaking excitedly about the "creative" process, Laforestrie was gesturing to the quick cuts in sound and video, while highlighting how the numerous tight shots of "Creil"—on train platforms and digital scrolls—were edited into the video to foreshadow Kanye's lyrics "that shit cray" from the track's hook. He and Leïla, thus "put the music right on the image"—linking the sound of Kanye's slang ("cray") to the pronounced sound of the Parisian suburb's name ("Creil").

Importantly, he justified the use of the track further, concluding "And, Jay Z was huge in Paris with Kanye. Everybody was singing this song at the time . . . and we just realized this was the music for this movie." The gestures to the sonic intensity and fever pitch of "Niggas in Paris" as a perfect match for the high-intensity visuals of their guerrilla political ad suggest that Laforestrie was indeed interested in something more that the "cray"/"Creil" wordplay and its implicit racialization of Paris's banlieue communities. This track, in Laforestrie's view, captured the spirit of the edited video and their whirlwind political tour through the banlieues. Despite the highly problematic (mis)application of the African American track "Niggas in Paris" to represent these postcolonial French communities, he (and purportedly Sy) felt that a global zeitgeist and an aesthetic synergy not only suggested, but *revealed*, that this was the perfect track—"we realized that it was exactly this music."

Why not use a French hip hop track by a local artist to represent this *banlieusard* politics? Because the swaggering ethos of this global hit was already in the air and perfectly captured that community's attitude. Sure, it would be controversial, but that's the point: it "gets the people *going*!" This is another side of NIP's pragmatic realpolitik—Laforestrie and Sy were willing to forego the careful focus-grouping of politically correct left-wing campaigns in favor of an energizing, DIY form of electioneering that used any means at their disposal. It might be "gross," and it might be that "no one knows what it means," but it is also "provocative" and "gets the people going."

Our thirty-minute interview ended with a look back on the legal maneuvering that went on behind the scenes after the guerrilla—and technically illegal—marketing campaign helped elect Hollande. Laforestrie continued with a bit of intrigue and a star-studded story he'd clearly been waiting to tell:

> Also, *something you don't know*, one day before the election, the head of Universal, Pascal Nègre, called me to say that I didn't have the right to use the music and he wanted me to destroy the movie and take it down from the internet. So, we had pressure from Pascal Nègre directly to say I want you to erase the

clip. And I said, I'm not really the producer, it's a viral clip. It's an artistic thing. It was a subject matter I knew quite well. So, I called Kevin Liles, you know, the former head of Def Jam, a founder of Def Jam, and he's a friend of mine. I called Kevin and said, I did this for François Hollande because we fight in the suburbs for young black people who Sarkozy was attacking. And Kevin said, okay that's cool. I'm gonna send it to Jay. And he said, yeah he liked the movie, we won't sue you. So, it wasn't a formal thing, but it was a good thing . . .

Laforestrie ended the thought, "so we left the movie [online] until the end of the campaign and we erased the movie after the victory of François Hollande."

Laforestrie concluded the story by recounting how the legal posturing continued after the election. Although Jay-Z agreed and in the end never did file charges against Laforestrie, Sy, or the campaign, Universal's Nègre continued to press a suit (probably for political as well as financial reasons, as the executive is reportedly a friend of Sarkozy's).[24] But as Laforestrie jokingly explained, neither he nor Sy were the producers or "main beneficiaries" of the video, as no money exchanged hands. That left Hollande as the main beneficiary—and as we are finding out with the forty-fifth president of the United States, heads of state are effectively above the law. "So," as Laforestrie put it, despite the barrage of threatening emails and letters "after a few weeks—it was off." He snapped his fingers to punctuate the end of the story before going on to recount a celebratory denouement: how, shortly after, he and Thomas Hollande were invited to the *Watch the Throne* tour in Paris on June 1, 2012, given the VIP treatment, and personally thanked for their work by Jay's long-time "consigliere," John Meneilly.[25] That shit Creil.

## "DON'T LET ME GET IN MY ZONE . . ."

"Niggas in Paris" ends with a profoundly disruptive coda that serves as a bridge to the next track and a transformational moment in the structure of the entire album. After the last lines of Ye's "gorilla" verse on the track and its "provocative" framing, and after Jay enters with what turns out to be a false restatement of the hook—"ball so hard motherfuckers wanna fine me"—we are treated to a signature Kanye *fuck you*. Just as we gear up for another statement of the beeping *Dirty South Bangaz* hook and the synth line seems to lead its octave rise to a final verse, we are instead treated to a rude awakening: an ear-splitting, fuzzed out, and grating bass pedal. As if this isn't enough, the unsettling pedal is further activated by a booming kick drum alternating with stabs of too-trebly white noise that is perfectly calculated to sound *horrible* against the rumbling low end.

After a full eight bars of this epically unlistenable sonic shitstorm, Kanye's voice reenters the track to inform us: "You are now watching the throne." Here, a heavenly chorus and quiet storm of I-vi-iii-II piano chords frame his lyrics in filigreed gold and gently place them on a pedestal. All the while, the shitstorm continues down below.

This perfectly crafted sonic middle finger casts the catchy banger in a new light. Indeed, apropos of this book's critical reading of a profoundly distracting pop artifact, it makes us wonder if Adorno was right. It should. Ye continues: "Don't let me get in my zone." He is daring us to look away. Are we in thrall to bullshit? Are we, as Adorno puts it, active participants in our own alienation, our own oppression? Here's our chance to look away, to break free. Are we victims of such "pseudo-individualization," of false consciousness?[26] Indeed, is my close reading of this album literally a study in self-deception? Fair questions all. But what would it mean if the power we were in thrall to was Black power? What if that bullshit—the opiate of this superstructure—was discovered to be Black? And worse, unapologetically so. What would white people do if they felt Black culture was taking over?

As it so happens, this type of unlistenable *deus ex machina* has become something of a "sonic signature" for Kanye.[27] From at least as early as the autotune and white noise experiments of his 2008 album *808s & Heartbreak*, Ye has dropped such ear-testing sonic ruptures with increasing regularity—purposely trying our patience and testing our commitment to and understanding of his musical vision. Indeed, his whole career has increasingly become something of a test of his fans' patience—from his Hurricane Katrina and Taylor Swift "outbursts" to his post-2016 Oval Office visits and maddening TMZ mischaracterization of slavery as "a choice."[28]

For our purposes here, the track most exemplary of this new ear-testing aesthetic from Kanye's wider oeuvre is the even more unlistenable beat to "On Sight" (2013), which begins with an aggressive, unstable, and noisy grind before Kanye threatens "how much do I not give a fuck / Let me show you right now . . ." Ye immediately makes good on the threat, inserting one of his typical old-school "chipmunk soul" non sequiturs—a sped-up sample of the gospel tune "He'll Give Us What We Really Need."[29] The chipmunk-soul respite only serves to make the beat more unlistenable on its return and prepares us for the sonically and conceptually upsetting voyage that awaits us on the full album, *Yeezus*.

Indeed, the first verse of that album's fourth track, "New Slaves," features a next-generation version of *Watch the Throne*'s argument over a sparse and mechanically dystopic beat. Centering on the mutuality of racism and capitalism, the track begins with a discussion of racialized access to clean water, which would prove prophetic regarding the 2014 Flint water crisis: "My momma was raised in the era when / Clean water was only served to the fairer skin." The verse continues, dripping with anger:

Doin' clothes, you woulda thought I had help
But they wasn't satisfied unless I picked the cotton myself
You see, it's broke nigga racism
That's that "don't touch anything in the store"
And it's rich nigga racism
That's that "come in, please buy more"

The urgent and indignant lines connect Black labor and chattel slavery directly to the racially policed realities of American consumer culture. The paradox is clear: in a country built on Black labor, Black people still have unequal, always racialized, access to the nation's material wealth. The passage ends with the fittingly essentialist line: "All you blacks want all the same things."

Given the increasingly grating and dystopic *noise* aesthetics of Kanye's beats—and the increasingly confrontational lyrics that accompany them—I want to suggest that this signature aesthetic has come to signify Kanye "in the zone." It is the sonic signature of an artist who "don't give a fuck"; an artist who doesn't care what we want, but thinks he knows "what we need"; an artist who dares us to turn away: "Who Gon Stop Me?" as he puts it on the album's ninth track. Indeed, Ye's increasingly idiosyncratic artistic praxis and this "in the zone" aesthetic, in particular, calls to mind J. S. Bach's *Musical Offering*, a collection of pieces written as a sort of game. Composed in response to a challenge from King Frederick the Great of Prussia to transform an unlistenable melody into a fugue, Bach went beyond the stated brief and sent the junk musical material back to the king as a wholly excessive set of beautiful, well-balanced, and carefully wrought canons, fugues, and other forms. In short, the musical tests that Ye seems to be setting for himself—and subjecting us to in recent years—demands that he make a hit out of anything; that he accept something akin to Michael Jordan's (failed) baseball test and turn lead into gold; or—apropos of the old hip hop aphorism—that he "turn nothing into something." In other words, through his noisy "in the zone" aesthetic, Kanye is demonstrating his mastery of form and then exceeding that mastery.

But unlike Bach's masterfully wrought crab cannons and aesthetically pleasing fugues, Kanye crafts a signal difference in his work—he demonstrates a mastery of form, but spits that form back at us with a sneer. Having mastered the Grammy formula for Album of the Year nominations for his first three albums—in 2005, 2006, and 2008 (a run bested only by Stevie Wonder, who was not only nominated for, but won the Grammy in 1974, 1975, and 1977)—2008's *808's and Heartbreak* marks a turn from "classic Kanye" toward experimental, *entitled* Kanye. Indeed, this is "In the Zone" Kanye. While we have seen glimpses of this aesthetic in the farthest reaches of his formal mastery thus far on *Watch The Throne*, the coda to "Niggas in Paris" gestures to something more. This "In the Zone" Kanye is "Deformation of Mastery" Kanye.

## "FEELING GOOD(?)": *BLACK MADNESS :: MAD BLACKNESS*

To better explain the affective content of "deformation of mastery"—like the sneer that marks the signal difference in the "Niggas in Paris" coda—let us briefly turn to a classic example. In the history of Black music there is perhaps no better example of "deformation of mastery" than Nina Simone's signature performance on "Feeling Good"—not coincidentally, a recording that Kanye samples as the basis for track 6, "New Day." Over the Nina lines "sun in the sky . . . breeze driftin' on by" Kanye begins that track *in medias res*:

And I'll never let my son have a ego
He'll be nice to everyone wherever we go
I mean I might even make him be Republican
So everybody know he love white people

Despite the breezy lyrics about "feelin' good" and ethereal filters that frame this particular Nina, the original track—despite its title and ostensible message—has an undercurrent of discontent that connects more directly to Kanye's lyrics of harbored resentments about his own life and resentments about the racial order.

Indeed, on Nina's 1965 "Feeling Good," the iconic singer, pianist, composer, and (in)famously militant performer ends the cut sounding like she's "feeling" more hell-bent on revenge than "good."[30] Or, rather, hidden behind the sweet sentiments conveyed by the words, there is another meaning—she is feeling good, but it's not for the reasons the words convey. It's not peace and contentment, but in many ways, the opposite. What we hear in Nina's voice is satisfaction; a hard-won satisfaction that sounds sweet . . . like revenge.

Nina's creative and productive use of anger on "Feeling Good" calls to mind Audre Lorde's "The Uses of Anger: Women Responding to Racism." In that keynote at the 1981 National Women's Studies Association Conference, Lorde explained how "every woman has a well-stocked arsenal of anger potentially useful against those oppressions, personal and institutional, which brought that anger into being. Focused with precision it can become a powerful source of energy serving progress and change."[31] Notwithstanding Lorde's focus on women's anger here—particularly *Black* women's righteous anger—and Kanye and Jay's problematic (at best) relationship to hip hop's sexisms, both structural and performed, this reading of the transformative power of a precise and targeted anger speaks directly to this space "in the zone" where anger can be transformed into positive change. Lorde continues, "Oppressed peoples are always being asked to stretch a little more, to bridge the gap between blindness and humanity. Black women are expected to use our anger only in the service of other people's salvation or learning. But that time is over. My anger has meant pain to me but it has also meant survival, and before I give it up I'm going to be sure that there is something at least as powerful to replace it on the road to clarity."

In her ground-breaking study *Black Madness :: Mad Blackness*, Therí Alyce Pickens examines Black speculative fiction to interrogate the discursive tropes and performed praxis around Black disability.[32] Citing recent work highlighting how narratives of madness also accrue to to Black musical performance, she writes:

Of late, critical race scholars La Marr Jurelle Bruce and Nicole Fleetwood examined the prevalence of disability in discourses surrounding Black celebrities Lauryn Hill and Rihanna, respectively, in a special issue of *African American Review,* edited by Soyica Colbert, on Black performance. They each argue that for these Black women entertainers disability—particularly madness—changes public perception of their voice. For Lauryn Hill, the use of crazy-as-insult makes it permissible to ignore her critiques of the music industry and its exploitation of her. For Rihanna, mobilizing craziness allows her some latitude in her creative and erotic projects.[33]

Indeed, Lauryn and Rihanna are just more recent examples in a long line of African American artists—especially women—whose careers have alternately been impacted by and/or used discourses of madness and "unhinged" anger. The line stretches back to Nina, Josephine Baker, and beyond, and Pickens's work can also help us understand the work of "mad" Black men from Kanye back to Charles Mingus and Buddy Bolden. [34]

Especially important for our prophetic purposes here, Pickens notes how such Black madness and mad Blackness "presages" and is a "bellwether" of our society—of our world. Drawing on the work of post-Fanonian scholars such as Anna Mollow and Harry Elam, she notes that Black madness is neither a "biological or psychosocial impairment." She continues:

> Rather, those who are Black and mad are societal bellwethers. Their madness either presages or pinpoints putative larger issues at stake. This idea rests on the politicization of both Blackness and madness, where either or both are primarily or solely political identities. Black madness then becomes revelatory for the rest of the world and the Black mad folks—real or imagined—stand in for an examination of what is happening.[35]

She concludes: "Their existence functions as an analysis *tout court*, an *explication de texte* that the world operates according to anti-Black logics." Black madness is not an outlier—someone else's individual problem. It is—as Fanon would have it—a symptom of a sick society.[36]

In his analysis of another black entertainer's struggles with celebrity and mental health, "Coming to Terms with Dave Chappelle," Roy Christopher cites the famed comedian's very same diagnosis:

> His [Chappelle's] intelligence has always been evident even in the crudest of his comedy. . . . Take his thoughts on the term "crazy" applied to celebrities: "The worst thing to call somebody is 'crazy'. It's dismissive. 'I don't understand this person, so they're "crazy."' That's bullshit. These people are not crazy. They're strong people. Maybe the environment is a little sick." As he told Blender the year before, "The public really enjoys the downfall of celebrities too much."[37]

As Pickens, Fanon, and Chappelle suggest, Black madness is a trope that serves to individualize and externalize what is, in fact, a societal sickness: anti-Blackness. And, to be sure, this mass sickness is most intensely felt when focused by the culture industry's power and projected onto the select few who transgress the unspoken rules around Black success.

In our Trumpist era of antiracist protest, Nina, Lauryn, Rihanna, and Dave's Black madness and mad Blackness are echoed in the mediatized frames of "rioting" and "looting" that obscure the antiracist revolt at hand and help white people close their eyes and ears to their own problems—frames that Black people know how to use. Indeed, we'll return to the antiracist (and antipatriarchal and anticapitalist) revolution that is already underway in the conclusion. For now, I want to suggest that the affective content of Nina's musical revenge on "Feeling Good"—this distilled sonic madness—is borne of the deformation of mastery. It's not good and it's not bad—but rather, *it's so bad that it's good* (or vice versa, really, for that matter). The peak example of this affective color in "Feeling Good" comes at the climax of Nina's masterful performance at the end of the cut—where she unleashes a steady stream of unapologetic swagger in the last lines and coda of the tune.

The tune was originally written by the British songwriting team of Newley and Bricusse for their 1964 production *The Roar of the Greasepaint, The Smell of the Crowd.* The title is a comic (and synesthetic) reference to vaudeville's theatrical masking practices—especially those of blackface minstrelsy. In the musical, the song is performed by a character known only as "the Negro" as first brought to life by the influential Guyanese-British performer, Cy Grant, and features the character claiming empathic connection with animals, insects, and inanimate objects ("Birds flying high, you know how I feel . . ."). Cy's original-cast recording nicely conforms to—indeed masters—the midcentury expectations of his largely white audience, with tasteful approximations of African American dialect and only slightly stilted blues phrasing. With all due respect to Cy (whose performance seems consciously modelled on Paul Robeson), Simone's recording—mere months later—completely deforms the mastery that the original demonstrates. She owned that song. Still does (Michael Bublé's version notwithstanding).

Important for us in this consideration is the fact that Simone not only mastered the melody and phrasing and reshaped it to suit her own aims, but that she could hear the "stage Negro" in that white-authored song, wanted no part in that stock character, and set to work on a subversive takedown of that character, its authors, and the culture industry that had made countless millions from decades of such misrepresentations.[38] When she sings the line "And *I* know how I feel," she completely inhabits it and takes control of it—you know she means it. She saw, in other words, a chance to deform that trope. And she knew just how to do it, simultaneously introducing a subtle and destabilizing poison into the character—and making a fat stack of cheddar in the process.

Nina's secret, of course, was that she could completely upend the meaning without changing a word. The secret was her voice (admittedly, not much of a secret, really). After delivering, with masterful elocution and almost too-authentic blues shading, all those pretty words about "freedom" from two men who have no idea what freedom might mean to their Black character, she delivers the poison. When Nina finally sings "Freedom is mine, and *I* know how I feel" she pours herself out into the "*I*" of the line; communicating more deeply than words could convey, a deep resentment for all of the decisions that have been made for her, for all of the (mis) representations that have been made of her, for all of the suffering that has yearned to gain voice in her. It is a performance that recalls the main argument of Scott Saul's study *Freedom is, Freedom Ain't*: that freedom ain't shit without suffering.[39]

So, when that line comes after all those pretty words, she juices the line "Freedom is mine, and *I* know how I feel" with the faintest hint of a blues growl. The rapturously improvised coda that brings Nina's "Feeling Good" to a close is itself something of a *fuck you*, sliding forcefully through a mind-bending range of modal environments and testing the limits of each of those palettes against the big band's cadential, stop-time chords. She's free, and *she* knows how she feels.

Fred Moten writes evocatively of such deformation of mastery—this doubling and redoubling—as intimately bound up in the interplay between the Enlightenment binaries I have tracked in this study. And importantly for this discussion of Nina's voice, he finds the greatest potential for such deformation and destabilization not in texts, but in the "phonic matter" of the voice—the "vocal exteriority, the extremity that is often unnoticed as mere accompaniment to (reasoned) utterance."[40] He writes of the double game that I am here calling "deformation" thus:

> Finally, the opposition between the vernacular and the modern, the black and the white, is to be thought precisely in that they are both, if they are real, the product of a miscegenative encounter that exists as a function of the difference between the actors and the internal difference of the encounter . . . with structure and æffect doubled and redoubled. But the deep-down love, the bone-deep love, convergence of death and love, memory and narrative (that's what recognition is), that accompanies the miscegenative origin of black/American identity is exceeded by another love: that of/for freedom. And freedom, here, is not the etiolation that comes as the emergence of individual voice; it is, rather, the ensemblic improvisation. . . . Something irreferable—before the ongoing exchange of poisonous gift and available only by way of the disconnection such exchange enforces and, as connection, undermines—lies in wait in cut, augmented, instrumentalized speech like a depth charge.[41]

It is this "poison"—this "depth charge" laying in wait—that best captures Nina's subversive deformation of mastery of "Feeling Good" and its retort to the stereotypically limiting idea of "freedom" that its authors penned. As we will see in the next chapter, this ineffable yet instrumentalized power of sound that is unleashed on Ye's "in the zone" coda will be key to understanding the following track, and the album as a whole.

## ". . . I'M DEFINITELY IN MY ZONE"

The "Niggas in Paris" coda continues to heat up as Kanye repeats the mantra "Don't let me get in my zone" two more times before boasting "These other niggas is lyin' / Actin' like the summer ain't mine." Here Jay interjects, from the left channel of the stereo field, "I got that hot bitch in my home." Ye responds from the right channel, concluding the couplet and the conversation, "You know how many hot bitches I own?" using another sexist red herring to refer to his "ownership" of the summer Billboard Hot 100 charts and picking up Jay's line of wordplay. After another string of

"Don't let me get in my zone" warnings Ye takes the reins fully, reveling in the spotlight until the track's end:

> The stars is in the building
> They hands is to the ceiling
> I know I'm 'bout to kill it
> How you know? I got that feeling

The end of "Niggas in Paris" is thus an ego trip. The track concludes:

> You are now watching the throne
> Don't let me into my zone
> Don't let me into my zone

The track ends at an arrival, with both Ye and Jay rapping: "I'm definitely in my zone" and the last "zone" echoing and receding into the beat's white noise. If there was any question whether Kanye has entered the zone, it is now confirmed. Kanye is definitely in his zone. "You are now watching the throne."

And, as we will see, this coda is a portal from the mastery of (white capitalist) form on "Niggas in Paris"—of Rolex, Audemar, Gucci, Louis, and Margiela—to the deformation of that mastery.

CHAPTER 5

# "Sophisticated Ignorance"

## *The Deformation of Mastery*

Meanwhile the wine glasses had flushed yellow and flushed crimson; had been emptied; had been filled. And thus by degrees was lit, half-way down the spine, which is the seat of the soul, not that hard little electric light which we call brilliance, as it pops in and out upon our lips, but the more profound, subtle and subterranean glow which is the rich yellow flame of rational intercourse. No need to hurry. No need to sparkle. No need to be anybody but oneself . . . in other words, how good life seemed, how sweet its rewards, how trivial this grudge or that grievance, how admirable friendship and the society of one's kind, as, lighting a good cigarette, one sunk among the cushions in the window-seat.

—VIRGINIA WOOLF, *A ROOM OF ONE'S OWN* (1929)

"Otis" begins with the rich Leslie-diffused tone of Booker T. Jones's Hammond M-3 organ supported by a slow and steady rim-shot pulse. After almost a full bar of the sustained organ chord, Otis Redding's soulful baritone finally enters with the line "It makes it easier. . . ." Recognizing the rhetorical direction of Redding's call, a piano responds, lightening the tone color and leading upward a step to a pivot chord that is doubled by Booker T's organ. Redding responds in turn, elaborating: ". . . easier to bear." As the piano and organ continue their upward motion, a guitar plays a sweep-picked and lilting line down to the release of the tonic; a return to "easy," stable ground. Redding confirms the arrival: "yeah."

From the harmonic rhetoric of the instrumental arrangement to the text's sense of midsentence conclusion, it becomes immediately apparent that "Otis" starts *in medias res.* Kanye West's production on the track famously dwells on this pivotal sample from the second minute of Redding's "Try a Little Tenderness," slowing down the original and dropping Booker T and the MG's accompaniment down a fourth to linger in its sonic nuance and romantic, soulful mastery. Indeed, throughout the track, the sample is held up for us to regard like a precious gem. Ye holds up "Tenderness" like Jay's proverbial diamond gesture ("throw ya diamonds up") and lets it spin, allowing his audience ample time to behold the pricey commodity, the costly sample.

Tom Breihan begins his July 21, 2011, Pitchfork review of "Otis" with the following critique-cum-compliment centered on the costly sample:

> Here's Jay-Z on the "Otis" intro: "It sounds so soulful! Don't you agree?" Well, yeah. If you're willing to plunk down enough money to sample "Try a Little Tenderness," *that'll happen.* But even if the sample works as a sort of audio money-flaunt, it's also a tough and hard chop from Kanye—Otis Redding's magnificent voice mostly limited to a couple of hellfire grunts, the song itself held to a sharp guitar stab.[1]

More than simply providing the raw materials for a hip hop beat, the Redding sample is a costly token of mastery, regarded with reverence—so much so that this, the fourth cut of *Watch the Throne,* would take on the first name of the sample's headline artist: "Otis."[2] Here, Kanye's production has his audience in thrall to his ostentatious display of wealth, to the classic sample, and as we will see, to his masterfully artistic deformation thereof.[3] We are now "watching the throne."

From a musical perspective, Redding's vocals over the course of the original source track are striking for the way they paint a picture of "tenderness" that, nonetheless, grows increasingly aggressive, full-throated, and rough—climaxing in the unbridled affect of Redding's gravel-toned yet soulful grunts and exhortations. The entirety of the 1966 Redding track is, in fact, constructed as something of a crescendo. It begins with the pastoral innocence of a tender trumpet and tenor sax introduction in gently intertwining counterpoint before slowly building in aesthetic energy and developing the conceptual argument over the course of the song. By track's end Redding leads a loud and rhythmically driving jam that is more raw than "tender."[4]

As such, it will be useful to listen to Jay and Ye's "Otis" with Redding's "Try a Little Tenderness" firmly established in our ears. Indeed, on "Otis," Jay and Ye are resignifying Redding's own mastery of form as exhibited on this classic soul track. Far from disrespecting it, they are showing how their music is indebted to Otis, Booker T, and their milieu of Black musicians—that of the soul and civil rights generation. Yet, as we will see, their twenty-first-century music must by necessity speak to their contemporary world, both socially and sonically.

In this final chapter I argue that Jay and Ye's resignification on "Otis" is a form of sonic and social subversion that Houston Baker terms "the deformation of mastery" in his influential *Modernism and the Harlem Renaissance.*[5] Baker's elaboration is worth citing at length:

> The Afro-American spokesperson who would perform a deformation of mastery . . . must transform an obscene situation, a cursed and tripled metastatus, into a signal self/cultural expression. The birth of such a self is never simply a coming into being, but always, also, a release from a BEING POSSESSED. The practice of a phaneric, diasporic expressivity is both a metadiscourse on linguistic investiture and a lesson in the metaphorical "worm holing" as it were—the tunneling out of the black holes of possession and "tight places" of old clothes, into perhaps, a new universe. . . .
>
> The deformation of mastery refuses a master's *nonsense.* It returns—often transmuting "standard" syllables—to the common sense of the tribe.[6]

While the mastery of form works subtly and slyly within the conditions of possibility, the deformation of mastery is a full-throated coming into being—a(n) (angry) cry of freedom.

Recalling Du Bois, the deformation of mastery is "when the black man begins to dispute the white man's title to certain alleged bequests of the Fathers in wage and position, authority and training." The deformation of mastery is "when his attitude toward charity is sullen anger rather than humble jollity." The deformation of mastery is "*when he insists on his human right to swagger and swear and waste.*" In this deformation "the spell is suddenly broken."[7] Indeed, though Baker doesn't cite Du Bois's "The Souls of White Folk" here, with mention of the "'tight places' of old clothes" his elaboration channels Du Bois's "So long, then, as humble black folk, voluble with thanks, receive barrels of old clothes from lordly and generous whites, there is much mental peace and moral satisfaction" that begins this memorable passage of self-righteous swagger.

Indeed, in another evocatively swaggering passage, Baker prefigures the deformational play of gorilla/guerrilla that we examined in "Niggas in

Paris." On this deformational weaponization of the racist trope, Baker further elaborates the difference between the mastery of form's sly subversion and the deformation of mastery's bluntly transformative work:

> Adopting a shorthand, we might say that the difference between the mastery of form and the deformation of mastery is that between a praying mantis, or rabbit (did you ever attempt to follow the movements of an autumn hare through sedge-brown, October woods?), and a gorilla.
>
> The mastery of form conceals, disguises, floats like a trickster butterfly in order to sting like a bee. The deformation of mastery, by contrast, is Morris Day singing "Jungle Love," advertising, with certainty, his unabashed *badness*—which is not always conjoined with violence. *Deformation* is a go(uer)rilla action in the face of acknowledged adversaries. It produces sounds radically different from those of, say, Sade, whose almost mumbled initial exposition gives way to subdued (but scandalously signifying) lyrics in "Smooth Operator."
>
> The deformation of mastery is fully at work in gorilla "display." Man—the master of "civilization"—enters forests and triggers a response.[8]

The passage's focus on Black sounds of radical difference calls to mind not only all the subhuman, beastly play on the album, but Kanye's ugly and conceited nasal "heh?" gestures.

More importantly, this "worm holing" to a "new self" of "unabashed *badness*" that is a rebirth to "the common sense of the tribe" is a transformation that we can now describe as an expression of "anti-anti-essentialism"—a critical project and artistic attitude that forges a humanity free from white Enlightenment universalism and all its lies. The term, which I have taken up and developed elsewhere, is elaborated by Gilroy through a tactical recovery of Amiri Baraka's "changing same." Gilroy writes:

> I believe it is possible to approach the music as a *changing* rather than unchanging same. Today, this involves the difficult task of striving to comprehend the reproduction of cultural traditions not in the unproblematic transmission of a fixed essence through time but in the breaks and interruptions that suggest that the invocation of tradition may itself be a distinct, though covert, response to the destabilizing flux of the postcontemporary world.[9]

Indeed, in his use of the geological term *phaneric* in defining the deformation of mastery, Baker is referring to igneous rocks—rocks made of solidified lava—that display clearly visible crystals.[10] The metaphor plays on this changing same, by highlighting how such essences are reborn and purified by going *through the fire.*

As we will see, the deformation of mastery on "Otis" is not directed at Otis Redding and his music *per se* but at his midcentury American capitalist habitus, its exchange economy metaphysics that equates love and things (in the right proportions), and its supplementation—the suggestion that love might suffice in lieu of material "things" (where "things" are posited as the preferred/normative romantic currency). This is the capitalist episteme that commoditized love and created Valentine's Day, champagne, red roses, and chocolate *bonbons* as we know them today—and as Jay and Ye will expound. This is the capitalist system that, indeed, invented romance as we understand it.[11] Redding has mastered these (white) bourgeois sensibilities, mastered these economics for his community, demonstrated this mastery of form on sound recording, and sold them back to his society to garner himself some agency. Jay and Ye, having already gamed the system, have other aims in mind.

## ECONOMIES OF LOVE ON "TRY A LITTLE TENDERNESS"

As the introductory horn duet winds to a conclusion on "Try a Little Tenderness" and the trumpet lethargically moans across the threshold, the electric guitar welcomes them home with the reassurance of a sweep-picked tonic chord and Redding delivers his earnest opening lines in an unhurried, rubato tempo:

> Oh, she may be weary
> Them young girls they do get wearied
> Wearing that same old shaggy dress, yeah yeah
> But when she gets weary
> Try a little tenderness, yeah yeah

Throughout the first verse Redding's heartfelt vocal lines elaborate the economics of love in a capitalist society. By centering the "old shaggy dress" Redding performs for his audience an accounting of the emotional value of material goods vis-à-vis romantic affection—especially given the inability of working men of limited means to provide "nice things" for the subjects of their affection. His earnestly considered advice is supported by low, sustained organ tones, like a Baptist preacher at the beginning of an invitation. From time to time the congregation—the organ, piano, and tenor sax—responds to his calls with short riffs and soulful affirmations.[12]

On the second verse, Booker T and the MG's heighten the dramatic energy, establishing a groove around rim shots on every beat. Redding continues, still supported by tasty and unobtrusive organ, piano, and guitar lines:

You know she's waiting
Just anticipating
For things that she'll never, never, never, never possess, yeah yeah
But while she's there waiting, without them
Try a little tenderness (half-spoken: that's all you gotta do)

Here, the musical aesthetic translates the yearning for "things" into sonic anticipation as Redding not only explains, but *performs* his theory about the value of love in a materialistic society—and the role of materialism in a love economy. In a capitalist society of winners and losers ("makers and takers"), he suggests, love compensates for those "*things* she'll never, never, never, never possess" as the tick-tock of the rim shots and the searching chords heighten our anticipation.

Although Redding's Stax-era soul and R&B version of "Try a Little Tenderness" is very different in musical style—indeed, in melody and harmony as well—it is worth pausing here to note that this song about *love and things* was written in 1933 by the British songwriting team of Jimmy Campbell, Reg Connelly, and Harry M. Woods at the height of the Great Depression. It became a global hit through recordings by Ray Noble (1933) and Bing Crosby (1934) during a time of calamitous economic turmoil and widespread poverty across Europe and the US.

While Noble's 1933 fox-trot version is nearly lyrically identical to the 1966 version (exceptions including a "shabby" rather than "shaggy" dress), Bing's version includes an entire rubato introduction highlighting the "hustle" and bustle of modern life in 1934.[13] The lyric begins, evincing a tragically quaint nostalgia for simpler times:

In the hustle of today
We're all inclined to miss
Those little things that mean so much:
A word, a smile, a kiss.
When a woman loves a man
He's a hero in her eyes
And a hero he can always be
If he'll just realize . . .

Here, the ur-crooner lingers on the last syllable, giving it the signature Bing treatment—a flipped, rising mordant a lilting step above the fifth. After a violin rises in chromatic resolution to end the introduction, Bing begins the song in earnest: "She may be weary. . . ." The added text makes explicit those other loving *actions* that can stand in for romantic *commodities*, those "little things that mean so much" and can cement the man's status as "hero in her eyes . . . if he'll just realize" that there's a tried-and-true plan for human intimacy in the age of global dehumanizing poverty: "just try a little tenderness."

If we track the tune from its 1933 genesis through its 1966 reinterpretation to its 2011 sampling, it becomes clear that the song must have had very similar purchase among its Great Depression (1929–), civil rights era (1954–), and Great Recession (2008–) audiences. To be sure, this savvy bit of advice must have seemed something of a game-changer for the men struggling to endure the demoralizing effects of these economic and cultural upheavals. Most likely, the words of Bing, Otis, Jay, and Ye eased the burden of poverty in a land of plenty. Or maybe they didn't . . .

Maybe they just came off as tired platitudes. Or, coming from the mouths of these entitled Black millionaires in particular, maybe they enraged "mainstream" (read: white) Americans. Maybe this sample, in the context of this track and its luxury rap album, just reminded them of the unfulfilled promises of the American Dream. Maybe it struck them as proof of the slow dismantling of the assurances afforded by the white privilege that underwrites the nation's public life. Maybe these Black millionaires just confirmed Arlie Russell Hochschild's conclusions in *Strangers in Their Own Land: Anger and Mourning on the American Right*—that Black success is hateful to conservative whites. That every Black success is viewed as "cutting in line."[14]

As we have seen, Jay and Ye's use of the song for their "luxury rap" album was much denigrated in its context of the global economic downturn—and not just by Donald Trump's silent (electoral) ~~majority~~ minority. As just one notable example, in his 1 September 2011 review for *Rolling Stone*, Jody Rosen opined:

> Such moments are too scarce on *Watch the Throne*: More often we hear about "big rocks" and "gold bottles"—which, by the way, rhymes with "scold models." In the midst of an early 21st-century Great Recession, the vicarious experience of opulence may be enough for Jay's and Kanye's millions of fans. But on a record this ambitious, this sonically bold, it's a shame two of music's greatest storytellers don't extend their gaze beyond their own luxe lives.[15]

Just like Breihan's Pitchfork review, Rosen's piece offers a modicum of begrudging respect (and admiration), but reflects the widely held critical opinion that the album was above all a chance for these two "haves" to have even more—a chance for talented millionaires to synergize and maximize their respective investments.

As I've argued, this widely publicized view is a fundamental misreading of an album that is, in fact, replete with deeply subversive forms of conspicuous consumption on a stunningly wide array of levels. As we will see, the recombination and resignification of this costly sample is yet another form of "critical excess"—a "deformation of mastery" with an explicitly political message that amounts to much more than a chance to "gaze" at "their own luxe lives." It is not in spite of the Great Recession that they perform this over-the-top accounting of "black excellence, opulence, decadence," but *because* of this historic failure of global capitalism. Even more importantly for our purposes here, however, is the fact that as I perform this cultural analysis of the 2011 album, global geopolitics are dangerously reminiscent of the mid-1930s in both political and cultural respects. Analyses of Trump's fascist and right-wing populist leanings are widely available—as are discussions of Brexit's dismantling of the postwar peace and broader right-wing trends across Europe.[16]

As I describe in the sections to come, on *Watch the Throne*, Jay and Ye deform "Tenderness" and its politics to bypass the discourse of humanity that was so central to civil rights politics and the rule of law; to bypass the cultural logic that allowed Otis Redding to appropriate and update, but not change, Bing Crosby's universalizing masculine message; and to bypass the discourse of Black respectability that laid the groundwork for everything from Motown becoming "the voice of young America" to the election of the nation's first Black president. As we know now, the Black respectability politics so famously framed in the album art for Kendrick Lamar's cover art for *To Pimp a Butterfly*—cover art that pits the stereotyped Black thugs of "America's nightmare" against the reality of its intelligent, decent, and *humane* Black president, Barack Obama—is dead. The November 8, 2016, election of Donald Trump as president of the United States issued a firm rejoinder to Black respectability politics just as it closed the door on the foregone conclusion that the nation would elect its first woman to the highest office in the land.

In Virginia Woolf's *A Room of One's Own* we are given a lucidly rendered taste of how humanity is a privilege.[17] In the first of her influential set of lectures at Cambridge's women's colleges (Newnham and Girton), the author describes the creature comforts that set the conditions of possibility to be "oneself." Writing in 1928, on the cusp of the Great Depression, Woolf describes a picturesque fall day in well-manicured (and well-policed) gardens and the sumptuous feast of a Cambridge (men's) college luncheon. She describes, in detail, the way the partridge, sole, salmon, and duckling were perfectly cooked and served and the way "the wine glasses had flushed yellow and flushed crimson; had been emptied; had been filled" before recounting the forgettable dinner in her own underfunded, unremarkable, and feminized communal dining hall later that same day.

In Woolf's rendering, the asymmetrical experience of the two spaces reveals something of the essence of privilege. Though the former scene is certainly set among the upper echelons, Woolf's opening story suggests that privilege need not revolve around the limits of excellence and opulence. Indeed, her main point is that true privilege resides in "the seat of the soul . . . not that hard little electric light which we call brilliance, as it pops in and pops out upon out lips, but the more profound, subtle and subterranean glow which is the rich yellow flame of rational intercourse. No need to hurry. No need to sparkle. No need to be anybody but oneself." The passage recalls Du Bois's passage from 1920's "The Souls of White Folk," which puts a different spin on "double consciousness"—on one's need to navigate an ever-asymmetrical society.

Indeed, on *Watch the Throne,* Jay and Ye always need to be "on." They are not afforded the privilege of being anything less than the best, anything but "brilliant"—even by their erstwhile fans at *Pitchfork* and *Rolling Stone.* As such, Jay and Ye perform stereotyped Blackness directly from subhuman to superhuman—from "Murder to Excellence" as track 10 puts it—with precious little time for the center space, that always already white (male) category: *humanity*. And as we're forced to witness the ongoing rebuke of Barack Obama—that paragon of Black respectability, of rationality, of humanity—and everything he stood for and worked for, I can't blame Jay and Ye for skipping the category of human for a second. Deform away.

As Steven Levitsky and Daniel Ziblatt put it in *How Democracies Die*: "History doesn't repeat itself. But it rhymes. The promise of history is that we can find the rhymes before it is too late."[18] In what follows, I attempt to do just that.

## CUTTING THE GEM: DEFORMING "TENDERNESS"

In the third verse of the sample source, "Tenderness," the bass walks down a fifth to establish a new tonal center on C major, further heightening the "waiting" and "anticipating" that Redding is singing about and giving the listener the sense that the stakes have just been raised. We're about to go somewhere.

> It's not just sentimental, no, no, no
> She has her grief and care, yeah yeah yeah
> But the *soft* words, they are spoke so gentle, yeah
> It makes it easier, easier to bear, yeah

Here, Redding's delivery grows more urgent, the timbre of his voice more rough-hewn. Indeed, on the word "soft" in the above couplet, Redding *growls*, his throat now contradicting the gentle "anticipation" and performative "soft words" about which he is advising us.[19] As we will see, this lyrically, musically, and performatively contradictory background on "Try a Little Tenderness" provides the springboard for Kanye's recomposition on "Otis"—and, notably, his refiguration of Redding's midcentury African American economics.

It is at this very moment in the original ("It makes it easier . . .") that Kanye starts his sample for "Otis." Here, between the first and second half of the last couplet above, Ye rightly recognizes that we have reached the first major structural arrival of Otis Redding's "Try a Little Tenderness": the surprise entrance of the rich and forceful organ chord. Indeed, this is the striking Hammond M-3 organ chord that I describe above—the Booker T attack that starts the Jay and Ye track. Most importantly, it is this organ entrance that highlights the takeaway—the *punch line*—of Redding's words of wisdom on the track, the lesson being: for people who have nothing, tenderness is priceless. Whether in the Great Depression, the civil rights era, the Great Recession, or today, a bit of loving tenderness makes poverty and quotidian struggle "easier to bear."

Here we can begin to consider the two tracks together. After the sweep-picking guitar line brings us back down to the "easy" stability of the tonic chord, "Otis" starts in earnest. As the horns lay down a soothing accompaniment of sustained chords to a cha-cha-chá piano accompaniment, Redding begins on the Jay and Ye track: "You won't regret it, no, no / Some girls they don't forget it / Love is their only happiness, yeah." After a couple organ stab interjections an otherwise unremarkable descending five-note piano line marks a chord change in the original. In Kanye's reconfiguration, however, this simple, step-wise gesture becomes a structural centerpiece. Here, Ye stops the source track and suspends the flow of time, incessantly looping the downward piano gesture while building in volume and skipping forward to a stuttering and glitchy reiteration of the word "squeeze" from the later line "Squeeze her, don't tease her, never leave her."

In skipping the "Tenderness" title lines—"But it's all so easy / All you gotta do is try, try a little tenderness, yeah / All you gotta do is, man, hold her where you want her"—Ye also skips the sonic buildup (and increasingly sexist subtext) that accompanies that text. In their stead, Jay breaks the fourth wall, entering the sonic frame and asking us, the audience: "Sounds so soulful, don't you agree?" Jay is talking about Otis's soulfulness, of course, but he's also commenting on Ye's signifyin(g) hypersoul on the track, for in sampling, deconstructing, and recombining "Tenderness" Kanye has taken the mastery of Otis Redding, Booker T and his MGs and catapulted them to the next level.[20] He has just deformed this cut, polished, and precious diamond. This is the "deformation of mastery"—an attitude and methodology that "refutes a master's *nonsense*. It returns—often transmuting 'standard' syllables—to the tribe," according to Baker's theory.[21] This "*nonsense*" is not the *content* of Redding's situated advice, but the *form* of the commodity that is supplementary to romantic affect and mimics human intimacy: the popular musical recording.

Indeed, we might also say that this deformational critique extends to the notated musical form of the published popular song as well. For not only is there a wealth of syllabic transformation in Kanye's deformation ("sque-sque-squeeze"), but a refutation of the searching harmonic rhetoric of the 1933 song—a return to "the tribe" of hip hop's harmonic stasis and rhythmic complexity.[22] Recalling Baker, here Ye has "transform(ed) an obscene situation, a cursed and tripled metastatus into a signal self/cultural expression." Ye has transformed Redding's need to transcend the capitalist economy of material things to express love in the context of poverty into a chart-topping celebration of Black wealth—*his* Black wealth. Ye has worm holed through the gendered and racialized palimpsest of poverty and possession in this classic track and "com[e] into being." Ye's swaggering deformation of "Try a Little Tenderness" on "Otis" is "a release from a BEING POSSESSED." This is no *cover* of the original—no sly mastery of its capitalist pop song form. It is an undoing of the original—a deformation of "Try a Little Tenderness." And as we will see, this deformation works not just musically, but conceptually, across both form and content, sound and ideology.

When, at long last, Ye lets the full line spin—"Squeeze her, don't tease her, never leave her"—the harmony rises stepwise, building tension, yearning, and anticipation and inverting the descending piano loop that leads up to Jay's first entrance. The first verse of the track thus begins: "I invented swag." In the background, Ye's beat settles into a driving yet harmonically static, urgent yet nonlexical loop of Redding's "got to, got to, na-na-na" from the track's climax. And like Ye's recombination of Otis's and Booker's demonstrated mastery on "Tenderness," in "transmuting" the common usage noun "swagger" into the nonnormative "swag," Jay situates himself in his genre frame and within the history of Black music more broadly.[23] Jay simultaneously draws on the trendiness of the word in the early 2000s, argues that his transmutation predates these usages, and claims that not only did he invent the word, but he invented the next-level swagger—the hyper-swagger (or ur-swagger)—that the term "swag" implies.

In light of the theoretical model of "Afro-American modernism" that Baker lays out in *Modernism and the Harlem Renaissance* and the present book's three-part analysis of cyclical—or better, spiraling—processes of full-circle-yet-next-level mastery, it will be worth returning to the Du Bois excerpt from "Souls of White Folk" in full.[24] In 1920, Du Bois explained hip hop's cultural inheritance of cultural critique and thug life thus:

> So long, then, as humble black folk, voluble with thanks, receive barrels of old clothes from lordly and generous whites, there is much mental peace and moral satisfaction. But when the black man begins to dispute the white man's title to certain alleged bequests of the Fathers in wage and position, authority and training; and when his attitude toward charity is sullen anger rather than humble jollity; *when he insists on his human right to swagger and swear and waste,—then the spell is suddenly broken. . . .*[25]

Here, Du Bois describes the unrefined and base "human right to swagger and swear, and waste." This swagger distinguishes the "humble-born" against the "lordly and generous whites," the "ignoble" against the "noble." Yet ninety-one years after the publication of *Darkwater,* Jay and Ye have "insisted," they have tasted success, they have attained the "position, authority, and training" of the upper class, they have sipped from the chalice of nobility. Yet, structurally, the spell of white supremacy is not broken. Nowhere close.

On *Watch the Throne*, the two moguls—the two modern-day royals—have exceeded the civilized norms and "moral satisfaction" of their caste. As we witnessed on "Niggas in Paris," they have mastered the ethos of the jet set and its *haute couture*. This is Baker's "mastery of form"—they know how to fit in, how to be heard, and how to prosper in a system designed to oppress them. They have mastered the racialized rules of Western capitalist democracy. On "Otis" they are out to deform that mastery. As such, we might say that here the vocal power and pure affect of the wordless climax to Redding's 1966 classic is beautifully recomposed, *acceding* to the aristocratic ideology of the European artistic tradition but *exceeding* that regal ethos to bypass Du Bois's uncouth "swagger"—and emerge, fully formed, in Jay's boastful paparazzi-ready "swag."

On "Otis," the critical excess of Jay's "swag" reinvents Du Bois's "swagger" to break "the spell of white supremacy" and take his rightful place alongside—or better, *above*—whites. Redding played to Euro-American rules of artistry and beauty and—like countless other Black American artists—captivated audiences globally and won the game during his century, yet never gained equality by any objective measure. Instead, Jay and Ye are out to performatively *exceed* the very logic of Europe and its whiteness. For these Black men, so recently deemed subhuman—and so often still treated as such—humanity is not the goal. Like "equality," humanity is the "master's *nonsense*"—that "universal" category so thoroughly defined and enforced as white as to be a trap.

Indeed, this postegalitarian logic is a central conceptual terrain in the recent and well-publicized debate between Cornell West and Ta-Nehisi Coates.[26] If we look closely at the politics that the two present and the cultural logics they represent, we can draw a line between West's old-guard view and the interracial coalition politics in pursuit of equality along class lines that has been central to the US Democratic Party's big tent. Though cast as insurgent, here West's support of Bernie Sanders's 2016 presidential campaign serves as illustrative. Though Coates ultimately suggested he'd vote for Sanders as well, he never fully supported the universalist "it's not race, it's class" argument that has been central to the (old) new Left since the civil rights movement. Indeed, Coates's position suggests that it is, in fact, about race.

In that regard, this twenty-first-century position is in line with Black Lives Matter—a mo(ve)ment that foregrounds the racialization and destruction of Black bodies. In brief, where West's Civil Rights ideology seeks equality under the law, Black Lives Matter just wants not to be shot. The "let's all be equal" dream has been revealed as just that: a dream. BLM moves past the lofty, idealistic, and ultimately abstract dream of equality to work on material concerns: namely stopping Black people from being killed by police and incarcerated in record numbers. In other words, as righteous as he himself conceives it, Cornel West's project is beholden to a universalism, steeped in the all-lives-matter ideology of hegemonic discourse dating back to the "all men are created equal" and "inalienable Rights" that *was then and is now* clearly little more than a bald-faced cover-up of a white-supremacist structure.[27]

No, the goal for the oppressed subhuman living within a system rigged against her is no longer humanity, but superhumanity, a superhumanity that utterly deforms our white-supremacist everyday through this spiral of mastery: subhuman—~~human~~—superhuman. Baker writes, "The Afro-American spokesperson who would perform a deformation of mastery . . . must transform an obscene situation, a cursed and tripled metastatus, into a signal self/cultural expression."[28] Indeed, this is the performed sub/superhumanity of "sophisticated ignorance," the spiraling paradox of "Drivin' Benzes with no benefits," the ambivalent tripling of "my other other Benz," and the critical excess of "I'm 'bout to call the paparazzi on myself" in the lines to come.

## CUTTING THE MAYBACH: THE "OTIS" VIDEO

If this "deformation of mastery" is not readily evident from Ye's musical recombination of "Try a Little Tenderness" or Jay's lyrical transmutation of "swagger," then a look at the visual narrative of Spike Jonze's video for "Otis" should prove conclusive.[29] As Booker T's rich organ chord enters the sonic frame, the video opens with a slow zoom shot of a black sedan flanked by five white-clad mechanics in what seems to be a warehouse back lot. A figure enters the visual frame from the right armed with a cutting torch spewing a foot-long blade of red-orange flame. Soon after, someone enters from the left carrying a massive circular saw. As the frame widens, we see the figure on the right look back over his shoulder, revealing that it's Jay. Indeed, the two artists distinguish themselves from the phalanx of mechanics not just by their cutting tools, but by their not being dressed for such work. Unlike the mechanics, they are dressed in loose-fitting dark pants and white tops, but more striking is the fact that Ye (the figure on the left) seems to be wearing a chunky gold bracelet while Jay, viewed in full profile, is revealed to be wearing a pair of classic red-and-black Jordans. These figures aren't Depression-era men looking to dispense or solicit romantic advice.

As Otis Redding sings the lines "You won't regret it, no, no / Some girls they don't forget it," the next shot moves from the cutting tools and the luxury goods to a close-up of the sedan's hood and grill. One of the mechanics moves from left to right in slow motion, unobscuring the car's double-M hood ornament and confirming that the car is a Maybach 57—a $350,000 luxury automobile. The next shot suggests putting two and two together as we see a helmeted mechanic taking a Sawzall to something . . . the Maybach's roof? In another shot sparks fly ominously over the open doors of the car. As Redding concludes the line "Love is their only happiness, yeah," we see a shot in a new outdoor setting where a massive American flag frames Ye dancing and Jay mouthing the lyrics in the foreground, as if to distract us from the ill-advised demolition work happening in the back lot.

In the next sequence, the edits come fast and furious as it becomes clear that, yes, the mechanics are breathing new life into to the term "chop shop." They are systematically disassembling the car, violently slashing through metal, removing the rear windshield, throwing unwanted scraps across the auto yard. And just as the visual rhythm gains speed and force,

Fig. 6. Still from the music video for "Otis" (dir. Spike Jonze). Ye and Jay approach the luxury car with cutting torch and circular saw.

the sonic rhythm grows frenetic and the dynamics louder—for this is the section in Ye's introduction where the descending five-note piano line gets looped incessantly, while the word "sque-sque-squeeze" stutters and glitches across the stereo field. In short, the moment when it becomes clear that Kanye is cutting that musical gem—"Tenderness"—is also the moment when it becomes clear that the luxury sedan—the Maybach—is being cut. The luxury commodity is being destroyed.

The video cuts back to Jay wearing an oversized Yankees cap in front of the oversized flag. He responds to Otis Redding's voice—and Ye's beat—as Ye goes bananas in the background: "Sounds so soulful, don't you agree?" More quick edits of auto parts being cut and tossed finally give way to a culminating shot: there, in rear profile, stands a car looking half *Back-to-the-Future* DeLorean and half demolition-derby bruiser. Alec Banks's *Highsnobiety* article on the video describes it thus: "Armed with a blowtorch and a Sawzall, the Maybach is instantaneously transformed into a Frankenstein-esque muscle car indicative of something that would have been suitable for the terrain in Mad Max."[30] The Maybach has not been destroyed, *per se*, it has been deformed. And like the "Tenderness" sample, this deformation takes the luxury item, cuts it, recombines it, and catapults it to a somewhat disturbing next level of artistry. To mark this culminating reveal—this deformation—the video and audio come into perfect alignment; just as a celebratory "oooooowwww!" issues from the sonic field—a Kanye scream—the new supercar spouts a burst of flame from a rear-mounted jet.

In the next frame Jay approaches the camera as Ye's beat settles into the new syncopated and driving loop of Redding's voice on "got to, got to, na-na-na." Jay grabs the camera and positions it *just . . . so* . . . as he delivers those first lines:

> Uh . . . I invented swag
> Poppin' bottles puttin' supermodels in the cab
> Proof: I guess I got my swagger back
> Truth: New Watch alert: Hublots
> Or the big-face Rollie, I got two of those
> Arm out the window through the city, I maneuver slow
> Cock back, snap back, see my cut through the holes

The lines pick up where "Niggas in Paris" left off, adding to the litany of name-dropped luxury brands (Gucci, Louis, Margiela . . .) the names of luxury time pieces: Hublots and Rollies. Notably, to these luxury items are added the hip hop *accoutrements par excellence*, champagne "bottles" and "supermodels"—the latter gaining physical presence in the music video.

As the supercar first streaks by, we see the drivers—Jay and Ye—in the front and four young women piled in back. Music videos have a long and deplorable history of objectifying women, but the supermodels named and depicted in this video rise (or better: sink) to a level of objectification so blatant as to clearly draw attention to their role as props in the video—a far cry from Otis's vision of humanizing tenderness. As we watch the throne on this, the album's fourth track, the spectacle of commodities trotted out through the first forty-five seconds includes the sample, the car, the gold bracelet, the Jordans, the bottles, the watches . . . and the models. Though nowhere as rich in luxury goods as "Niggas in Paris," this fourth track sets up the "luxe life" well. But as we've already seen, on "Otis," these objects don't quite function or behave as we might expect them to.

Here, the "snap back" cap mentioned at the verse's end is illustrative. In positioning the camera *just . . . so* . . . Jay frames his face and his cap, which had been front-facing but is now, notably, backward. Although the cap doesn't appear to be a standard plastic mesh snap back, it is clearly an adjustable model with a strap clearly protruding in this close-up. The confluence of lyric and image here reminds us that it is artists like Jay who have taken budget commodities such as the cheap foam-and-plastic "snap back" version of the "on-field" fitted wool caps and turned them into desirable fashion accessories.

To be sure, this is cultural labor common to popular media icons. James Dean famously transformed Levi Strauss's denim work pants into a cultural commodity for the new demographic market category of "teenagers," but it is worth noting how Black musics have launched a thousand styles and products, from Jazz Age flapper dresses and Swing Era bobby socks to MJ's leather jackets, Hammer's pants, and Kanye's pink Polos, to name just a very, very few.[31] What these commodities have in common is their resignification by the wearer. In hip hop culture, if you want to embody swag you don't just wear an item, you *rock it*. In the video for "Otis," Jay doesn't just wear a Yankees cap, he *rocks* a Yankees snap back. In each shot, it is clear Jay has pulled down, tilted, turned, or otherwise reset the angle of the cap on his head—this is the "cock back" of the lyric. In that introductory shot before "I invented swag" Jay isn't just telling us about his role in the birth of "swag," he is performing it for us. It's not whether you wear something, or what you wear, it's how you wear it—even, we might suppose, if it's a "shaggy" or "shabby" dress.

## CATALOGING PARADOX, PERFORMING SUPERHUMANITY

The balance of "Otis" sees Jay and Ye lyrically and rhetorically performing the paradox-laden *critical excess* that we hear in the sonic transmutation of the track, "Tenderness," from the introduction and see in the visual de- and reformation of the video's chop shop. As we track this critical excess I want to keep in mind the binary collapsing sub/superhuman structure of Jay and Ye's critique on the track—and throughout the album. In particular, I want to consider the stereotypes of Blackness that the two highlight and subvert through Homi Bhabha's theorization of a "third space" that "subverts any binary or sublatory ordering of power and sign," "endows it with a strategic motion," "and initiates a space of intercutting that articulates politics/psyche, sexuality/race. It does this in a relation that is differential and strategic rather than originary, ambivalent rather than accumulative, doubling rather than dialectical."[32] That is, I want us to be insistently dialectical in our analysis of the relationality of the rhetorically polarized paradoxes—like "sophisticated ignorance"—that Jay and Ye set up for us. Further, I want us to examine how every contradiction—like "I'm 'bout to call the paparazzi on myself"—that they set up is strategically calculated to exact maximum damage on our preconceptions. Indeed, these paradoxical constructions "transform an obscene situation, a cursed and tripled metastatus, into a signal self/cultural expression."[33]

The first superhuman paradox that requires our attention is the *ill* takedown of Kanye's perceived competitors in the rap game: "I adopted these niggas, Philip Drummoned 'em / Now I'm 'bout to make 'em tuck they whole summer in." As he suggests on track 11, "Made in America," the album was an unfair intervention into the rap industry and the *Billboard* charts that rely on success in the lucrative summer airplay hustle and market for sales. He raps:

> Niggas hustle every day for a beat from Ye
> What I do? Turn around gave them beats to Jay
> And I'm rapping on the beat they was supposed to buy
> I guess I'm getting high off my own supply.

The lines suggest that the collaborative album by hip hop's top two artists had an oxygen-sucking impact on the summer market. What's more, this impact was compounded by the fact that Ye's beats not only laid the foundation for the album's massive success, but robbed other artists of the foundations for their own success. As Ye summarizes, the move is a dangerous one, tantamount to a drug pusher using his own product.

What is particularly striking in this construction, however, is Ye's verbification of the name "Philip Drummond"—the name of the rich white father character of two underprivileged adopted Black boys on the wildly popular late 1970s and early 1980s sit-com, *Diff'rent Strokes*. The rhetorical play here is structured around the fact that Ye is taking on the role of the rich white daddy of his competitors, competitors he equates with the show's ghetto kids. Thus, Ye is here performing anti-anti-essentialism: he is a Black man playing a white dad to Black boys—a "differential and strategic rather than originary" doubling, as Bhabha would have it.

The following couplets continue the paradoxical, doubling play, entering a third space that Bhabha's "evil eye/I" might not see coming. Ye raps:

They say I'm crazy, well I'm 'bout to go dumb again
They ain't see me 'cause I pulled up in my other Benz
Last week I was in my other other Benz
Throw ya diamonds up 'cause we in this bitch another 'gain.

The rhetorical construction of "my other Benz" here conforms to the excessive wealth we've come to expect on the album, but then strategically exceeds that excess with the unimaginable (and apparently invisible) image of "my other other Benz." That's three Benzes. And in the context of this album, that's not just more excess, that's *critical excess*, a form of performative excess that critiques and undermines the capitalist logic of excess. What's more, this construction is notably framed as a "crazy" one; an *irrational* one. Indeed, as we have seen, Kanye has been known to be "crazy"—a public perception and mediatized meme stretching back to his veering off-script during a Hurricane Katrina telethon, wherein he shocked his cohost Mike Myers by stating the obvious: "George Bush doesn't care about black people."[34]

Here Jay stays in the visual register, picking up the flow of contradictions with the line "Photoshoot fresh, looking like wealth / I'm 'bout to call the paparazzi on myself." The line is tailor-made for our reality-TV age with its reality-TV president, coining for the "new gilded age" a highly managed standard of freshness—"photoshoot fresh," a fresh that gives the visual impression of wealth. Looking so good, Jay admits his desire to further manage his image with the help of the much-maligned photographers who are, in fact, the lifeblood of the twenty-four-hour TMZ-style mediasphere. But surely celebrities don't call the paparazzi on themselves, *do they*? In this case, the line is constructed as a contradiction, but ultimately revealed as part and parcel of the self-reinforcing, wag-the-dog dialogue that feeds the media economy—a symptom of a deeply ambivalent and solipsistic hypercapitalism that looks primed to eat itself.

Jay's verse continues the track's ongoing catalog of contradictory play with two couplets that give the verses a more weighty and overtly political cast.

Flee in the G450 I might surface
Political refugee asylum can be purchased

Uh, everything's for sale, I got five passports
I'm never going to jail.

Beginning with the image of the Gulfstream private jet, Jay imagines himself a "political refugee," albeit an apparently wealthy one. While the line seemed something of a conceit in the Obama era, it has the ring of prophesy in Trump's America. Further, the track goes on to set up the paradox "asylum can be purchased" before detailing the range of goods available to the ultrawealthy. If everything is for sale, as it would now seem to be, surely one can buy asylum. Perhaps for someone who has two big-face Rollies and three Benzes, five passports isn't out of the question.

On Ye's second verse the political turns to the religious and artistic.

I made "Jesus Walks" I'm never going to hell
Couture level flow, it's never going on sale
Luxury rap, the Hermès of verses
Sophisticated ignorance, write my curses in cursive

In citing his first major success as a recording artist, the top-20 hit "Jesus Walks" from his Grammy-nominated album *College Dropout*, Ye simultaneously references his critical accolades and the fact that he achieved them on the back of a track steeped in Christian imagery and scripture—something of a paradox in itself.

Yet it is the following couplet that best summarizes the binary collapsing rhetorical play on the track. Riffing on the "Couture level flow" of the previous line (everything might be *for* sale, but some things never go *on* sale), Ye here invents the new category of "Luxury rap." Notably, his rhetoric suggests that he does so in both *content and form*—the album is *about* luxury and is, *itself*, a luxury good like something from the Parisian high-fashion house Hermès. The gilded geometric patterns of the Givenchy artwork for the album are a primary case in point here, giving the material artifact of the album (or its digital version) a unique bling.

Most importantly, the line "Sophisticated ignorance, write my curses in cursive" confirms that this performative collapsing of binaries is central to the conception and realization of the album at every level. Sophistication is the demonstration of worldly experience and cultivation while ignorance is the lack thereof. Yet we know exactly what Kanye *means*. Surely the very idea of "luxury rap" is a paradox. This is street music. Hip hop is famously "something from nothing." But in the mental picture of Kanye writing his "fucks," "niggas," and "bitches" in cursive, he (literally? literarily?) flips the script on our received—and often cultivated—image of the ignorant foul-mouthed rapper and reminds us that he is a critically acclaimed, commercially successful, and remarkably enduring artist—as is his collaborator, Jay-Z. This performance of "sophisticated ignorance" is, thus, not a reversion to essentialist tropes of Black ignorance, it is a *through the fire* expression of anti-anti-essentialism. Here, Ye is cultivating this ignorance, deforming the obscene, racist perception of that ignorance, and worm holing through to a "signal self/cultural expression"—a critical excess.

On the next verse, Jay picks up where he left off, and takes up a thread from Ye's boastful discussion of his experience with borders: "I get it custom, you a customer / You ain't 'customed to going through customs / You ain't been nowhere huh?" Picking up on the Latin American train of thought after Ye's concluding joke "I'm done, I'll hit you up mañanaaah," Jay begins, "Welcome to Havana / Smoking Cubanos with Castro in cabanas." The line resonates with one of my favorite postcolonial paradoxes from Nas's landmark album *Illmatic*, in which the Queensbridge MC raps:

I sip the Dom P, watchin' Gandhi til I'm charged then
Writin' in my book of rhymes all the words past the margin.[35]

The classic lines from "The World Is Yours" (1994) prefigure Jay's cigars with Castro, offering up the cognitive dissonance of Nas sipping Dom Perignon while watching another anticolonial activist on film—in order to gain inspiration for his art. Despite their perceived incongruities—class struggle with a spa treatment—the swaggering, deformed images are perfect encapsulations of critical excess.

Indeed, in asking Jay about a similar incongruity, the *Village Voice* reporter, Elizabeth Mendez Berry, inspired the MC to respond to such contradictory "bad looks" in a verse. [36] Jay recounts the story in *Decoded*—a story relating "the struggle" to "the hustle":

> After we listened to the album the reporter came up to me and said the strangest thing: "You don't feel funny?" I was like, *Huh?*, because I knew she meant funny as in weird, and I was thinking, *Actually, I feel real comfortable; this is one of the best albums of my career.* . . . But then she said it again: "You don't feel funny?

You're wearing that Che T-shirt and you have–" she gestured dramatically at the chain around my neck. "I couldn't even concentrate on the music," she said. "All I could think of is that big chain bouncing off of Che's forehead." The chain was a Jesus piece—the Jesus piece that Biggie used to wear, in fact. It's part of my ritual when I record an album: I wear the Jesus piece and let my hair grow till I'm done.[37]

Like the ritual Nas describes in "The World Is Yours," Jay's creative process also seems to involve a contradictory mashup of bling and resistance. But as Jay describes, when Mendez Berry's article came out, she called him on it—including the critique: "When he rocks his Guevara shirt and a do-rag, squint and you see a revolutionary. But open your eyes to the platinum chain around his neck: Jay-Z is a hustler."[38]

In *Decoded* Jay responds: "Wow. I could've dismissed her as a hater; I remember her going on about 'bling-bling,' which was just too easy, and, honestly, even after reading her essays I was mostly thinking, 'It's a T-shirt. You're buggin.' But I was fascinated by the piece and thought some more about what she was saying. It stuck with me and that night I turned it around in my head." As he describes, the article ultimately inspired Jay to add a second verse to "Public Service Announcement." In that verse, Jay responds with opening lines that make the connection between the struggle and the hustle—tying Che Guevara to another icon of resistance who has been commodified on T-shirts. The verse in question includes the lines:

I'm like Che Guevara with bling on, I'm complex
I never claimed to have wings on
Nigga, I get my "by any means" on whenever there's a drought
Get your umbrellas out because that's when I brainstorm

With the line "I get my 'by any means' on" Jay connects the Latin American revolutionary to the African American revolutionary Malcolm X—owning the contradictions, the complexities.

The section from *Decoded* on these perceived hypocrisies concludes with a gesture of conciliation to those complexities being an "honest" thing, a human thing.

The journalist was right, though. Images aren't everything, and a T-shirt doesn't change who you are. Like I said in the song "Blueprint 2," *cause the nigger wear*

> *a kufi, it don't mean that he is bright.* For any image or symbol or creative act to mean something, it has to touch something deeper, connect to something true. I know that the spirit of struggle and insurgency was woven into the lives of the people I grew up with in Bed-Stuy, even if in sometimes fucked up and corrupted ways. Che's failures were bloody and his contradictions frustrating. But to have contradictions—especially when you're fighting for your life—is human, and to wear the Che shirt and platinum and diamonds together is honest. In the end I wore it because I meant it.

While my main aims in this study have centered on the cultural discourses this album has drawn on and the impact it has generated—holding the question of intentionality at arms-length—the passage from *Decoded* gives us some perspective on the external pressures and internal questions that hip hop artists like Jay and Ye are confronted with. Indeed, this story essentially opens *Decoded*, beginning the book's part 1 under the title, "The Revolutionary T-Shirt."

Immediately following his chillin-with-Castro line, Jay thus follows up with a nod of solidarity to all the Cuban, Mexican, and Dominican "plugs" ("connections") he knows. Implicating Latino Americans—including "illegal" ones—in his critique of excess, he continues:

> Driving Benzes, with no benefits
> Not bad, huh, for some immigrants?
> Build your fences, we digging tunnels
> Can't you see? We gettin' money up under you.

The verse is particularly prophetic from the standpoint of the "big, beautiful wall" that would become the centerpiece of Trump's campaign, but also notable here are the valences of above and below that structure the imagery. Notably, it also recalls Baker's description of the deformation of mastery as a practice of "tunneling out of the black holes of possession and 'tight places' of old clothes, into perhaps, a new universe"—of "worm holing."[39] The couplets confirm the reality of borders: the more unequal the realities between the two sides, the greater and more violently goods, capital, and people will flow across.

Ye gets the last word on this track, asking us to visualize the private jets circumventing national borders and imagining the paradox of a bumper sticker on a Maybach. Here, Ye gestures, point blank, to the target of his ostentatious display of Black wealth with the concluding jibe "As you can see, we done bodied [destroyed] the damn lames / Lord, please let them accept the things they can't change." The line points directly at those white Americans who view every Black, Latino, and Asian success as "cutting in line"—turning that Christian inheritance back on itself. Ye finishes the thought, reprising the recurrent "sham/pain" theme, now as "And pray that all of their pain be champagne." Right on cue, James Brown enters with a gesture that is equal parts jarring scream and soulful melisma. Part nightmare and part dream. The conclusion seems clear: it is neither. And it is both. From this elevated perspective the primal "pain" of subhumanity is of a kind with the "champagne" of superhumanity. Or, to refigure my paraphrase of Scott Saul's *Freedom Is, Freedom Ain't*, champagne ain't shit unless you've tasted pain.[40]

## THE SCREAM

The concluding scream on "Otis" is of a kind with Fred Moten's trenchant examination of the phonic materiality of Black performance in the opening to his *In the Break*, "Resistance of the Object: Aunt Hester's Scream." There Moten introduces his binary collapsing hermeneutic device, "in the break," as an investigation into "a radically exterior aurality that disrupts and resists certain formations of identity and interpretation by challenging the reducibility of phonic matter to verbal meaning or conventional musical form."[41] Central to his thinking about phonic materiality—and Black performance writ large—is the work of Saidiya Hartman, who in her *Scenes of Subjection: Terror, Slavery, and Self-Making in Nineteenth-Century America*, sets her sights on the ways that subjectivities are *born* in subjugation. In beginning his analysis of irreducible, yet meaningful, phonic matter with a consideration of "Aunt Hester's Scream"—Frederick Douglass's most chilling recounting of racial brutality—Moten turns to Hartman's description of that *birth*.[42] Hartman's *Scenes of Subjection* begins:

> The "terrible spectacle" that introduced Frederick Douglass to slavery was the beating of his Aunt Hester. It is one of the most well-known scenes of torture in the literature of slavery, perhaps second only to Uncle Tom's murder at the hands of Simon Legree. By locating this "horrible exhibition" in the first chapter

> of his 1845 *Narrative of the Life of Frederick Douglass,* Douglass establishes the centrality of violence to the making of the slave and identifies it as an original generative act equivalent to the statement "I was born." The passage through the blood-stained gate is an inaugural moment in the formation of the enslaved. In this regard it is a primal scene.[43]

Hartman goes on to explain her aim to find new ways to understand anti-Black racial terror without spectacularizing Black suffering, and thus rehearsing and inducing a familiar, performative indignation. Instead, writes Hartman,

> What concerns me here is the diffusion of terror and the violence perpetrated under the rubric of pleasure, paternalism, and property. Consequently, the scenes of subjection examined here focus on the enactment of subjugation and the constitution of the subject and include the blows delivered to Topsy and Zip Coon on the popular stage, slaves coerced to dance in the marketplace, the simulation of will in slave law, the fashioning of identity, and the process of individuation and normalization.[44]

I cite Hartman at some length here, because both the "primal scene" of this screaming birth into slavery with its violent "passage through the blood-stained gate" and the "individuation"—the "subjection"—that Hartman describes are of a piece with Baker's work on the deformation of mastery. Where Hartman's focus is on the birth scream—the announcement "I was born"—as the coming into form of a slave subject, Baker describes deformation's "birth of such a self" as "never simply a coming into being, but always, also, a release from a BEING POSSESSED." Baker's birth is a "metaphorical 'worm holing' as it were—the tunneling out of the black holes of possession and 'tight places' of old clothes, into perhaps, a new universe." Hartman marks the "generative" process of becoming possessed, while Baker marks the process of release from possession.

Together, the two passages mark a fitting encapsulation of this book's argument that *Watch the Throne* collapses the subhuman into the superhuman. While the primal scene of slave subjection transforms the human into the subhuman, the deformation of mastery—of slavery—transforms the subhuman into the new universe of the superhuman. And notably, both generative processes of possession and release from possession are marked by the scream. For Moten and Baker, both entry into slavery and exit from it are marked by the "radically exterior aurality" and irreducible "phonic material"—similarly sounded because they both mark a *break* from humanity. "The deformation of mastery refuses a master's *nonsense.* It returns—often transmuting 'standard' syllables—to the common sense of the tribe."[45] As such, James Brown's scream at the end of "Otis" is a doubled scream—a scream of pain-in-joy. It is a "sham-pain" scream because its freedom knows terror. And further, it is an *anti-anti-essentialist* scream because it is an utterance that refuses the conditions of possibility that constrain even the mastery of form. It is the "Big Payback" of James Brown, the "Feeling (*hell-bent on revenge*) Good" of Nina Simone, the "unabashed *badness*" of Morris Day, and it is the "I'm definitely in my zone" swag of Jay-Z and Kanye West.

I can't speak for Jay and Ye, but it is my view that this deformation of mastery is more than a simple assertion of superhumanity and is instead a tactic that forces the issue—a tactic of critical excess. For what we really want is to break past these categories into a real humanity—a humanity not bound up in Enlightenment binaries—the binaries encoded in Jay and Ye's breathless catalog of Western universalist paradoxes. Recalling Sylvia Wynter's "embattled humanism," my view—and my hope—is that critical excess is a strategy that battles its way to real humanity, to real freedom. If *Watch the Throne*'s performance of "Black excellence, opulence, decadence" proves to be the self-fulfilling prophesy that I hope and helps topple our faith in capitalism, we have a chance to make ours the *Last Gilded Age.*

# Conclusion

## Black Noise: *Re-composition in the Last Gilded Age*

In composition, to produce is first of all to take pleasure in the production of differences. Musicians foresaw this new concept. For example, in the language of jazz, to improvise is "to freak freely." A freak is also a monster, a marginal. To improvise, to compose, is thus related to the idea of the assumption of differences, of the rediscovery and blossoming of the body.

—JACQUES ATTALI, *NOISE: THE POLITICAL ECONOMY OF MUSIC* (1977/1985)

At the December 2018 conference, "Recognition, Reparation, and Reconciliation," the Cameroonian philosopher and activist Achille Mbembe delivered a keynote entitled "The Trauma of the World and the World as Trauma." The feminist literary scholar Jacqueline Rose summarized the talk thus in a 2019 piece for the *London Review of Books*:

> Mincing no words, he spoke of the "traumatogenic" institutions of capitalism and liberal democracy which to this day have never delivered racial equality, and of the "genocidal unconscious," which turns humans, first among them the racial "other," into disposable commodities. A more viable future will emerge, he suggested, only out of rupture, only if we begin by recognizing the brokenness all around.[1]

The talk, she explains, was centered on the urgent need for "a new political subject."

Indeed, in the recorded video of the talk, Mbembe offers a reconsideration of Frantz Fanon's views on violence in the service of anticolonial liberation. Now that we have better access to the famed anticolonial activist's psychoanalytic writings, he explains, we can see that Fanon was as interested in healing as he was in armed revolution. Pivoting on Fanon's thinking about healing practices of "political interiority"—and Stefano Harney, Fred Moten, and others' scholarship on "fugitivity"—Mbembe goes on to outline a program for what such a new subject would look like.[2] Speaking of specifically African American healing and repair of "infrastructures of survival," Mbembe described how these "repertoires of practices of survival"—"traditions of dispersing one's self, knowing when to retreat, knowing when to come out, when to shut up, when to speak"—are key to this new subject. Mbembe explains:

> To get out of the hole and to break through the wall, the captured subject must actively engage in a relation of multiple doubles and multiple selves. He or she must develop an extraordinary capacity to become imperceptible, to continually shift from one self to its alternate, to inhabit the tiniest of cracks and fissures. He or she must know how and when to become like everybody else, how and when to be nobody, when to be alone, when to hide, when to no longer have anything to hide, when to become unfindable, and when to rush to the other side in order to meet one's double. These micromovements, these micropostures were essential because survival depended on being able to inhabit multiple selves, often at the *same time*.[3]

Indeed, this new subjectivity based on Afrodiasporic traditions draws on the "practices of survival" that Du Bois describes as the "second sight" of double consciousness.

What's more, it bears a striking resemblance to Ralph Ellison's musical description of African American multiplicity in his classic, *Invisible Man*.

> Invisibility, let me explain, gives one a slightly different sense of time, you're never quite on the beat. Sometimes you're ahead and sometimes behind. Instead of the swift and imperceptible flowing of time, you are aware of its nodes, those points where time stands still or from which it leaps ahead. And you slip into the breaks and look around.[4]

Mbembe's "cracks and fissures" and Ellison's "breaks" both serve to multiply doubleness and turn a shortcoming into a tactical advantage. Further, both Mbembe and Ellison center *improvisation* in these figurations of a nimble and dynamic subject—a key point to which we will return.

In *Bodies in Dissent*, Daphne Brook's masterful examination of the intersectional work that Black women performed on nineteenth- and early-twentieth-century European stages, the scholar details how these highly visible founders of popular culture turned their African American traumas into transformative art. Referencing the historical trauma of the Middle Passage and scientific racism's dehistoricization of African people—and echoing Ellison's resultant "slightly different sense of time"—Brooks writes:

> Erupting, then, out of this putative "stillness," Afro-alienation is thus encoded with the traumas of self-fragmentation resulting from centuries of captivity and subjugation. Yet it also manifests the counter-normative tactics used by the marginalized to turn the horrific historical memory of moving through oceanic space while "suspended in time" not only into a kind of "second sight," as Du Bois would have termed it, but also into a kind of dissonantly enlightened performance.[5]

What's more, Brooks connects this "dissonantly enlightened performance," borne of double consciousness, to the "enlivened position" that Elin Diamond describes as "looking at being looked at ness," thus "calling attention to the hypervisibility and cultural constructions of Blackness in transatlantic culture."[6]

This "dissonant enlightenment" is precisely what I argue Jay and Ye have performed for us on *Watch the Throne*—a mastery of enlightenment that is then deformed; a deformation of mastery. As I have argued, the album performs for us a deconstruction of the Enlightenment category of the human—laying bare the paradox of how that "universalist" category obscures the bifurcating reality of its subhuman and superhuman investments and hierarchies.[7] Indeed, in detailing how capitalism assigns value to different "classes of people" from the "overall category of the human," Mbembe refers to that great Enlightenment thinker Alexis de Tocqueville, who understood the term "indivisible" in the US national-ideological context to imply this capitalist/democratic hierarchy. That is, argues Mbembe, for Tocqueville and his contemporaries in that great experiment of American democracy, "indivisible" referred to the indivisibility of the white race.[8] Tocqueville makes this much clear in his landmark *Democracy in America* (1835)—democracy and capitalism are for whites alone.[9]

Jay and Ye's performance on *Watch the Throne* highlights this fundamental paradox of Western "universalist" democracy, deforms it, and spits it back out for all to see. Through their critical excess of that contradiction, "Black capitalism," their performance instrumentalizes this deconstruction of the human subject in order to dethrone the West. Further, they take the celebrity hypervisibility powered by the white gaze, connect it to those "counter-normative tactics" produced over centuries of fugitivity, and fashion from the paradox of popular music's commercial authenticity a performance that entertains while it critiques—music that revels as it destroys. The paradox of luxury rap thus brings the logic of popular music—that is, the logic of racial capitalism—to its logical conclusion: the end of capitalism, the end of whiteness, the end of Europe. It is through this unseemly performance of critical excess that Jay and Ye resolve the paradox of racial capitalism on the unlikely terrain of popular music.

## RE-COMPOSITION: THE NEW JONGLEURS

Keeping in mind Mbembe's "multiple doubles," and adding to it Du Bois's "second sight," Ellison's evocative "breaks," and Brooks's "enlightened dissonance," I want to recall all of the doubling, flipping, and deformation on *Watch the Throne* and return to Attali's "double game." As we consider the Afrodiasporic repertoires of survival that will build this new subjectivity, I also want to refigure Attali's predictions of the future to show us where he got it wrong—and where he almost got it right in his thinking about "composition."

In a section from the final chapter of Attali's *Noise* titled "Representation and Composition: The Return of the Jongleurs," the critical theorist outlines his own prophesy of the future of music—and his own vision of a new political subjectivity. Notably, in a section titled "'Uhuru'—The Failure of the Economy of Free Music," he spends considerable time highlighting the possibilities of improvised free jazz like that of Chicago's Association for the Advancement of Creative Musicians (AACM), but ultimately suggests that "the sound of free jazz, like the violent wing of the black movement, has failed in its attempt to break with repetition."[10] While the free jazz movement was on the right track as a highly localized "meeting of black popular music and the more abstract theoretical explorations of European music"—a move that "eliminated the distinction between popular music and learned music"—he concludes (not unproblematically) that the movement ultimately failed because it didn't circulate in the dominant media networks. He explains: "since this noise was not inscribed on the same level as the messages circulating in the network of repetition, it could not make itself heard."[11]

It is immediately after this section on free jazz that Attali lays out his alternative vision—a vision centered on new modes of musical production and a new jongleur figure. He writes: "Along with this search for another power in repetition, continuing this mutation in the economy of music, there is a reappearance of very ancient forms of production." These are the forms of the jongleur—truly creative musicians "who live on the margins of culture," he explains, quoting Revault d'Allones. Here he details what he means by the new mode that he heralds as "composition," going on to describe the rise of noncommercial and community-centered musicking practices—DIY artists and amateur ensembles, the invention of new instruments and new collective modes of composition, and—notably—the sing-along karaoke records known then as *Minus One*.

This new mode of "composition," he concludes, "does not constitute, therefore, a new form of popular music, but rather a new practice of music among the people. Music becomes the superfluous, the unfinished, the relational." Echoing social media's collapse of art and artist that I described in chapter 3, he continues, "it even ceases to be a product separable from its author. It is inscribed within a new practice of value. . . . By subverting objects, it heralds a new form of the collective imaginary, a reconciliation between work and play."

And here's where Attali's comments really begin to heat up the observational space that *Watch the Throne*—and hip hop praxis more broadly—focuses for us. He writes, "Although these new practices may faintly resemble those of the medieval jongleurs, they in fact constitute a break with" what Attali refers to as the "sacrificial, representative, and repetitive" modes of musical economy—the modes that prophesied the respective economic orders of times past. He clarifies:

> [B]efore the advent of recording and modern sound tools, the jongleurs were *the collective memory*, the essential site of cultural creation, *and the circulation of information from the courts to the people*. Recording stabilized the musical work and organized its commercial stockpiling. But now the field of the commodity has been shattered and a direct relation between man and his milieu is being reestablished.[12]

As I suggested at the outset of this book, this description of musicians as "the collective memory" and source of information for the community resonates uncannily with hip hop's deeply intertextual practices of community-making—of cultural memory-making—and the "street reporting" of the "black CNN."[13] What's more, the description calls to mind the Afrocentric search for meaning and recovery of history that led early exponents of hip hop culture to seek out and find resonance in the figure of the West African griot—a figure who not only sings *of* the people, but *sings the people.*

This connection between hip hop's street reporting and African oral traditions has been of enduring value in suturing those cracks and filling those crevices in African America's African prehistory and is of profound import for how hip hop sustains community today. Indeed, albums like *Watch the Throne* create spaces for community—for connections to be made and for cultural debates to be played out and negotiated. But here I want to turn from the social parallels that we can find between the jongleur and the MC and shift our focus to the fascinating musical parallels between Attali's descriptions of "composition" and the contours of hip hop praxis.

Detailing his theory that we can glimpse the outline of an emergent economic order in the organization of music—from "sacrificial, representative, and repetitive" to this new DIY order of "composition," he explains, "if representation is tied to printing (by which the score is produced), and repetition to recording (by which the record is produced), composition is tied to the instrument (by which music is produced). We may take this as a herald of considerable future progress, in the production and in the invention of new instruments." This invention is of key importance to Attali's theorization. But these instruments and their technologies, he says, must be truly new. "Inducing people to compose using predefined instruments cannot lead to a mode of production different from that authorized by those instruments. That is the trap. The trap of false liberation through the distribution to each individual of the instruments of his own alienation." Instead, "like representation and repetition, composition needs its own technology as a basis of support for the new form of value. While recording was intended as a reinforcement for representation, it created an economy of repetition. As with the preceding codes, the technology upon which composition is based was not conceived for that purpose." Enter the turntable, instrument of the DJ.[14]

Perhaps the most widely influential impact of hip hop praxis on music-making has been its upending and opening up of the recorded artifact. Indeed, in hip hop, recordings are no longer static "works" but raw materials to be re-worked, re-framed, and re-composed—as we saw with Kanye's cutting and deformation of "Try a Little Tenderness" in chapter 5. The turntable has been turned from a semiotically stable playback device to a rich and diverse site of musical creation and meaning-making—from an overinscribed object to an active and improvising subject. This is a subject that not only creates meaning but re-creates meaning (and, yes, *deforms* the meanings of "mastered" recordings).

Taken together with Attali's almost comical focus on the "Minus One" karaoke record as a major musical breakthrough, we can see that hip hop praxis fits his description perfectly—even those commercially produced "sing-along" records were used in a way different than intended. They provided the conceptual model for the band "minus one"—you!—but hip hop refused to use that "sing-along" technology as intended and refigured that technology too. Enter rapping, art of the MC.

These commercially produced "predefined instruments"—from turntable to 808 to iPhone—are thus torn from their intended use. They are, for many, no longer instruments of alienation. In this way, hip hop flips the script on the master's tools.[15] Indeed, this is the essence of my argument about Jay and Ye's *Watch the Throne*. Well-meaning leftists have been struggling against the oppressive, objectifying, traumatogenic structures of capitalism since at least 1848. Where has that led? What if, instead of fighting against this totalizing beast, we taught it how to complete its work? To borrow a fitting line from the Wu-Tang Clan, what if we sewed its asshole closed and kept feedin' it, and feedin' it, and feedin' it?[16] (Sorry). This is critical excess. An excess that leads to death.

George Lipsitz writes of hip hop's ability to work both within and against the system in this way in his *Dangerous Crossroads*:

> One might conclude that this reliance of post-colonial culture on existing economic and cultural forms can at best lead only to subordinate rather than autonomous reforms. That possibility certainly exists. But the desire to work through existing contradictions rather than stand outside them represents not so much a preference for melioristic reform over revolutionary change, but rather *a recognition of the impossibility of standing outside totalitarian systems of domination.* Attempts to create liberated zones, cooperatives, "socialism within one coun-

> try," and counter-cultural communes have all failed because of the hegemonic power of capitalists within the world economic system. Although still useful as a means of raising consciousness, these strategies have been largely superseded by forms of struggle that engage in what Gramsci called the war of position (an effort to build a counter-hegemonic alliance) rather than what he termed the war of maneuver (the effort to seize state power).[17]

This simultaneously working within and against—this "war of position"—is of course, what Mbembe is talking about. This is Brooks's "enlightened dissonance." Indeed, this is Paul Gilroy's "counterculture of modernity." While these theoretical models might align most readily with Baker's "mastery of form," I hope to have shown that the "deformation of mastery" pushes through this mastery of white codes and not only carves out a space for agency in which to work against our racial capitalist hegemony, but tunnels under and through that structure so aggressively that it destabilizes its very foundations.

Indeed, hip hop and its Afrodiasporic inheritance has never worked outside the system. Its resignifying of "predefined instruments" through the detritus of the culture industry confirms this for us. But it has learned to work in and against the system; it has learned repertories of resistance and "traditions of dispersing one's self," such as "knowing when to retreat, knowing when to come out, when to shut up, when to speak," "when to become like everybody else, how and when to be nobody, when to be alone, when to hide, when to no longer have anything to hide, when to become unfindable, and when to rush to the other side in order to meet one's double."[18] Indeed, it is this final aggressive (bum-)rushing to meet one's double that I argue characterizes the deformation of critical excess.

These are the repertories of hip hop's new subjectivity. And these are the praxes of this new music—what I want to call, instead of Attali's "composition," "re-composition"—a multiplying daily practice of becoming. As Lipsitz puts it (riffing on Gilroy, riffing on Ellison): "The ability to find that identity of passions and turn it into a diasporic conversation informing political struggles in similar but not identical circumstances has enabled peoples of African descent to survive over the centuries; it may now also hold the key to survival for the rest of the world as well."[19] This is our challenge today: for *all of us* to put those Afrodiasporic "repertoires of practices of survival" into action; to follow hip hop's lead and take up a new and ever-unfinished subjectivity of *re-composition*.

### *Black Noise*

As I have shown, I am not the first to have made this case about the repertories of survival that are encoded in Black musical performance. Be it Baker, Mbembe, Du Bois, Moten, Lipsitz, Brooks, Gilroy, or Ellison's wonderful construction "the real secret of the game is to make life swing," the legacy of Afrodiasporic arts and letters records the performative healing of this counterhegemonic subjectivity in brilliant detail.[20] Afrodiasporic artists and thinkers have long considered these repertories to be key in the foundation of a new subjectivity. Less remarked upon is the fact that Attali's prognostications *have* been drawn on by hip hop scholars. Indeed, as I suggested at the outset of this book, one of the first landmarks in the field of hip hop studies, Tricia Rose's *Black Noise: Rap Music and Black Culture in Contemporary America*, is about just that: the prophetic power of *Black* noise.

Although she doesn't center Attali's work in that foundational book, it is through the concept of "noise" that Rose takes up Attali's ideas about the disruptive power of music and applies it to hip hop. Responding directly to Attali, Adorno, and the more recent (white) postmodernist critique of Fredric Jameson, she also corrects Attali and addresses post-Marxist mischaracterizations of Black music's repetitive structures, noting that "repetition cannot be reduced to a repressive, industrial force."[21] Most importantly, recalling Lipsitz, of whom she was a student, Rose takes up the idea of hip hop as "a blueprint" for survival in chapter 2 of her foundational study, where she writes of hip hop's potential for "social dislocation and rupture"—of *deformation*. Echoing Attali, she writes:

> These effects at the level of style and aesthetics suggest affirmative ways in which profound social dislocation and rupture can be managed and perhaps contested in the cultural arena. Let us imagine these hip-hop principles as a blueprint for social resistance and affirmation: create sustaining narratives, accumulate them, layer, embellish, and transform them. However, be also prepared for rupture, find pleasure in it, in fact, plan on social rupture. When these ruptures occur, use them in creative ways that will prepare you for a future in which survival will demand a sudden shift in ground tactics.[22]

I save Rose's foundational argument as the last best example in a long line of Afrodiasporic work on the need to "make life swing" because it is the present rupture that needs tending to immediately.

And it is now, in our present rupture, that we have a chance to shift our tactics. Indeed, thanks to people of color from the hip hop generation—foremost among them, women and queer activists like BLM's Alicia Garza—this shift is already happening. As that colleague of mine suggested on the eve of 11/9—and the fascist nightmare that we're currently enduring—"if Trump wins, socialism is back on the table. Maybe we have to hit rock bottom to see the way forward."

As I suggested in the introduction to this book, he was right. Socialism is indeed now back on the table. With the election of the congresswomen Alexandria Ocasio-Cortez, Ilhan Omar, Ayanna Pressley, and Rashida Tlaib—dubbed "the Squad"—and the centering of progressive proposals such as the Green New Deal and Medicare for All for which they and others have pressed, the Left is on the rise. Indeed, two of its heroes—Bernie Sanders and Elizabeth Warren—polled among the top three candidates for Democratic nominee for president of the US in the 2020 election. Now that the emperor has his new clothes, we can see the US for what it is—what marginalized communities have been arguing for decades—a racial-capitalist empire. The dog-whistling is no longer needed; the trolls have crawled out from under their rocks and we know where we stand. We know who we are as a nation. Indeed, with the rise of American-style fascism around the world—Bolsonaro, Duterte, Orbán, Erdoğan, and Johnson—we can see the contours of a geopolitical realignment. And, for all the suffering and loss of life that has accrued and accelerated since the election of Donald Trump on 11/9/2016, one positive has become clear: we can't go back. Today, white, suburban baby boomers are talking about white privilege. Today, white supremacy is no longer an academic theory. Today, socialism is back on the table.

As I have argued in this book, *Watch the Throne* interrogated this house of cards and sensed this social rupture on the horizon, leveraging its manifest paradoxes in creative and generative ways. Indeed, its strategy of luxury rap—of critical excess—certainly marks a sudden shift in tactics. Let us hope that this deformation of mastery is the right kind of tactic—and be prepared for more sudden shifts. Let us find pleasure in its comedy and its tragedy. But let us also find creative ways to take these ideas and create from them *our own set of tactics*—our own "repertoires of practices of survival"—to build a new, more just, equitable, and sustainable world.

## "BURNT TO THE GROUND": KILLER MIKE AND HIP HOP'S ROLE

As I write this conclusion in the early summer of 2020 America is burning. Added to our already surreal context of a global pandemic with a nation in thrall to alt-right power and its crippling fear, the world watched a white police officer kneel on a Black man's neck—George Floyd's neck—for nine minutes until he stopped breathing. Now America is burning. If we use this moment right, Rome will burn—the throne will fall.

We are now in the midst of rupture. The time for Mbembe's "repertoires of practices of survival"—of Rose's "sudden shift in ground tactics"—has come. With the organizing praxis of Occupy, Black Lives Matter, and Me Too, America is ready to seize this moment of rupture. America is ready to end our racial capitalist patriarchy. This hegemony can and must die. Now is our moment to slip the noose of our dehumanizing neoliberal system, turn to an equitable future, and make this the *last gilded age*.

On 29 May 2020, in the midst of the revolutionary fallout from the killing of George Floyd, Killer Mike, of Atlanta hip hop duo Run the Jewels, spoke to his community with other local leaders on live television. He implored his community to use the killing—and the anger it generated—as a generative political moment. In a tear-filled stream of righteous anger, he explained, "it is the responsibility of us to make this better right now. We don't want to see one officer charged, we want to see four officers prosecuted and sentenced. We don't want to see Targets burning, we want to see the system that sets up for systemic racism burnt to the ground."[23] Knowing his influence on this community—knowing hip hop's influence—local government officials and community leaders had asked Killer Mike to make a statement calling for peace. Indeed, Mike is something of a new breed of Black capitalist himself, nodding in his remarks to both Atlanta-based global businesses like CNN and Coca-Cola and the "over 50 restaurants owned by black women" in the city as part of his address.[24]

But Mike also referenced the Black women and men who organized before him and emphasized that "it wasn't just Doctor King and people dressed nicely who marched and protested to progress this city and so many other cities." He used this rupture and the platform it provided to express his anger, reject the politics of respectability, and "plot" his community's revenge—at the ballot box. He continued:

> So, my question for us, on the other side of this camera, is after it burns, will we be left with char, or will we rise like a phoenix out of the ashes that Atlanta has always done? Will we use this as a moment to say that we will not do what other cities have done, and in fact, we will get better than we've been . . .
>
> So, we have an opportunity now because I'm mad. I don't have any good advice. What I can tell you is that if you sit in your homes tonight instead of burning your home to the ground, you will have time to properly plot, plan, strategize, and organize and mobilize in an effective way.

He went on, laying out his tactics through anger and tears:

> Two of the most effective ways is first taking your butt to the computer and making sure you fill out your Census so that people know who you are and where you are. The next thing is making sure you exercise your political bully power and going to local elections and beating up the politicians that you don't like.

Killer Mike's plea for the deformation of our racist, capitalist, and patriarchal neoliberal order is clear. Indeed, his plea for peace—by "beating up the politicians that you don't like"—exceeds the political mastery of form. The T-shirt he wore for the televised address read "KILL YOUR MASTERS." This "mad as hell" plea to "beat up the politicians" at the ballot box is a deformation of mastery.[25]

As Mike's remarks make clear, hip hop has a pivotal role in our present moment of rupture. Hip hop can burn down, but hip hop can also build up. As Tricia Rose suggests, hip hop can offer us a "a blueprint for social resistance and affirmation." Hip hop can "create sustaining narratives, accumulate them, layer, embellish, and transform them . . ." And as she urges us, "When these ruptures occur, use them in creative ways that will prepare you for a future in which survival will demand a sudden shift in ground tactics."[26]

Let us hope that Killer Mike's "phoenix out of the ashes" prophesy comes to pass. Let us hear hip hop's *Black noise* and work creatively to re-compose our future from the present rupture. *Watch the Throne* may have predicted the end of our racial capitalist patriarchy, but it is up to us to make it happen.

## "SEA LEGS": THE NEW 1619 PROJECT

As I close this conclusion on the ways that scholars of *Black* noise have identified in the practices of Afrodiasporic performance tools to recompose the world in moments of rupture—moments such as our present *break*—it bears repeating that hip hop tracks themselves offer myriad ways of turning trauma into transfiguration. As we have seen, in addition to its destructive work, *Watch the Throne* offers a number of resignifications that flip the script on oppression and hold the potential to turn shortcomings into tactical advantages. One such track from Killer Mike's landmark collaboration with producer-turned-MC, El-P—*Run the Jewels* (2013)—holds a particularly fitting encapsulation of such doubled resignifications that seems a perfect point of embarkation from this book's transatlantic analysis of *Watch the Throne*—that album's fifth track, "Sea Legs."[27]

"Sea Legs" begins by conjuring an oceanic sonic space of waves crashing onto shore, as undulating synth tones underscore a feeling of instability. El-P enters with lines that establish the track's themes of swaggering iconoclasm: "Really fell out the lane with this shit / Man, print this shit: I'm a misfit." He further elaborates the scene with maritime imagery, before revealing the subversive nature of his "misfit"—or "freak," as Attali would have it—tactics, rapping: "I move through the room like an animal fooling a master."

After the first verse, Killer Mike delivers a hook that perfectly models Daphne Brooks's "dissonant enlightenment," performing those "misfit," "freak," "counter-normative tactics used by the marginalized to turn the horrific historical memory of moving through oceanic space . . . into a kind of 'second sight,' as Du Bois would have termed it."[28] Moving from the Black Atlantic to the shore, Mike sings:

> Trying not to walk crooked while this anchor's dropped
> But I been out on them choppy waves and it's hard to say
> Where this land begins and that water stops
> I got sea legs
> I got sea legs
> I got sea legs

The track thus elaborates the difficulty of moving between the asymmetries of double consciousness—between the even ideals of universalism and the disorienting realities of racial inequality. But hidden behind hook's stated attempt "not to walk crooked" on solid ground is the performed recognition that this experience of "them choppy waves" has prepared him for everything. He's got "sea legs."

Having one's "sea legs" is, of course, an expression usually reserved to express the mastery of balance (and intestinal fortitude) once acclimated to travel by ship. Yet, here—and throughout his verse on the track—Mike is gesturing to the fact that this hard-won ability at sea also serves him well on land. The continuing presence of the undulating and uncertain waves gives him an ability to be always ready to "continually shift from one self to its alternate," to "inhabit the tiniest of cracks and fissures," to "know how and when to become like everybody else, how and when to be nobody, when to be alone, when to hide, when to no longer have anything to hide, when to become unfindable, and when to rush to the other side in order to meet one's double" as Mbembe puts it.[29] These "choppy waves" have given him a valuable improvisational ability. These "choppy waves" have given him a mastery of uncertainty. These "choppy waves" have given his "sea legs" dynamism, limberness, and sway. These experiences of "oceanic space"—of trauma—have given him a certain swagger: the "misfit"/ "freak" swag that El-P opens with.

On the verse that follows this hook, Killer Mike expands on the tactical power of this oceanic swag—his own "repertoires of practices of survival."

> Real shit, I came for the jewels
> I'm the killer of kings and fools
> I'm the reason the season for treason starts this evening
> And this evening, the odds ain't even

Here he begins riffing on the "Run the Jewels" name—an expression at once of theft, control, and excellence—again in the Attalian jongleur language of sub- and superhumanity ("kings and fools"). And in a line of masterfully assonance-rich wordplay, he gives voice to the "odd" and choppy reality of universal "even"-ness.

Indeed, the very next line—"People praying to the gods, but the gods ain't even listening"—Mike seems to echo the "What's a god to a nonbeliever" nihilism of Jay and Ye's "No Church in the Wild" while continuing the "odds ain't even" wordplay. The track's devil-may-care elaboration of his merciless sea legs swag continues:

There will be no "mercy me's"
There will be no reprieve for the thieves
There will be no respect for the thrones
No master mastered these bones

If we didn't know better, it might even seem that this track is a direct response to *Watch the Throne* and its discourses of nobility, excellence, and mastery—a subtle targeting of Jay and Ye's throne and (crown) jewels. Or maybe . . . not so subtle. The verse continues:

Your idols all are my rivals, I rival all of your idols
I stand on towers like Eiffel, I rifle down all your idols
Niggas will perish in Paris, niggas is nothing but parrots
I write for the writers that write for the liars that impress you and your parents

Here, with the line "Niggas will perish in Paris," Mike makes the target crystal clear. With its takedown of European nobility discourses, "god is dead" ethos, and "Niggas . . . in Paris" punch line—and in the context of this track's 2013 release, just less than two years after the release of *Watch the Throne*—it is abundantly clear that Jay and Ye's luxury rap album is the target. Indeed, with its line about "parrots" and "liars," Mike throws an insinuation of ghostwriters into the mix, questioning Jay and Ye's very authorship.

But more than just targeting Jay and Ye's "jewels"—swinging the sword of Damocles and claiming the throne for himself—Mike here seems more intent on destroying the very system of "kings and fools" that undergirds this aristocracy. As statues and "idols" fall from Cape Town, South Africa to Bristol, UK to Richmond, VA in the wake of the Rhodes Must Fall and Black Lives Matter movements, it seems too that Jay and Ye must be knocked off their pedestals. Like Yasiin Bey's "Niggas in Poorest," he and El-P's "Sea Legs" builds upon the iconoclasm of *Watch the Throne* in ways that make their end game more explicit—the end of our racial capitalist patriarchy.

Indeed, like the studied iconoclasm of "I rifle down all your idols" and his "Phoenix from the ashes" address in the summer of 2020, the lead single from his 2020 album *RTJ4* (*Run the Jewels 4*), continues "Killer" Mike's message that he is "the killer of kings and fools."[30] Playing again on the

Eurocentric critique, "I stand on towers like Eiffel," the track is titled "Ooh La La" and includes the lines:

> Fuck a king or queen and all of they loyal subjects
> I pull my penis out and piss on they shoes in public
> People, we the pirates, the pride of this great republic
> No matter what you order, mo'fucker, we what you're stuck with

Indeed, with the mention of "pirates," the recent track even seems to build upon the "oceanic" concepts of "Sea Legs"—those tactical repertoires of subversion borne of the "horrific historical memory" of the Middle Passage that resonate in the sonic and rhetorical contours of Black Atlantic cultural performance.

* * *

I highlight this continuity between 2011's *Watch the Throne*, 2013's *Run the Jewels*, and 2020's RTJ4 at some length in concluding this book, not only to show us the tactical discourses and contest of ideas in the world of hip hop artistry but to illustrate the ways that close reading practices—such as those modelled in these pages—can throw into high relief music's power to shape our world. Cultural artifacts and performances do have material relevance. They do create responses. Our words matter. Our performances matter. Our music matters.

Knowingly or unknowingly, consciously or unconsciously, culture is the terrain on which the future is contested and written—especially in the ineffable contours and resonances of musical sound. If Jacques Attali hoped to prove one thing in his audacious historical study of music's prophetic force, it was that music is not a superstructural *effect*, but a socioeconomic *cause*. "Music is prophecy. Its styles and economic organization are ahead of the rest of society because it explores, much faster than material reality can, the entire range of possibilities in a given code. It makes audible the new world that will gradually become visible, that will impose itself and regulate the order of things."[31] In this way, Attali asks us to flip the script on how we understand culture.

This is the inversion that Lipsitz suggests when he asks us to reimagine hip hop through the lens of Gramsci's "war of position." As he, like Mbembe, suggests, Afrodiasporic performance like hip hop's *Black* noise "has enabled peoples of African descent to survive over the centuries." And further, "it may now also hold the key to survival for the rest of the world as well."[32]

For the last forty years we have been witness to hip hop's prophesy. Be it in the re-compositional turntable practices of Kool Herc or the "new jongleur" street reporting of Melle Mel's "Message," hip hop has shown us what is to come while pulling back the curtain on the last 400 years. In this historical moment, political projects like Black Lives Matter and historical projects like Nikole Hannah Jones's 1619 Project have helped us wake up to a reality that hip hop artists have long prophesied. It is now time to not just hear, but to heed the messages that hip hop artists have been performing for decades. It is now time to fashion a new 1619 Project by *acting* on hip hop's prophecy, "by recognizing the brokenness all around," by working with these prophetic voices on the margins of society, by following their lead in fashioning new tactics, new repertoires of survival, and new subjectivities. It's time for us—*all of us*—to learn from hip hop's *Black* noise and do the work of re-composing our future. It's time for us all to find our "sea legs" in this destabilizing moment of rupture and possibility.

# NOTES

## INTRODUCTION

1. W. E. B. Du Bois, *Darkwater: Voices from Within the Veil,* chapter II, "The Souls of White Folk," 55–56. (New York: Harcourt, Brace and Company, 1920), http://www.gutenberg.org/files/15210/15210-h/15210-h.htm. Italics are my own.

2. Thanks to my peer review readers for their understanding and encouragement—and for their challenges and recommendations. Sometimes, the oft-maligned "Reader 2" is the scholar's best friend. Despite their questions and challenges, this, their phrase—"capitalism's death dance"—showed a deep understanding of this book's critical work and has shaped its published form.

3. Rupert Neate, "World's Witnessing a New Gilded Age as Billionaires' Wealth Swells to $6tn," *The Guardian,* Oct. 26, 2017, https://www.theguardian.com/business/2017/oct/26/worlds-witnessing-a-new-gilded-age-as-billionaires-wealth-swells-to-6tn; David Huyssen, "We Won't Get Out of the Second Gilded Age the Way We Got Out of the First," *Vox,* Apr. 1, 2019, https://www.vox.com/first-person/2019/4/1/18286084/gilded-age-income-inequality-robber-baron

4. Houston Baker, *Blues, Ideology and Afro-American Literature: A Vernacular Theory* (Chicago: University of Chicago Press, 1984), 10. Houston A. Baker Jr., *Modernism and the Harlem Renaissance* (Chicago: University of Chicago Press, 1987). We'll return to this meta-methodology in chapter 1.

5. Justin D. Burton, "The Roots, *Undun,* Def Jam 001678202, 2011; Kanye West and Jay-Z, *Watch the Throne.* Roc-A-Fella/Roc Nation/Def Jam 001542602, 2011," *Journal of the Society for American Music* 7, no. 3 (2013): 343–47. Justin Burton, *Posthuman Rap* (Oxford: Oxford University Press, 2017).

6. Tricia Rose, *Black Noise: Rap Music and Black Culture in Contemporary America* (Hanover, NH: Wesleyan University Press, 1994); Robin D. G. Kelley, *Race Rebels: Culture, Politics, and the Black Working Class* (New York: Free Press, 1994); Eithne Quinn, *Nuthin' but a "G" Thang: The Culture and Commerce of Gangsta Rap* (New York: Columbia University Pres 2005); Loren Kajikawa, *Sounding Race in Rap Songs* (Berkeley: University of California Press, 2015).

7. Kelley, *Race Rebels,* 192.

8. Kelley, *Race Rebels*, 189.

9. Kelley, Race Rebels, 194. The critique also jibes with Lipsitz and Rose's assessments of hip hop's "war of position." Jordanna Matlon has written a compelling summary of such scholarship on the commodifications of Black masculinity and subversions thereof, linking Kelley's work in *Race Rebels* to Theresa Runstedtler's work on heavyweight Jack Johnson, Mark Anthony Neal's "analysis of Jay-Z's self-branding as an 'elite 'product,'" and Greg Tate's work on Blackness as "capitalism's original fetish object," noting his point that "the Black body, and subsequently Black culture, has become a hungered-after taboo item and a nightmarish bugbear in the badlands of the American racial imagination." Jordanna Matlon, "Black Masculinity Under Racial Capitalism," *Boston Review* (July 16, 2019), http://bostonreview.net/race/jordanna-matlon-black-masculinity-under-racial-capitalism. See also Jordanna Matlon, "Racial Capitalism and the Crisis of Black Masculinity," *American Sociological Review* vol. 81, no. 5:1014–1038; Theresa Runstedtler, *Jack Johnson, Rebel Sojourner* (Berkeley: University of California Press, 2012); Mark Anthony Neal, *Looking for Leroy* (New York: NYU Press, 2013); Greg Tate, *Everything but the Burden* (New York: Penguin/Random House, 2003).

10. Kendra Salois, "Forum: Religion & Hip Hop," *Performance, Religion and Spirituality* 2, no. 1 (2019), 73–74. Salois continues, "But one of the counter-arguments here is this claim, implicitly or explicitly, that it can't be possible to maintain a critique once you have that kind of wealth. And within that claim I think is this assumption that we hold hip hop artists as individuals, as musicians of colour, or as musicians dedicated to an Afro-diasporic form, to a higher ethical standard than we hold others. That we get to critique them in turn if they've reached a point where they embody a rebuke to our system, which is just racist and unfair."

11. Jacques Attali, *Noise: The Political Economy of Music*, trans. Brian Massumi (Minneapolis: University of Minnesota Press, 1985 [1977]), 12. Italics in original.

12. Etienne Balibar, "Racism as Universalism," in *Masses, Classes, Ideas: Studies on Politics and Philosophy Before and After Marx* (New York: Routledge, 1994).

13. Burton's key point of reference is Sylvia Wynter's work, where "the bioeconomic conception of the human" becomes a particularly useful iteration of "neoliberal humanism." David Scott, "The Re-Enchantment of Humanism: An Interview with Sylvia Winter," *Small Axe: A Caribbean Journal of Criticism* 4, no. 2 (September 2000): 160. See also Rosi Braidotti, *The Posthuman* (Malden, MA: Polity Press, 2013) and N. Katherine Hayles, *How We Became Posthuman: Virtual Bodies in Cybernetics, Literature, and Informatics* (Chicago: University of Chicago Press, 1999).

14. Cedric Robinson, Black Marxism: *The Making of the Black Radical Tradition* (Chapel Hill: University of North Carolina Press, 1983), 9.

15. Robinson, *Black Marxism*, 26.

16. Roy Christopher, *Dead Precedents: How Hip-Hop Defines the Future* (New York: Penguin Random House, 2019), 12–13.

17. Cheryl L. Keyes, *Rap Music and Street Consciousness* (Urbana: University of Illinois Press, 2002); Catherine M. Appert, *In Hip Hop Time: Music, Memory, and Social Change in Urban Senegal* (New York: Oxford University Press, 2018).

18. Attali, *Noise*, 141.

19. Elisabeth Mahoney, "The Black CNN: When Hip Hop Took Control," *The Guardian*, June 25, 2010, https://www.theguardian.com/tv-and-radio/2010/jun/25/black-cnn-hip-hop-took-control; see also Tricia Rose, *Black Noise*, 99–124.

20. Attali, *Noise*, 4. He writes: "as we shall see, if it is true that the political organization of the twentieth century is rooted in the political thought of the nineteenth, the latter is almost entirely present in embryonic form in the music of the eighteenth century."

21. Rose, *Black Noise*, 72–73.

22. Rose, *Black Noise*, 71.

23. See the introduction to Jeff Todd Titon's influential textbook, *Worlds of Music: An Introduction to the Musics of the World's Peoples* (Belmont, CA: Cengage, 2008), 18.

24. J. Griffith Rollefson, CIPHER grant proposal (ERC CoG, 2018), 1–6, https://europeanhiphoporg.files.wordpress.com/2018/06/ercconsolidatorgrant-2018-rollefson-fullapp.pdf

25. Rose, *Black Noise*; Imani Perry, *Prophets of the Hood: Politics and Poetics in Hip Hop* (Durham: Duke University Press, 2004).

26. Rose, *Black Noise*, 72–73.

27. See Russell Potter, *Spectacular Vernaculars: Hip-Hop and the Politics of Postmodernism* (Albany, NY: SUNY Press, 1995). For discussions of "golden age thinking" and the "good hip hop/bad hip hop binary," see J. Griffith Rollefson, *Flip the Script: European Hip Hop and the Politics of Postcoloniality* (Chicago: University of Chicago Press, 2017), 7, 9, 231.

28. Gayatri Chakravorty Spivak, "Scattered Speculations on the Subaltern and the Popular" in *An Aesthetic Education in the Era of Globalization* (Cambridge, Mass.: Harvard University Press, 2012), 429–31.

29. Brad Evans and Gayatri Chakravorty Spivak, "When Law Is Not Justice," *New York Times* (July 13, 2016). Thanks to Kira Thurman for calling the phrase "affirmative sabotage" to my attention in her talk with Alex Ross. Kira Thurman and Alex Ross, "Alex Ross and Kira Thurman on Afro-Wagnerism for Popular Music Books in Process Series," September 22, 2020. https://www.youtube.com/watch?v=lVA862NDiD4&ab_channel=EricWeisbard

30. Rollefson, *Flip the Script*.

31. Du Bois, *The Souls of Black Folk* (New York: Modern Library, 2003 [1903]).

32. Du Bois, *Darkwater*, 55. My italics.

33. Theodore W. Allen, *The Invention of the White Race, Volume One: Racial Oppression and Social Control* (New York: Verso, 1994), 194.

34. Jay-Z and Kanye West, *Watch the Throne* (Roc-A-Fella Records 2011). While other versions of the album are in circulation, this book focuses on the original 12+1-track release.

35. Salois, "Forum: Religion & Hip Hop," 74.

36. Jean-Vincent Russo, "Le clip branché de Hollande cartonne aux USA: Le

candidat socialiste François Hollande est devenu un sujet de conversation chez les branchés américains," on *20min.ch*, 12 April, 2012, https://amp.20min.ch/fr/story/le-clip-branche-de-hollande-cartonne-aux-usa-746095560254

37. See the conclusion to Rollefson, "Hip Hop as Martial Art: Towards a Political Economy of Violence in Rap Music," *Oxford Handbook of Hip Hop Music Studies* (Oxford: Oxford University Press, 2018).

38. Ta-Nehisi Coates, *Between the World and Me* (New York: Spiegel and Grau, 2015), 11.

39. *Rolling Stone* editors, "Obama Goes on Record to Call Kanye West a 'Jackass,'" *Rolling Stone,* April 12, 2012, https://www.rollingstone.com/music/music-news/obama-goes-on-record-to-call-kanye-west-a-jackass-204727/. *Rolling Stone* reports, when asked "Kanye or Jay-Z?" by *Atlantic Monthly* interviewer David Samuels, Obama replied, "Jay-Z," clarifying, "'Although I like Kanye. He's a Chicago guy. Smart. He's very talented.' The reporter then asks, 'Even though you called him a jackass?' referring to Obama's off-the-record comments about West that were leaked from a 2009 interview with CNBC. Obama's response: 'He *is* a jackass. But he's talented.'"

40. The tweet about Trump's "dragon energy"—and fallout from it—is at https://twitter.com/kanyewest/status/989179757651574784?lang=en

41. Kanye West, "Amazing," on *808s & Heartbreak* (Def Jam/Roc-A-Fella 2008). My emphasis.

42. The video is worth another look. https://www.youtube.com/watch?v=HHckZCxdRkA

43. Astra Taylor, "Time's Up for Capitalism. But What's Next," *The Nation,* May 6, 2019, https://www.thenation.com/article/democracy-environment-astra-taylor/

44. The reference is, of course, to *The Sound of Music*—but just as women who don't conform to gender roles, Berndt Ostendorf wrote long ago of the problem of Black people being reduced to the dehumanizing (and essentializing) binary of "problem or victim." Berndt Ostendorf, "Celebration or Pathology? Commodity or Art? The Dilemma of African-American Expressive Culture," *Black Music Research Journal* 20, no. 2 (Autumn 2000).

45. Chapter 2 will necessarily track some of the most recent developments with regard to Kanye's gospel turn in the "Sunday Service," but by and large, the analysis will track the music and political discourses most relevant to the album's cultural work. One case in point: I've never watched *Keeping Up with the Kardashians.*

46. Frantz Fanon, *Toward the African Revolution,* trans. Haakon Chevalier (New York: Grove Press, 1964), 53. Of the Algerian case Fanon writes, "If psychiatry is the medical technique that aims to enable man no longer to be a stranger to his environment, I owe it to myself to affirm that the Arab, permanently an alien in his own country, lives in a state of absolute depersonalization." See also "The North African Syndrome" (3–16), a section that concludes with the line "Don't push me too far"—a line that resonates with and circulates throughout hip hop praxis to this day.

47. Daphne Brooks, *Bodies in Descent: Spectacular Performances of Race and Freedom, 1850–1910* (Durham: Duke University Press, 2006).

48. Audre Lorde, "Uses of Anger: Women Responding to Racism," in *Sister*

*Outsider: Essays and Speeches by Audre Lorde* (Berkeley: Crossing Press, 2007) 124–33.

49. Attali, 4.

50. Indeed, in this context, I can't help but think of the first hip hop album that really made me think: Public Enemy's 1989, *Fear of a Black Planet*—an album that also proved prophetic of our current "you will not replace us" moment. Public Enemy, *Fear of a Black Planet,* Def Jam 1990. I wasn't hip to *It Takes a Nation of Millions*, I was still listening to Kool Moe Dee and DJ Jazzy Jeff and the Fresh Prince in the eighties.

51. Chris Cillizza, "It's Not the Economy, Stupid," https://edition.cnn.com/2018/09/17/politics/trump-economy-poll/index.html

52. We'll look into this reception more closely in the coming chapters.

53. Regarding my claim that Black people won the 1990s "culture wars"—and the backlash it inspired—the high-profile trial of O. J. Simpson offers one case in point.

54. We can again offer Kanye as an example in this regard, judging from the (white) backlash to the "Taylor Swift Affair," in which Kanye aggressively supported a video by Beyoncé over that of the white (then) country artist, Swift. Hollie McKay, "Kanye West Told to Leave VMAs After Upsetting Taylor Swift," *Fox News*, September 14, 2009, https://www.foxnews.com/story/kanye-west-told-to-leave-vmas-after-upsetting-taylor-swift. Constance Grady, "How the Taylor Swift–Kanye West VMAs Scandal Became a Perfect American Morality Tale: The Fraught Legacy of the 2009 VMAs Explained," *Vox*, August 26, 2019, https://www.vox.com/culture/2019/8/26/20828559/taylor-swift-kanye-west-2009-mtv-vmas-explained

55. *The New York Times Magazine*'s 1619 Project is exemplary of this movement. The project website explains: "The 1619 Project is an ongoing initiative from the New York Times Magazine that began in August 2019, the 400th anniversary of the beginning of American slavery. It aims to reframe the country's history by placing the consequences of slavery and the contributions of black Americans at the very center of our national narrative." *New York Times Magazine* editors, "The 1619 Project," *New York Times Magazine* (August 2019), https://www.nytimes.com/interactive/2019/08/14/magazine/1619-america-slavery.html.

56. Coates, *Between the World and Me*, 11.

57. Martin Luther King, NBC News interview with Sander Vanocur, 1967, https://www.nbcnews.com/video/martin-luther-king-jr-speaks-with-nbc-news-11-months-before-assassination-1202163779741?cid=sm_npd_nn_tw_ma&fbclid=IwAR2-4dbIS1W-_jwOXObKwh8ntGNZxmC2Nmdmw_pxzePNlbfp86NuZP2S3V0

58. Arlie Russell Hochschild, *Strangers in Their Own Land: Anger and Mourning on the American Right* (New York: The New Press, 2016).

59. Du Bois, Black Reconstruction in America, introduction by David Levering Lewis (New York: The Free Press, 1992 [1935]), 700.

60. Carol Anderson, "The Policies of White Resentment," *New York Times,* August 5, 2017, https://www.nytimes.com/2017/08/05/opinion/sunday/white-resentment-affirmative-action.html

61. During the congressional hearings that ultimately impeached the forty-fifth president of the United States, Stanford law professor Pamela Karlan explained,

with what now seems dangerous faith in democracy and the rule of law in the US, "Contrary to what President Trump has said, Article 2 does not give him the power to do anything he wants. . . . The Constitution says there can be no titles of nobility, so while the president can name his son Barron, he can't make him a baron." Ashley Feinberg, "Republicans Invade Barron Trump's Privacy, Drag Him into Politics," *Slate*, Dec 4, 2019, https://slate.com/news-and-politics/2019/12/republicans-invade-barron-trumps-privacy-drag-him-into-politics.html

62. Emily Yahr, "Billboard Said Lil Nas X's 'Old Town Road' Wasn't Country Enough. Then Billy Ray Cyrus Stepped In," https://www.washingtonpost.com/arts-entertainment/2019/03/29/billboard-pulled-lil-nas-xs-viral-old-town-road-country-chart-it-ignited-controversy/?utm_term=.9e6be5613be4

63. Elias Leight, "Lil Nas X's 'Old Town Road' Was a Country Hit. Then Country Changed Its Mind," *Rolling Stone*, March 26, 2019, https://www.rollingstone.com/music/music-features/lil-nas-x-old-town-road-810844/

64. Of course, "country" music has a much more complicated and racially co-implicated history itself—as shown in Karl Hagstrom Miller, *Segregating Sound: Inventing Folk and Pop Music in the Age of Jim Crow* (Durham: Duke University Press, 2010), and Diane Pecknold, ed., *Hidden in the Mix: The African American Presence in Country Music* (Durham: Duke University Press, 2013). Nonetheless, for the purposes of the present industry-centered analysis, the characterization holds.

65. Thanks to Loren Kajikawa for stressing the fear of sonic miscegenation at play here. See also Miller, *Segregating Sound*.

66. See Miller, *Segregating Sound*. Indeed, the racialized structures of the culture industries are well-documented in the academic literature.

67. Fanon, *Black Skin*, 148.

68. Jonah Weiner, "Niggas in Practice: Jay-Z, Gwyneth Paltrow, and When White People Can Say the Word," *Slate*, June 12, 2012, http://www.slate.com/articles/arts/music_box/2012/06/gwyneth_paltrow_and_niggas_in_paris_is_it_ever_ok_for_white_people_to_use_the_word_.2.html

69. Houston A. Baker Jr., *Modernism and the Harlem Renaissance* (Chicago: University of Chicago Press, 1987).

## CHAPTER 1

1. The track is produced by West with 88 Keys and Mike Dean.

2. Phil Manzanera, "K-Scope" on *K-Scope* (Polydor 1978).

3. Thanks to Mary J. King for her help with this and other transcriptions.

4. Thomas Hobbes, *Leviathan*, ed. by Richard Tuck (Cambridge: Cambridge University Press, 1996) [1651]. See also chapter 8 of Rollefson, *Flip the Script*, 210.

5. Rollefson, *Flip the Script*, 7.

6. In his book *Decoded*, Jay gestures to the film *Gladiator* as inspiration for its classic script-flipping, slave-turned-master subversion. Shawn Carter, *Decoded* (New York: Spiegel and Grau, 2010). See also Frederick Jackson Turner,

"The Significance of the Frontier in American History," in *Annual Report of the American Historical Association* (1893), 197–227, https://www.historians.org/about-aha-and-membership/aha-history-and-archives/historical-archives/the-significance-of-the-frontier-in-american-history

7. As countless people of color and critics of Eurocentrism have suggested, the "Western civ" model that begins with ancient Greece obscures the Mycenaean and Athenian indebtedness to Phoenician, Mesopotamian, Egyptian, and Nubian civilizations.

8. Plato, *Euthyphro,* trans. Benjamin Jowett. http://classics.mit.edu/Plato/euthyfro.html

9. Dayo Olopade, "How the (Dr. Cornel) West Was Won," *The Root,* October 20, 2009, https://www.theroot.com/how-the-dr-cornel-west-was-won-1790870470; see also Cornel West, *Brother West: Living and Loving Out Loud* (New York: Smiley Books, 2010), 277.

10. Kool Moe Dee, "Wild Wild West" on *How Ya Like Me Now* (Jive 1988).

11. Dan-El Padilla Peralta, "From Damocles to Socrates: The Classics in/of Hip Hop," *Eidolon,* June 8, 2015, https://eidolon.pub/from-damocles-to-socrates-fbda6e685c26

12. Lauryn Hill (Fugees), "Zealots" on *The Score* (Ruffhouse/Columbia 1996).

13. Carter, *Decoded,* 168.

14. The tricky contours of this tightrope (of Blackness and Black success) is given performative elaboration on Janelle Monáe, "Tightrope" on *The ArchAndroid* (Wondaland Arts Society/Bad Boy Records, 2010).

15. As with Kanye West's "Horus" reference, Padilla Peralta also addresses hip hop's myriad African and Egyptological renderings.

16. Padilla Peralta, "From Damocles to Socrates."

17. Kanye West, "Power" on *My Beautiful Dark Twisted Fantasy* (2010).

18. Houston Baker, *Blues, Ideology and Afro-American Literature: A Vernacular Theory* (Chicago: University of Chicago Press, 1984), 10.

19. I discuss the intentional fallacy and the power of this unfinishedness in my hip hop pedagogy article, J. Griffith Rollefson, "'Yo Nací Caminando': Community-Engaged Scholarship, Hip Hop as Postcolonial Studies, and Rico Pabón's Knowledge of Self," *Journal of World Popular Music* 5, no. 2 (Double Special Issue: Hip Hop Activism and Representational Politics), eds. Adam Haupt, Quentin Williams, and H. Samy Alim (Winter 2018).

20. Homi Bhabha, *The Location of Culture* (London: Routledge Classics, 1994), 55; Meiling Jin, "Strangers on a Hostile Landscape," in *Watchers and Seekers, eds.* R. Cobham and M. Collins (London: The Women's Press, 1987), 126–27; Ralph Ellison, *Invisible Man* (New York: Random House, 1952).

21. Here, Bhabha is borrowing from Derrida's "supplementarity"—a concept that also resonates with "critical excess." Regarding the slippage between seeing and hearing here, please see chapter 8 of Rollefson, *Flip the Script.*

22. Attali, *Noise,* 12. Italics in original.

23. All of the album art images discussed here can be accessed at this book's companion website, www.criticalexcess.org, and in the August 2011 *Rolling Stone*

preview. *Rolling Stone* editors, "Jay-Z and Kanye West's 'Watch the Throne' Album Artwork: Preview the packaging Givenchy's Riccardo Tisci designed for the album's physical release," *Rolling Stone*, August 10, 2011, https://www.rollingstone.com/music/music-lists/jay-z-and-kanye-wests-watch-the-throne-album-artwork-14035/watch-the-throne-inside-artwork-90977/

24. The flag artwork will appear again in the video for "Otis."

25. Kanye has a history of interest in so-called "glitch art," as evidenced on his 2009 video for "Welcome to Heartbreak (ft. Kid Cudi)."

26. Honoré de Balzac, *Père Goriot* (New York: W. W. Norton, 1997).

27. Go ahead and listen (1:45–1:49 on the track). I'm not making this up. Also, now's probably a good time for this reminder/disclaimer: You don't have to like what they do, but you can't dismiss their work as thoughtless.

28. Alexander Weheliye, "'Feenin': Posthuman Voices in Contemporary Black Popular Music," *Social Text* 20, no. 2: 21–47.

29. Rollefson, "Hip Hop as Martial Art: A Political Economy of Violence in Rap Music," in *The Oxford Handbook of Hip Hop Music*, ed. Justin D. Burton and Jason Lee Oakes (Oxford: Oxford University Press, 2018), 17. See also Mark Katz, *Groove Music: The Art and Culture of the Hip Hop DJ* (New York: Oxford University Press, 2012).

30. Jeff Chang, *Can't Stop, Won't Stop: A History of the Hip Hop Generation* (New York: St. Martin's Press, 2005).

31. Attali, *Noise*, 144.

32. Fanon, *Black Skin*, 45

33. Fanon, 3.

34. Attali, *Noise*, 12.

35. Writers for the 99%, *Occupying Wall Street: The Inside Story of an Action That Changed America* (New York: Independent, 2011). For a critical race studies perspective on the Occupy Movement, see Emahunn Raheem Ali Campbell, "A Critique of the Occupy Movement from a Black Occupier," *Black Scholar* 41, no. 4 (2011).

36. Romain Gavras, dir., "No Church in the Wild" video (2012), https://www.youtube.com/watch?v=FJt7gNi3Nr4. The video turns out to have been shot in Prague.

37. Rollefson, *Flip the Script*, 195–225.

38. David Scott, "The Re-Enchantment of Humanism: An Interview with Sylvia Wynter," *Small Axe* 8 (September 2000), 119–207.

39. Wynter, in Scott, "The Re-Enchantment of Humanism," 159–60.

40. Wynter, in Scott, "The Re-Enchantment of Humanism," 160.

41. Marilynne Robinson, "What Kind of Country Do We Want?" *New York Review of Books,* June 11, 2020, https://www.nybooks.com/articles/2020/06/11/what-kind-of-country-do-we-want/

42. David Harvey, "Neoliberalism as Creative Destruction," *Annals of the American Academy of Political and Social Science*, vol. 610 (Special Issue: NAFTA and Beyond: Alternative Perspectives in the Study of Global Trade and Development) (Mar. 2007), 23.

43. Aaron Robertson, "The Year Afropessimism Hit the Streets?: A Conversation at the Edge of the World," Lithub.com (August 27, 2020). https://lithub.com/the-year-

afropessimism-hit-the-streets-a-conversation-at-the-edge-of-the-world/. See also Orlando Patterson, *Slavery and Social Death* (Cambridge, MA: Harvard University Press, 2018).

44. Frank B. Wilderson III, *Afropessimism* (New York: Liveright Publishing, 2020), 164.

## CHAPTER 2

1. In a 2014 entry on the fan site, KanyeToThe.com, commenter "everybody-noname" writes "My gf said it seems it has been taken from the series Dexter. I can't confirm because I did not watch it at the time." https://www.kanyetothe.com/forum/index.php?topic=1953913.0

2. https://www.whosampled.com/sample/113628/Jay-Z-Kanye-West-Frank-Ocean-No-Church-in-the-Wild-Orchestra-Njervudarov-Tristessa/

3. Elmer Bernstein, "Main Title and Calvera" from *Magnificent Seven: Original Motion Picture Soundtrack* (Goldwyn Studios, 1960).

4. That's a Mos Def reference for ya.

5. For more on Beyoncé's voice and industry pull, see the recent special issue on Beyoncé, ed. Marquita R. Smith, in *Popular Music and Society* 42 (2019).

6. Kelley, *Race Rebels*, 194.

7. See Alondra Nelson, "Introduction: Future Texts," *Social Text* 20, no. 2 (2002); Weheliye, "'Feenin'"; Kodwo Eshun, *More Brilliant than the Sun: Adventures in Sonic Fiction* (London: Quartet, 1998). I track these critical approaches and renderings of musical Afrofuturism—including a focus on "anti-anti-essentialism"—at length in "The 'Robot Voodoo Power' Thesis: Afrofuturism and Anti-Anti-Essentialism from Sun Ra to Kool Keith," *Black Music Research Journal* 28, no. 1 (Special Issue: *Becoming: Blackness and the Musical Imagination*), ed. Guthrie P. Ramsey Jr. (Spring 2008).

8. Marcia Dunn, "Jack King: NASA official who performed hundreds of countdowns and became celebrated as 'the Voice of Apollo 11,'" *The Independent*, 16 June 2015, https://www.independent.co.uk/news/people/news/jack-king-nasa-official-who-performed-hundreds-of-countdowns-and-became-celebrated-as-the-voice-of-10324520.html

9. Genius.com prefers the latter reading, though the line sounds more like the former (to my ear). Indeed, the main entry on the line jumps to the conclusion that it is a reference to Kanye's famed feud with country-pop artist Taylor Swift. https://genius.com/Jay-z-and-kanye-west-lift-off-lyrics

10. Phife on "We Can Get Down" on *Midnight Marauders* (Jive/RCA 1993).

11. Yes, Lauryn Hill is the exception. Don't worry, we'll get to Lauryn.

12. In the run-up to the 2016 presidential election, Donald J. Trump explained, "I could stand in the middle of Fifth Avenue and shoot somebody and I wouldn't lose any voters." Lauren Aratani, "Trump couldn't be prosecuted if he shot someone on Fifth Avenue, lawyer claims," October 23, 2019, https://www.theguardian.com/

us-news/2019/oct/23/donald-trump-immune-shoot-fifth-avenue-murder. Jay references South Shore Drive—Ye's home turf—on track 5, "Gotta Have It."

13. In fact, the line "five, four" doubles sonically as "if I fall" in Jay's presentation—thus underscoring the Dale Earnhardt reference.

14. Sun Ra, "Outer Spaceways Incorporated" on *Pictures of Infinity*, Black Lion Records, Polydor (BLP 30103, 2460 106), 1971.

15. *Space Is the Place*, dir. John Coney (Plexifilm 1974).

16. Sun Ra, *It's After the End of the World: Sun Ra and His Intergalactic Research Arkestra Live at the Donauschingen and Berlin Festivals* (BASF 1972). For more on this and broader Afrofuturist discourses around humanity, see Rollefson, "The Robot Voodoo Power Thesis: Afrofuturism and Anti-anti-essentialism from Sun Ra to Kool Keith." *Black Music Research Journal* 28, no. 1 (Spring 2008).

17. Berndt Ostendorf, "Celebration or Pathology? Commodity or Art? The Dilemma of African-American Expressive Culture," *Black Music Research Journal* 20, no. 2, Special Issue: European Perspectives on Black Music (Autumn, 2000), 217–36.

18. Ostendorf, "Celebration," 217.

19. Ostendorf, "Celebration," 217.

20. The sample is a particularly appropriate one, as it is taken from a Black director's film. Robert Townsend, *The Five Heartbeats* (Twentieth Century Fox, 1991). De La Soul, "Patti Dooke" on *Buhloone Mindstate* (Tommy Boy, 1993).

21. Karl Marx, *The 18th Brumaire of Louis Bonaparte* (New York: International Publishers, 1852).

22. Swamp Dogg, *I'm Not Selling Out / I'm Buying In* (Sonet/Takoma 1981).

23. *New York Times*, "Black Supporters of President Under Fire," October 17, 1972: 29, https://www.nytimes.com/1972/10/17/archives/black-supporters-of-president-under-fire-sammy-davis-a-key-target.html

24. My emphasis.

25. Earl Ofari Hutchinson, "The Continuing Myth of Black Capitalism," *The Black Scholar: Journal of Black Studies and Research* 23, no. 1 (1993), 20.

26. Hutchinson, "The Continuing Myth," 18.

27. Fanon, *Black Skin, White Masks*, 4.

28. Audre Lorde, *The Master's Tools Will Never Dismantle the Master's House* (New York: Penguin Classics, 2018).

29. Derecka Purnell, "Jay-Z has crossed the picket line with his NFL deal," *The Guardian*, Aug 19, 2019, https://www.theguardian.com/commentisfree/2019/aug/19/sorry-jay-z-racial-justice-corporations-billionaires

30. Fanon, *Black Skin, White Masks*, 5.

31. White, *From Jim Crow to Jay-Z*; Eric Lott, *Love and Theft: Blackface Minstrelsy and the American Working Class* (New York: Oxford University Press, 1993); David R. Roediger, *The Wages of Whiteness: Race and the Making of the American Working Class* (New York: Verso, 1999); Matthew Frye Jacobson, *Whiteness of a Different Color: European Immigrants and the Alchemy of Race* (Cambridge: Harvard University Press, 1999).

32. Jamiles Lartey, "Ta-Nehisi Coates Quits Twitter After Public Row with Cornel West," *The Guardian*, Dec. 20, 2017, https://www.theguardian.com/books/2017/dec/20/

ta-nehisi-coates-quits-twitter-after-public-row-with-cornel-west. For a more detailed overview of these recurring oppositional frames in the Harlem Renaissance, see Tobi Haslett, "The Man Who Led the Harlem Renaissance—and His Hidden Hungers," *New Yorker*, May 21, 2018, https://www.newyorker.com/magazine/2018/05/21/the-man-who-led-the-harlem-renaissance-and-his-hidden-hungers. See also Amiri Baraka, *Blues People: The Negro Experience in White America and the Music that Developed from It* (New York: William Morrow, 1963), and Amiri Baraka, *Black Music* (New York: William Morrow, 1968).

33. Lartey, "Ta-Nehisi Coates Quits Twitter."

34. Fanon, *Black Skin, White Masks*, 4.

35. Baker, *Modernism and the Harlem Renaissance*, 15–16. My emphasis.

36. Miles White, *From Jim Crow to Jay-Z: Race, Rap, and the Performance of Masculinity* (Urbana: University of Illinois Press, 2011), 80.

37. Du Bois, "The Souls of White Folk."

38. Donald Byrd, "(Fallin' Like) Dominoes" on *Places and Spaces* (Blue Note 1975).

39. Ralph Ellison, "An American Dilemma: A Review" 1944. https://teachingamericanhistory.org/library/document/an-american-dilemma-a-review/

40. Kelley, 194. The critique also jibes with Lipsitz and Rose's assessments of hip hop's "war of position."

41. Sun Ra, *Sun Ra: A Joyful Noise*, dir. Robert Mugge, Rhapsody Films (1980). See also Rollefson, "The Robot Voodoo Power Thesis."

42. Week 10 of Kanye's "Sunday Service" was originally at https://www.youtube.com/watch?v=rasILMsJiD0. It is now at https://www.youtube.com/watch?v=L2mu4jLhETk

43. *Irish Mirror* editors, "Kendall Jenner and Kanye West Join Hillsong Church for Midweek Service," *The Irish Mirror*, Apr. 25, 2019, https://www.irishmirror.ie/showbiz/celebrity-news/kendall-jenner-kanye-west-join-14579904

44. Thanks to contemporary worship music scholar Monique Ingalls for her tremendous help in guiding my reading in this area.

45. Nathaniel P. Grimes, "The Racial Ideology of Rapture," *Perspectives in Religious Studies* issue 3 (Fall 2016), 212.

46. Grimes, "Racial Ideology": 216.

47. Matthew Paul Turner, "The Rapture: The Theological Idea that Inspired 'The Leftovers,'" *Daily Beast*, July 12, 2017, https://www.thedailybeast.com/the-rapture-the-theological-idea-that-inspired-the-leftovers?ref=scroll

48. Grimes, "Racial Ideology," 219.

49. Grimes, "Racial Ideology," 211.

50. In addition to the "Christian trilogy," there was a 2018 album titled *Ye* that foregrounded Ye's mental health issues—including on the album art, which read: "I hate being Bi-Polar its awesome."

51. Ben Roazen, "Kanye West's Sunday Service—a Religious Experience or a Cult?" *OkayPlayer.com* (19 April 2019). https://www.okayplayer.com/music/kanye-west-sunday-service-coachella-what-is-it.html

52. Gil Scott-Heron, "Whitey on the Moon," on *Small Talk At 125*th *and Lenox* (Flying Dutchman, 1970).

53. Natalie Wolchover, "'One Small Step for Man': Was Neil Armstrong Misquoted?" Space.com, August 27, 2012, https://www.space.com/17307-neil-armstrong-one-small-step-quote.html

54. Kenneth Chang, "How NASA's Astronauts Became Space X's Customers," *New York Times,* May 26, 2020, https://www.nytimes.com/2020/05/26/science/spacex-launch-nasa.html

55. Lisa Yaszek, "An Afrofuturist Reading of Ralph Ellison's *Invisible Man,*" *Rethinking History* 9, nos. 2/3 (2005); Nelson, "Introduction: Future Texts"; Weheliye, "'Feenin'"; Kodwo Eshun, *More Brilliant than the Sun;* Rollefson, "The 'Robot Voodoo Power' Thesis."

## CHAPTER 3

1. Josh Gordon and Will Speck, directors, *Blades of Glory* (Dreamworks 2007).

2. The Black Eyed Peas, "My Humps" on *Monkey Business* (A&M 2005).

3. The point resonates with the widespread (and deeply ironic) belief that Obama was successful because of his race. See Rollefson, *Flip the Script*, 90.

4. Andy Greene, "Bill Withers: The Soul Man Who Walked Away," *Rolling Stone*, April 14, 2015, https://www.rollingstone.com/music/music-news/bill-withers-the-soul-man-who-walked-away-111535/

5. Michael Lee, "Why Michael Jordan's last shot in 1998 made everything that followed irrelevant," *Yahoo Sports*, 14 June 2018, https://sports.yahoo.com/michael-jordans-last-shot-made-everything-followed-irrelevant-202019275.html

6. Ostendorf, "Celebration or Pathology?"

7. Ronald Radano, "Hot Fantasies: American Modernism and the Idea of Black Rhythm," in *Music and the Racial Imagination* (Chicago: University of Chicago Press, 2000), 459. My italics. In the article Radano examines the historical circumstances in which expressions of African American "hot" rhythm were "marketed as expressions of a racially inherited rhythmic gift." This hotness "traced the meanings of African-American music across the twentieth century, from the swing sensibility of early jazz to the funk and groove of hip hop."

8. Radano, "Hot Fantasies," 475.

9. Radano, "Hot Fantasies," 474.

10. Miles White, *From Jim Crow to Jay-Z*; Eric Lott, *Love and Theft.*

11. Radano, "Hot Fantasies," 459.

12. Reverend W. A. Donaldson and Congregation, "Baptizing Scene (1959)," field recording by Alan Lomax on *Sounds of the South (Southern Folk Heritage Series)* (Atlantic, 1961).

13. The full recording is worth listening to in gauging West's thinking about counterposing the two tracks.

14. W. E. B. Du Bois, *Darkwater,* chapter I, "The Shadow of Years."

15. Martin Luther King Jr., NBC News interview with Sander Vanocur, 1967.

16. James Reese Europe, *James Reese Europe and the 369*th *US Infantry "Hell*

*Fighters" Band, Featuring Noble Sissle, the Complete Pathé Recordings* (IAJRC CD 1012, 1996 [1919]).

17. Du Bois, "Close Ranks," *The Crisis* (July 1918), 505. Special thanks to my colleague and J. R. Europe scholar Dave Gilbert for leading me to these sources. See his *The Product of Our Souls: Ragtime, Race, and the Birth of the Manhattan Musical Marketplace* (Chapel Hill: University of North Carolina Press 2016).

18. Du Bois, "Returning Soldiers," *The Crisis* (May 1919): 506.

19. Langston Hughes, "The Negro Artist and the Racial Mountain," *The Nation* (1926).

20. DuBois, "Returning Soldiers," 506.

21. See Michelle Alexander's incisive *The New Jim Crow: Mass Incarceration in the Age of Colorblindness* (New York: New Press, 2010).

22. Moten, *In the Break: The Aesthetics of the Black Radical Tradition* (Minneapolis: University of Minnesota Press, 2003), 34.

23. NAACP Website, "Criminal Justice Fact Sheet." https://www.naacp.org/criminal-justice-fact-sheet/

24. In the 2009–10 season the Nets started 0 for 18, the worst start in the history of the NBA.

25. The theme of ownership also gains a valence of considered misogyny in the conclusion to Jay's verse, as the MC cautions a fashion model, "Bitch behave." The ugly and well-crafted lyric performs a layered signification, pivoting from model to dog on the word "bitch" and reprimanding the model just as he might an animal.

26. Langston Hughes would critique the "ideology of uplift" in his piece, "The Negro Artist and the Racial Mountain," *Langston Hughes Review* 4, no. 1 (Spring 1985): 1–4. Paul Allen Anderson, *Deep River: Music and Memory in Harlem Renaissance Thought* (Durham: Duke University Press, 2001).

27. Mary Kate and Ashley Olson, "You're Invited to Mary-Kate and Ashley's Sleepover Party" (1995), https://www.youtube.com/watch?v=k6DA_WwO90c. Thanks to my 2012 graduate seminar *European Hip Hop and the Politics of Postcoloniality* at UC Berkeley for suggesting this reading.

28. Jonah Weiner, "Niggas in Practice: Jay-Z, Gwyneth Paltrow, and When White People Can Say the Word," *Slate* (12 June 2012). http://www.slate.com/articles/arts/music_box/2012/06/gwyneth_paltrow_and_niggas_in_paris_is_it_ever_ok_for_white_people_to_use_the_word_.2.html

29. Fanon, *Towards the African Revolution*, 53.

30. Ricky Saiz, dir., "Apeshit" video (2018), https://www.youtube.com/watch?v=kbMqWXnpXcA

31. 2 Live Crew, *As Nasty as They Wanna Be* (Luke/Atlantic Records, 1989).

32. Kimberlé Williams Crenshaw, "Beyond Racism and Misogyny: Black Feminism and 2 Live Crew," *Boston Review* (December 1991), http://bostonreview.net/race-gender-sexuality/kimberle-w-crenshaw-beyond-racism-and-misogyny

33. Crenshaw, "Beyond Racism and Misogyny."

34. Henry Louis Gates Jr., "2 Live Crew Decoded: Rap Music's Use of Street

Language in Context of Afro-American Cultural Heritage Analyzed," *New York Times*, June 19, 1990. The full text of Gates's published defense of 2 Live Crew is available at http://www.english.upenn.edu/~jenglish/Courses/gates.htxx

35. Crenshaw, "Beyond Racism and Misogyny."

36. Martin Iddon and Melanie Marshall, eds., *Beyonce: At Work, On Screen, and Online* (Bloomington: Indiana University Press, 2021).

37. Amy Vidor and Caroline Barta, "What on Earth Do Beyoncé, This Sphinx, and Napoleon Have in Common?," ThinkingInPublic.org, June 18, 2018, https://thinkinginpublic.org/story/what-on-earth-do-beyonce-this-sphinx-and-napoleon-have-in-common/

## CHAPTER 4

1. Thanks to social anthropologist Yusef J. Carter for introducing me to this track in my 2012 UC Berkeley seminar, "European Hip Hop and the Politics of Postcoloniality."

2. Sharief Easterling, "Niggas in Poorest," *Huffpost*, March 12, 2012, https://www.huffpost.com/entry/mos-def-yasiin-bey-niggas-in-poorest_b_1336929

3. While we might find fault with Easterling's characterization of Bey as "never really a confrontational MC," given the recorded archive of the rapper's critically minded work (that often calls out our capitalist, racist, and sexist society and its aggressors, sometimes by name), it seems that the point here is that Bey rarely got overly engaged in hip hop "beefs" with other artists.

4. Rupert Neate, "World's Witnessing a New Gilded Age"; David Huyssen, "We Won't Get Out of the Second Gilded Age."

5. Yasiin Bey (Mos Def), "Niggas in Poorest," https://www.youtube.com/watch?v=jfMx-miPtms. The "darkened" Queen Elizabeth comes at 2:16 in the video clip—along with the lines "Prince Williams ain't do it right if you ask me / If I was him I'd put some *black up in my family.*"

6. For a close reading of such misreadings, see chapter 5 of Rollefson, *Flip the Script*: "M.I.A.'s 'Terrorist Chic': Black Atlantic Music and South Asian Postcolonial Politics in London," 93–138.

7. Attali, *Noise*, 12. Italics in original.

8. Burton, "The Roots, *Undun*. Def Jam 001628202, 2011; Kanye West and Jay-Z, *Watch the Throne*. Roc-A-Fella/Roc Nation/Def Jam 001542602, 2011," 343–47. See also Burton, *Posthuman Rap*.

9. Joseph Winters, "Contemporary Sorrow Songs: Traces of Mourning, Lament, and Vulnerability in Hip Hop," *African American Review* 46, no. 1 (Spring 2013): 9–20. Winters writes in detail of the cultural and political work that the spirituals performed.

10. Moten, *In the Break*, 55.

11. In the interest of full disclosure, I was a Hillary supporter and voter. And for me, while I preferred Bernie's policy platform, it came down to a matter of race—I

didn't trust Bernie to take seriously the specific concerns of people of color. (Nor did I trust that he would win—and, of course, there's the rub.)

12. Leïla Sy and Bruno Laforestrie, "48H AVEC FH" video (2012). The clip has been removed from the internet based on copyright violations but a write-up can be found at Slate.fr editors, "François Hollande en banlieue au son de Niggas in Paris (VIDEO)," Slate.FR (23 April 2012), https://www.slate.fr/france/53893/francois-hollande-niggas-in-paris-video?amp

13. Jean-Vincent Russo, "Le clip branché de Hollande cartonne aux USA."

14. For more on French cultural politics, see chapter 1 of Rollefson, *Flip the Script*, "'*J'accuse*': Hip Hop's Postcolonial Politics in Paris," 19–33.

15. Killer Mike, "Episode 1: Living Black," *Trigger Warning with Killer Mike* (Netflix 2019). See, for instance, episode 1, which examines the difficulty in trying to live a life that works intentionally to support Black-owned businesses.

16. Rollefson, *Flip the Script*, 147.

17. Libération editors, "François Hollande, en clip sauce rap américain," (Net Campagne: Batailles de tweets, outils de mobilisation en ligne, parodies et clips: l'actu de la net-campagne) *Libération*, April 10, 2012, https://www.liberation.fr/france/2012/04/10/francois-hollande-en-clip-sauce-rap-us_810748

18. Slate.fr editors, "François Hollande en banlieue au son de Niggas in Paris (VIDEO)."

19. Bruno Laforestrie, personal interview, June 12, 2019.

20. See Rollefson, *Flip the Script*, chapter 1: "*J'accuse*."

21. *L'Afro* editors, "Interview: Leïla Sy: Portrait musical de la réalisatrice, pilier du mouvement hip-hop," *L'Afro* (26 December 2015). https://lafrolesite.wordpress.com/2015/12/26/interview-leila-sy-portrait-musical-de-la-clippeuse-dun-certain-rap-francais/

22. It is also important to note that I was unable to interview Leïla Sy for this book.

23. Emphasis in the original spoken interview.

24. Renaud Dély and Didier Hassoux, *Sarkozy et l'argent roi* (Paris: Calmann Lévy 2008).

25. "Though Meneilly is essentially a business manager, Jay Z refers to him as a consigliere," Zack O'Malley Greenburg wrote of Meneilly in his book, *Empire State of Mind* (New York: Penguin Random House, 2011). Stephanie Smith, "Top 'Consigliere' John Meneilly Leaves Jay Z's Team," *Page Six*, May 29, 2014, https://pagesix.com/2014/05/29/top-consigliere-john-meneilly-leaves-jay-zs-team/

26. Theodor Adorno (with George Simpson), "On Popular Music," *Studies in Philosophy and Social Science* (New York: Institute of Social Research, 1941), 17–48, http://www.icce.rug.nl/~soundscapes/DATABASES/SWA/On_popular_music_1.shtml. Adorno writes, "Pseudo-individualization, for its part, keeps them in line by making them forget that what they listen to is already listened to for them, or 'pre-digested.'"

27. Justin Williams, *Rhymin' and Stealin': Musical Borrowing in Hip-Hop* (Ann Arbor: University of Michigan Press, 2013). See Williams for an expert discussion of "sonic signatures" in hip hop.

28. Benjamin Lee and Ben Beaumont-Thomas, "Kanye West on Slavery: 'For 400 Years? That Sounds Like a Choice,'" *The Guardian*, May 2, 2018, https://www.theguardian.com/music/2018/may/01/kanye-west-on-slavery-for-400-years-that-sounds-like-a-choice

29. Holy Name of Mary Choral Family, "Sermon (He'll Give Us What We Really Need)," on *He'll Give Us What We Really Need* (Delta 1986).

30. Nina Simone, "Feeling Good," on *I Put a Spell on You* (Philips 1965).

31. Audre Lorde, "The Uses of Anger: Women Responding to Racism" (1981) (conference keynote address reprinted at https://www.blackpast.org/african-american-history/1981-audre-lorde-uses-anger-women-responding-racism/)

32. Therí Alyce Pickens, *Black Madness :: Mad Blackness* (Durham: Duke University Press, 2019). We'll also look at the work of Daphne Brooks in concluding.

33. Pickens, *Black Madness :: Mad Blackness*; La Marr Jurelle Bruce, "'The People Inside My Head, Too': Madness, Black Womanhood, and the Radical Performance of Lauryn Hill," *African American Review* 45, no. 3 (Special Issue: On Black Performance, ed. Soyica Colbert) (Fall 2012), 371–89; Nicole Fleetwood, "The Case of Rihanna: Erotic Violence and Black Female Desire," *African American Review* 45, no. 3 (Special Issue: On Black Performance, ed. Soyica Colbert) (Fall 2012), 419–35.

34. The story of Buddy Bolden is somewhat foundational in this regard. In his *The History of Jazz*, Ted Gioia explains: "In March of that year (1906), he was arrested after assaulting his mother-in-law with a water pitcher—an event that led to the only newspaper articles mentioning this jazz icon during his lifetime. A second arrest, in September, and a third one the following March resulted in Bolden's being declared legally insane and committed to an asylum in Jackson. For the next twenty-four years, Bolden remained at this institution, his condition deteriorating into pronounced schizophrenia." That the famed "first jazz musician" would first garner press attention for outlandishly dangerous behavior rather than for his world-changing musical practice is telling in this early twentieth-century context. Gioia, *The History of Jazz*, second edition (New York: Oxford University Press, 2011), 35.

35. Pickens, *Black Madness :: Mad Blackness*.

36. Fanon, *Toward the African Revolution*, 3–16, 53.

37. Roy Christopher, "Coming to Terms with Dave Chappelle," RoyChristopher.com (January 17, 2019). https://roychristopher.com/coming-to-terms-with-dave-chappelle/.

38. For more on Nina's musical politics, see also chapter 5, "Soul Intact: CORE, Conversions, and Covers of 'To Be Young, Gifted and Black,'" of Shana L. Redmond, *Anthem: Social Movements and the Sound of Solidarity in the African Diaspora* (New York: NYU Press, 2014); Tammy Kernodle, "'I Wish I Knew How It Would Feel to Be Free': Nina Simone and the Redefining of the Freedom Song of the 1960s," *Journal of the Society for American Music* 2, no. 3 (2008): 295–317. Kernodle writes of "the raw, gritty texture and anger that defined Simone's vocals" in her freedom songs (313–14).

39. Scott Saul, *Freedom Is, Freedom Ain't: Jazz and the Making of the Sixties* (Cambridge: Harvard University Press, 2005)..

40. Moten, *In the Break*, 34–35.

41. Moten, *In the Break*, 71.

## CHAPTER 5

1. Tom Breihan, *Pitchfork* (21 July 2011). https://pitchfork.com/reviews/tracks/12266-otis/. Italics in the original.

2. Indeed, the track's full title in track listings is something of a double homage. The liner notes read "Otis feat. Otis Redding." Liner notes, *Watch the Throne,* 5.

3. For much more on the foundational role of sampling in hip hop—and its myriad valences—see Joseph G. Schloss, *Making Beats: The Art of Sample-Based Hip Hop* (Middletown, CT: Wesleyan University Press, 2004), and Williams, *Rhymin' and Stealin'*.

4. In fact, by track's end Redding's unbridled soul is not enough of a sonic exclamation point, and Ye turns to another sample, James Brown's melismatic scream on his 1974 "Don't Tell a Lie About Me and I Won't Tell the Truth on You."

5. Houston A. Baker Jr., *Modernism and the Harlem Renaissance* (Chicago: University of Chicago Press, 1987).

6. Baker, *Modernism,* 56.

7. Du Bois, "The Souls of White Folk," in *Darkwater: Voices from within the Veil* (1920).

8. Baker, *Modernism,* 50.

9. Paul Gilroy, "Sounds Authentic: Black Music, Ethnicity, and the Challenge of a 'Changing Same,'" *Black Music Research Journal* 11, no. 2 (Autumn 1991).

10. Baker writes, "Rather than concealing or disguising in the manner of the *cryptic* mask (a colourful mastery of codes), the phaneric mask is meant to advertise." The deformation of mastery thus "distinguishes rather than conceals." Baker, *Modernism,* 51. Hobart M. King, "Igneous Rocks" on Geology.com, https://geology.com/rocks/igneous-rocks.shtml. Baker's wide-ranging study also calls on a zoological usage of *phaneric* from H. B. Cott's "Animal Form in Relation to Appearance," in *Aspects of Form: A Symposium on Form in Art and Nature,* ed. Lancelot Law Whyte (Bloomington: Indiana University Press, 1951), 43.

11. See Eva Illouz, *Consuming the Romantic Utopia: Love and the Cultural Contradictions of Capitalism,* (Berkeley: University of California Press, 1997). Janice Radway, *Reading the Romance: Women, Patriarchy, and Popular Literature* (Chapel Hill: University of North Carolina Press. 1984).

12. For a diverse and lucent set of discussions about soul's sonic and performative roots in the Black church, see Monique Guillory and Richard C. Green, eds., *Soul: Black Power, Politics, and Pleasure* (New York: New York University Press, 1998).

13. The imprint on the 78 recording of Ray Noble's New Mayfair Dance Orchestra performing "Try a Little Tenderness—Slow Fox Trot" (1933) for RCA Victor's HMV ("his master's voice") imprint reads: "Recorded in Europe."

14. Arlie Russell Hochschild, *Strangers in Their Own Land: Anger and Mourning on the American Right* (New York: The New Press, 2016).

15. Jody Rosen, "Jay Z and Kanye West's *Watch the Throne,*" *Rolling Stone,* September 1, 2011.

16. For one illustrative historical analysis of post-Weimar Germany and its resonances today see Charles S. Maier, "In Merkel's Crisis, Echoes of Weimar," *New York Review of Books*, December 4, 2017, http://www.nybooks.com/daily/2017/12/04/in-merkels-crisis-echoes-of-weimar/

17. Virginia Woolf, *A Room of One's Own* (New York: Harcourt Brace & Co., 1929).

18. Steven Levitsky and Daniel Ziblatt, *How Democracies Die* (New York: Crown, 2018).

19. Fred Moten, *In the Break*. As we have seen, one of Moten's main aims in the study is to work across the form/content and music/politics binaries and suggest that "the senses . . . have become theoreticians in their immediate practice" (11–12). Here, Moten's work will provide a touchstone to help us hear how these performative slippages theorize in their own right, sometimes in line with the textual rhetorics, sometimes diverging from them.

20. For a masterful explanation on the central role of introductions in Black musics, see Alexander Weheliye, *Phonographies: Grooves in Sonic Afro-Modernity* (Durham: Duke University Press, 2005). For a description of his concept of "hypersoul" see Weheliye, "Feenin."

21. Baker, *Modernism and the Harlem Renaissance*, 56. Stress in the original.

22. See also Kofi Agawu's "Tonality as a Colonizing Force in African Music," CIRMMT Distinguished Lectures in the Science and Technology of Music, May 29, 2014, https://www.cirmmt.org/activities/distinguished-lectures/agawu; and Baraka, *Blues People* and *Black Music*.

23. For a discussion of genre frames vis-à-vis performativities, see Philip Auslander, "Performance Analysis and Popular Music: A Manifesto," *Contemporary Theatre Review* 14, no. 1 (2004): 5.

24. Indeed, this idea of the spiral of mastery owes much to Amiri Baraka's concept of the "changing same" and Paul Gilroy's recombination thereof.

25. Du Bois, "The Souls of White Folk."

26. Larkey, "Ta-Nehisi Coates Quits Twitter."

27. For further explication of this postegalitarian politics, see Rollefson, "Hip Hop as Martial Art: A Political Economy of Violence in Rap Music," in *Oxford Handbook of Hip Hop Music Studies*, eds. Justin Burton and Jason Oakes (Oxford: Oxford University Press, 2018), http://www.oxfordhandbooks.com/view/10.1093/oxfordhb/9780190281090.001.0001/oxfordhb-9780190281090-e-11; and Rollefson, "The Robot Voodoo Power Thesis."

28. Baker, *Modernism and the Harlem Renaissance*, 56.

29. Spike Jonze, "Otis" video (2011), https://www.youtube.com/watch?v=BoEKWtgJQAU.

30. Alex Banks, "The Story Behind the Heavily Modified Maybach in Jay Z & Kanye West's 'Otis' Video," *HighSnobiety*, January 7, 2016, https://www.highsnobiety.com/2016/01/07/jay-z-kanye-west-maybach/. Ironically (or perhaps fittingly), it was reported that the "modified" Maybach sold for only $60,000 at an auction benefitting Save the Children. The article continues in the conflicted admiration vein of the previous reviews and concludes citing yet another conflicted review: "While contemporary

and commercially viable hip-hop releases have always relied on a sense of consumerism to push popular street narratives that illustrate a 'rags to riches' ascent, *Watch the Throne* fanned the flames with a style of 'luxury rap' that felt more akin to a Sotheby's auction catalog than anything else. With notable mentions of brands like Hermés, Audemars Piguet, Rolex, Gucci, Louis Vuitton, Maison Martin Margiela, Christian Louboutin, Dries Van Noten, Lanvin, COMME des GARÇONS and more, it should come as little surprise that *Spin* noted of the album, 'The elitism, the narcissism, the relentless capitalism, [and] the smug yet undeniable greatness.'"

31. Robin D. G. Kelley, *Yo Mama's Dysfunktional! Fighting the Culture Wars in Urban America* (Boston: Beacon Press, 1998). Kelley picks apart the value judgments about (African American) culture, labor, and play vis-à-vis paid work.

32. Bhabha, *The Location of Culture* (London: Routledge Classics, 1994), 55. See also Chela Sandoval's *Methodology of the Oppressed* (Minneapolis: University of Minnesota Press, 2000) for an elaboration of the idea of strategic "differential consciousness."

33. Baker, *Modernism and the Harlem Renaissance*, 56.

34. Kanye West, "Bush Doesn't Care About Black People," https://www.youtube.com/watch?v=zIUzLpO1kxI.

35. Nas, "The World Is Yours" on *Illmatic* (Columbia 1994).

36. The story is recounted in an article by another *Voice* reporter, Zach Baron, in his "How a Village Voice Reporter Helped Write the Second Verse of Jay-Z's 'Public Service Announcement,'" *Village Voice,* November 4, 2010, https://www.villagevoice.com/2010/11/04/how-a-village-voice-reporter-helped-write-the-second-verse-of-jay-zs-public-service-announcement/. Many thanks to Loren Kajikawa for this and countless other leads that were central to the development of this study.

37. Jay-Z, "The Revolutionary T-Shirt," in *Decoded,* 23–26.

38. Elizabeth Mendez Berry, "The Last Hustle," *Village Voice,* November 25, 2003. An archived version of the Mendez Berry article is at https://www.villagevoice.com/2003/11/25/the-last-hustle/3/

39. Baker, *Modernism and the Harlem Renaissance*, 56.

40. Scott Saul, *Freedom Is, Freedom Ain't.*

41. Moten, *In the Break*, 6.

42. Frederick Douglass, *Narrative of the Life of Frederick Douglass, An American Slave*, ed. Henry Louis Gates Jr., in *The Classic Slave Narratives* (New York: Mentor Books, 1987).

43. Saidiya Hartman, *Scenes of Subjection: Terror, Slavery, and Self-Making in Nineteenth-Century America* (Oxford: Oxford University Press, 1997).

44. Hartman, *Scenes of Subjection.*

45. Baker, *Modernism and the Harlem Renaissance*, 56.

## CONCLUSION

1. Jacqueline Rose, "One Long Scream," *London Review of Books* 41, no. 10 (23 May 2019): 10–14.

2. Stefano Harney and Fred Moten, *The Undercommons: Fugitive Planning & Black Study* (New York: Minor Compositions, 2013).

3. Achille Mbembe, "The Trauma of the World and the World as Trauma," paper delivered at the conference "Recognition, Reparation and Reconciliation," December 14, 2018, https://recognitionreparationandreconciliation2018.co.za/videos-saturday/. Emphasis in spoken/performed original.

4. Ralph Ellison, *Invisible Man* (New York: Random House, 1952), 6–7.

5. Daphne Brooks, *Bodies in Descent,* 5.

6. Daphne Brooks, *Bodies in Descent,* 5. Brooks cites Elin Diamond, *Unmaking Mimesis: Essays on Feminism and Theater* (London: Routledge 1997), 52.

7. George Lipsitz, *The Possessive Investment in Whiteness* (Philadelphia: Temple University Press, 1998).

8. Mbembe, "The World as Trauma and Trauma as the World."

9. Alexis de Tocqueville, *Democracy in America, English edition,* ed. Eduardo Nolla, trans. James T. Schleifer (Indianapolis: Liberty Fund, 2012).

10. Attali, *Noise,* 140.

11. Attali, *Noise,* 140.

12. Attali, *Noise,* 141. My Italics.

13. Mahoney, "The Black CNN"; Rose, *Black Noise,* 99–124.

14. Indeed, enter the drum machine, sampler, digital audio workstation, mobile phone, internet applications, and other recent developments—which have been incessantly toyed with, reprogrammed, hacked, and otherwise redeployed in and through hip hop culture. See Schloss, *Making Beats*; Mark Katz, *Groove Music: The Art and Culture of the Hip-Hop DJ* (New York: Oxford University Press, 2012); *Capturing Sound: How Technology Has Changed Music* (Berkeley: University of California Press, 2004).

15. Lorde, *Master's Tools.*

16. Wu-Tang Clan, "Method Man," on *Enter the Wu-Tang (36 Chambers)* (Loud Records 1993).

17. George Lipsitz, *Dangerous Crossroads* (New York: Verso, 1994), 35. My italics.

18. Achille Mbembe, "The Trauma of the World and the World as Trauma." Emphasis in spoken/performed original.

19. Lipsitz, *Dangerous Crossroads,* 33.

20. Ellison, "What America Would Be Like Without Blacks," *Time Magazine,* April 6 1970, 109–10. The full passage reads: "Without the presence of Negro American style, our jokes, tall tales, even our sports would be lacking in the sudden turns, shocks and swift changes of pace (all jazz-shaped) that serve to remind us that the world is ever unexplored, and that while a complete mastery of life is mere illusion, *the real secret of the game is to make life swing.* It is its ability to articulate this tragic-comic attitude toward life that explains much of the mysterious power and attractiveness of that quality of Negro American style known as 'soul.' An expression of American diversity within unity, of Blackness with whiteness, soul announces the presence of a creative struggle against the realities of existence."

21. Rose, *Black Noise,* 71.

22. Rose, *Black Noise*, 39.

23. The full transcript of Killer Mike's remarks is at https://www.rev.com/blog/transcripts/rapper-killer-mike-speech-transcript-during-atlanta-protests

24. As mentioned in chapter 4, episode 1 of Killer Mike's Netflix show *Trigger Warning with Killer Mike*, "Living Black," promoted Black-owned businesses.

25. CNN, "Killer Mike's Emotional Plea to Atlanta Protesters," May 29, 2020, https://edition.cnn.com/videos/us/2020/05/30/killer-mike-atlanta-protesters-george-floyd-vpx.wgcl

26. Rose, *Black Noise*, 39.

27. Run the Jewels, "Sea Legs" on *Run the Jewels* (Fool's Gold/Big Dada, 2013).

28. Daphne Brooks, *Bodies in Descent*, 5.

29. Achille Mbembe, "The Trauma of the World and the World as Trauma."

30. Run the Jewels, "Ooh La La" on *RTJ4* (Jewel Runners/BMG, 2020).

31. Attali, *Noise*, 11.

32. Lipsitz, *Dangerous Crossroads*, 33.

# BIBLIOGRAPHY

Adorno, Theodor (with George Simpson). "On Popular Music." In *Studies in Philosophy and Social Science* (New York: Institute of Social Research, 1941). http://www.icce.rug.nl/~soundscapes/DATABASES/SWA/On_popular_music_1.shtml

Agawu, Kofi. "Tonality as a Colonizing Force in African Music," CIRMMT Distinguished Lectures in the Science and Technology of Music, May 29, 2014, https://www.cirmmt.org/activities/distinguished-lectures/agawu

Alexander, Michelle. *The New Jim Crow: Mass Incarceration in the Age of Colorblindness.* New York: New Press, 2010.

Allen, Theodore W. *The Invention of the White Race, Volume One: Racial Oppression and Social Control.* New York: Verso, 1994.

Anderson, Carol. "The Policies of White Resentment" *New York Times*, August 5, 2017, https://www.nytimes.com/2017/08/05/opinion/sunday/white-resentment-affirmative-action.html

Anderson, Paul Allen. *Deep River: Music and Memory in Harlem Renaissance Thought.* Durham: Duke University Press, 2001.

Appert, Catherine M. *In Hip Hop Time: Music, Memory, and Social Change in Urban Senegal.* New York: Oxford University Press, 2018.

Aratani, Lauren. "Trump couldn't be prosecuted if he shot someone on Fifth Avenue, lawyer claims." *The Guardian*, October 23, 2019, https://www.theguardian.com/us-news/2019/oct/23/donald-trump-immune-shoot-fifth-avenue-murder

Attali, Jacques. *Noise: The Political Economy of Music.* Translated by Brian Massumi. Minneapolis: University of Minnesota Press, 1985 [1977].

Auslander, Philip. "Performance Analysis and Popular Music: A Manifesto." *Contemporary Theatre Review* 14, no. 1 (2004).

Baker, Houston A. *Blues, Ideology and Afro-American Literature: A Vernacular Theory.* Chicago: University of Chicago Press, 1984.

Baker, Houston A. *Modernism and the Harlem Renaissance.* Chicago: University of Chicago Press, 1987.

Balibar, Etienne. "Racism as Universalism." In *Masses, Classes, Ideas: Studies on Politics and Philosophy Before and After Marx.* New York: Routledge, 1994.

de Balzac, Honoré. *Père Goriot.* New York: W. W. Norton, 1997.

Banks, Alex. "The Story Behind the Heavily Modified Maybach in Jay Z & Kanye

West's 'Otis' Video." *HighSnobiety,* January 7, 2016, https://www.highsnobiety.com/2016/01/07/jay-z-kanye-west-maybach/

Baraka, Amiri (LeRoi Jones). *Blues People: The Negro Experience in White America and the Music that Developed from It.* New York: William Morrow, 1963.

Baraka, Amiri (LeRoi Jones). *Black Music.* New York: William Morrow, 1968.

Baron, Zach. "How a *Village Voice* Reporter Helped Write the Second Verse of Jay-Z's 'Public Service Announcement.'" *Village Voice,* November 4, 2010, https://www.villagevoice.com/2010/11/04/how-a-village-voice-reporter-helped-write-the-second-verse-of-jay-zs-public-service-announcement/

Bhabha, Homi. *The Location of Culture.* London: Routledge Classics, 1994.

Braidotti, Rosi. *The Posthuman.* Malden, MA: Polity Press, 2013.

Breihan, Tom. *Pitchfork,* 21 July 2011, https://pitchfork.com/reviews/tracks/12266-otis/

Brooks, Daphne. *Bodies in Descent: Spectacular Performances of Race and Freedom, 1850–1910.* Durham: Duke University Press, 2006.

Bruce, La Marr Jurelle. "'The People Inside My Head, Too': Madness, Black Womanhood, and the Radical Performance of Lauryn Hill." *African American Review* 45, no. 3 (Special Issue: On Black Performance, ed. Soyica Colbert) (Fall 2012): 371–89.

Burton, Justin D. "The Roots, *Undun.* Def Jam 001628202, 2011. Kanye West and Jay-Z, *Watch the Throne.* Roc-A-Fella/Roc Nation/Def Jam 001542602, 2011." *Journal of the Society for American Music* 7, no. 3 (2013): 343–47.

Burton, Justin. *Posthuman Rap.* Oxford: Oxford University Press, 2017.

Campbell, Emahunn Raheem Ali. "A Critique of the Occupy Movement from a Black Occupier." *The Black Scholar* 41, no. 4 (2011).

Carp, Alex. "Slavery and the American University." *New York Review of Books* (7 February 2018). Columbia University & Slavery project website: https://columbiaandslavery.columbia.edu/content/about-project

Carter, Shawn. *Decoded.* New York: Spiegel and Grau, 2010.

Chang, Jeff. *Can't Stop, Won't Stop: A History of the Hip Hop Generation.* New York: St. Martin's Press, 2005.

Chang, Kenneth. "How NASA's Astronauts Became Space X's Customers." *New York Times,* May 26, 2020, https://www.nytimes.com/2020/05/26/science/spacex-launch-nasa.html

Christopher, Roy. "Coming to Terms with Dave Chappelle." RoyChristopher.com (January 17, 2019). https://roychristopher.com/coming-to-terms-with-dave-chappelle/.

Christopher, Roy. *Dead Precedents: How Hip-Hop Defines the Future.* New York: Penguin Random House, 2019.

Cillizza, Chris. "It's Not the Economy, Stupid," https://edition.cnn.com/2018/09/17/politics/trump-economy-poll/index.html

Coates, Ta-Nehisi. *Between the World and Me.* New York: Spiegel and Grau, 2015.

Coney, John, dir. *Space Is the Place.* Plexifilm 1974.

Cott, H. B. "Animal Form in Relation to Appearance." In *Aspects of Form: A Symposium* on Form in Art and Nature, edited by Lancelot Law Whyte. Bloomington: Indiana University Press, 1951.

Crenshaw, Kimberlé Williams. "Beyond Racism and Misogyny: Black Feminism and 2 Live Crew." *Boston Review,* December 1991, http://bostonreview.net/race-gender-sexuality/kimberle-w-crenshaw-beyond-racism-and-misogyny

Dély, Renaud, and Didier Hassoux. *Sarkozy et l'argent roi.* Paris: Calmann Lévy 2008.

Diamond, Elin. *Unmaking Mimesis: Essays on Feminism and Theater.* London: Routledge 1997.

Douglass, Frederick. *Narrative of the Life of Frederick Douglass, An American Slave,* edited by Henry Louis Gates Jr. The Classic Slave Narratives. New York: Mentor Books, 1987.

Du Bois, W. E. B. *The Souls of Black Folk.* New York: Modern Library, 2003 [1903].

Du Bois, W. E. B. "Close Ranks," *The Crisis,* July 1918: 505.

Du Bois, W. E. B. "Returning Soldiers," *The Crisis,* May 1919: 506.

Du Bois, W. E. B. *Darkwater: Voices from Within the Veil.* New York: Harcourt, Brace and Company, 1920. http://www.gutenberg.org/files/15210/15210-h/15210-h.htm

Du Bois, W. E. B. *Black Reconstruction in America,* introduction by David Levering Lewis. New York: The Free Press, 1992 [1935].

Dunn, Marcia. "Jack King: NASA official who performed hundreds of countdowns and became celebrated as 'the Voice of Apollo 11.'" *The Independent,* 16 June 2015, https://www.independent.co.uk/news/people/news/jack-king-nasa-official-who-performed-hundreds-of-countdowns-and-became-celebrated-as-the-voice-of-10324520.html

Easterling, Sharief. "Niggas in Poorest." *Huffpost,* 12 March 2012, https://www.huffpost.com/entry/mos-def-yasiin-bey-niggas-in-poorest_b_1336929

Ellison, Ralph. "An American Dilemma: A Review." In *Shadow and Act.* New York: Random House, 1964. Originally written in 1944, for Carnegie Corporation. https://teachingamericanhistory.org/library/document/an-american-dilemma-a-review/

Ellison, Ralph. *Invisible Man.* New York: Random House, 1952.

Ellison, Ralph. "Blues People." In *Shadow and Act.* New York: Vintage, 1964.

Ellison, Ralph. "What America Would Be Like Without Blacks." *Time Magazine,* April 6 1970.

Eshun, Kodwo. *More Brilliant than the Sun: Adventures in Sonic Fiction.* London: Quartet, 1998.

Evans, Brad and Gayatri Chakravorty Spivak, "When Law Is Not Justice" *New York Times* (July 13, 2016).

everybodynoname, *KanyeToThe.com,* https://www.kanyetothe.com/forum/index.php?topic=1953913.0

Fanon, Frantz. *Black Skin, White Masks* (Peau noire, masques blancs). Translated by C. L. Markham. London: Pluto Press, 1986 [1952].

Fanon, Frantz. *Toward the African Revolution.* Translated by Haakon Chevalier. New York: Grove Press, 1964.

Feinberg, Ashley. "Republicans Invade Barron Trump's Privacy, Drag Him into

Politics." *Slate*, Dec 4, 2019, https://slate.com/news-and-politics/2019/12/republicans-invade-barron-trumps-privacy-drag-him-into-politics.html

Fleetwood, Nicole. "The Case of Rihanna: Erotic Violence and Black Female Desire." *African American Review* 45, no. 3 (Special Issue: On Black Performance, ed. Soyica Colbert) (Fall 2012): 419–35.

Gates Henry Louis Jr. "2 Live Crew Decoded: Rap Music's Use of Street Language in Context of Afro-American Cultural Heritage Analyzed." *New York Times*, 19 June 1990, http://www.english.upenn.edu/~jenglish/Courses/gates.htxx

Gilbert, Dave. *The Product of Our Souls: Ragtime, Race, and the Birth of the Manhattan Musical Marketplace*. Chapel Hill: University of North Carolina Press, 2016.

Gilroy, Paul. *The Black Atlantic: Modernity and Double Consciousness*. Cambridge, MA: Harvard University Press, 1993.

Gilroy, Paul. "Sounds Authentic: Black Music, Ethnicity, and the Challenge of a 'Changing Same.'" *Black Music Research Journal* 11, no. 2 (Autumn 1991).

Gilroy, Paul. "Why Harry's Disoriented about Empire." *The Guardian*, 18 January 2005.

Gopal, Priyamvada. "Yes, We Must Decolonise: Our Teaching Has to Go Beyond Elite White Men." *The Guardian*, 27 October 2017.

Grady, Constance. "How the Taylor Swift–Kanye West VMAs Scandal Became a Perfect American Morality Tale: The Fraught Legacy of the 2009 VMAs Explained." *Vox*, August 26, 2019, https://www.vox.com/culture/2019/8/26/20828559/taylor-swift-kanye-west-2009-mtv-vmas-explained

Greene, Andy. "Bill Withers: The Soul Man Who Walked Away." *Rolling Stone*, April 14, 2015, https://www.rollingstone.com/music/music-news/bill-withers-the-soul-man-who-walked-away-111535/

Grimes, Nathaniel P. "The Racial Ideology of Rapture." *Perspectives in Religious Studies*, issue 3 (Fall 2016).

Guillory, Monique, and Richard C. Green, eds. *Soul: Black Power, Politics, and Pleasure*. New York: New York University Press, 1998.

Hagstrom Miller, Karl. *Segregating Sound: Inventing Folk and Pop Music in the Age of Jim Crow*. Durham: Duke University Press, 2010.

Hall, Stuart. "Old and New Identities, Old and New Ethnicities." In *Culture, Globalization and the World System: Contemporary Conditions for the Representation of Identity*. Binghamton: State University of New York, 1991.

Harney, Stefano, and Fred Moten. *The Undercommons: Fugitive Planning & Black Study*. New York: Minor Compositions, 2013.

Hartman, Saidiya. *Scenes of Subjection: Terror, Slavery, and Self-Making in Nineteenth-Century America*. Oxford: Oxford University Press, 1997.

Harvey, David. "Neoliberalism as Creative Destruction." *The Annals of the American Academy of Political and Social Science* vol. 610 (Special Issue: NAFTA and Beyond: Alternative Perspectives in the Study of Global Trade and Development) (March 2007).

Haslett, Tobi. "The Man Who Led the Harlem Renaissance—and His Hidden Hungers." *New Yorker*, May 21, 2018, https://www.newyorker.com/magazine/2018/05/21/the-man-who-led-the-harlem-renaissance-and-his-hidden-hungers

Hayles, N. Katherine. *How We Became Posthuman: Virtual Bodies in Cybernetics, Literature, and Informatics*. Chicago: University of Chicago Press, 1999.

Hobbes, Thomas. *Leviathan, or The Matter Former and Power of a Common Wwealth Ecclesiastical and Civil*, edited by Richard Tuck. Cambridge: Cambridge University Press, 1996 [1651].

Hochschild, Arlie Russell. *Strangers in Their Own Land: Anger and Mourning on the American Right*. New York: New Press, 2016.

Hughes, Langston. "The Negro Artist and the Racial Mountain." *The Langston Hughes Review* 4, no. 1 (Spring 1985 [1926]).

Hutchinson, Earl Ofari. "The Continuing Myth of Black Capitalism." *The Black Scholar: Journal of Black Studies and Research* 23, no. 1 (1993).

Huyssen, David. "We Won't Get Out of the Second Gilded Age the Way We Got Out of the First." *Vox* (1 April 2019), https://www.vox.com/first-person/2019/4/1/18286084/gilded-age-income-inequality-robber-baron

Iddon, Martin, and Melanie Marshall, eds. *Beyonce: At Work, On Screen, and Online*. Bloomington: Indiana University Press, 2021.

Illouz, Eva. Consuming the Romantic Utopia: Love and the Cultural Contradictions of Capitalism. Berkeley: University of California Press, 1997.

*Irish Mirror* editors. "Kendall Jenner and Kanye West Join Hillsong Church for Midweek Service." *Irish Mirror*, 25 April 2019, https://www.irishmirror.ie/showbiz/celebrity-news/kendall-jenner-kanye-west-join-14579904

Jacobson, Matthew Frye. *Whiteness of a Different Color: European Immigrants and the Alchemy of Race*. Cambridge, MA: Harvard University Press, 1999.

Jin, Meiling. "Strangers on a Hostile Landscape." In *Watchers and Seekers, edited by* R. Cobham and M. Collins. London: The Women's Press, 1987.

Kajikawa, Loren. *Sounding Race in Rap Songs*. Berkeley: University of California Press, 2015.

Katz, Mark. *Capturing Sound: How Technology Has Changed Music*. Berkeley: University of California Press, 2004.

Katz, Mark. *Groove Music: The Art and Culture of the Hip Hop DJ*. New York: Oxford University Press, 2012.

Kelley, Robin D. G. *Race Rebels: Culture, Politics, and the Black Working Class*. New York: Free Press, 1994.

Kelley, Robin D. G. *Yo Mama's Dysfunktional! Fighting the Culture Wars in Urban America*. Boston: Beacon Press, 1998.

Kernodle, Tammy. "'I Wish I Knew How It Would Feel to Be Free': Nina Simone and the Redefining of the Freedom Song of the 1960s," *Journal of the Society for American Music* 2, no. 3 (2008): 295–317.

Keyes, Cheryl L. *Rap Music and Street Consciousness*. Urbana: University of Illinois Press, 2002.

Killer Mike. Remarks on George Lloyd protests (transcript). Rev. com, 30 May 2020, https://www.rev.com/blog/transcripts/rapper-killer-mike-speech-transcript-during-atlanta-protests

Kincaid, Jamaica. *A Small Place*. New York: Penguin, 1988.

King, Hobart M. "Igneous Rocks" on Geology.com, https://geology.com/rocks/igneous-rocks.shtml

King, Martin Luther. NBC News interview with Sander Vanocur, 1967, https://www.nbcnews.com/video/martin-luther-king-jr-speaks-with-nbc-news-11-months-before-assassination-1202163779741

Laforestrie, Bruno. Personal interview, 12 June 2019.

*L'Afro* editors. "Interview: Leïla Sy: Portrait musical de la réalisatrice, pilier du mouvement hip-hop." *L'Afro*, 26 December 2015, https://lafrolesite.wordpress.com/2015/12/26/interview-leila-sy-portrait-musical-de-la-clippeuse-dun-certain-rap-francais/

Lartey, Jamiles. "Ta-Nehisi Coates Quits Twitter After Public Row with Cornel West." *The Guardian*, 20 December 2017, https://www.theguardian.com/books/2017/dec/20/ta-nehisi-coates-quits-twitter-after-public-row-with-cornel-west

Lee, Benjamin, and Ben Beaumont-Thomas. "Kanye West on Slavery: 'For 400 Years? That Sounds Like a Choice.'" *The Guardian*, 2 May 2018.

Lee, Michael. "Why Michael Jordan's Last Shot in 1998 Made Everything that Followed Irrelevant." *Yahoo Sports*, 14 June 2018, https://sports.yahoo.com/michael-jordans-last-shot-made-everything-followed-irrelevant-202019275.html

Leight, Elias. "Lil Nas X's 'Old Town Road' Was a Country Hit. Then Country Changed Its Mind." *Rolling Stone*, 26 March 2019.

Levitsky, Steven, and Daniel Ziblatt. *How Democracies Die*. New York: Crown, 2018.

*Libération* editors. "François Hollande, en clip sauce rap américain" (Net Campagne: Batailles de tweets, outils de mobilisation en ligne, parodies et clips: l'actu de la net-campagne). *Libération*, 10 April 2012, https://www.liberation.fr/france/2012/04/10/francois-hollande-en-clip-sauce-rap-us_810748

Lipsitz, George. *Dangerous Crossroads*. New York: Verso, 1994.

Lipsitz, George. *The Possessive Investment in Whiteness*. Philadelphia: Temple University Press, 1998.

Lorde, Audre. "Uses of Anger: Women Responding to Racism." In *Sister Outsider: Essays and Speeches by Audre Lorde*. Berkeley: Crossing Press, 2007 [1981].

Lorde, Audre. *The Master's Tools Will Never Dismantle the Master's House*. New York: Penguin Classics, 2018.

Lott, Eric. *Love and Theft: Blackface Minstrelsy and the American Working Class*. New York: Oxford University Press US, 1993.

Mahoney, Elisabeth. "The Black CNN: When Hip Hop Took Control." *The Guardian*, 25 June 2010.

Maier, Charles S. "In Merkel's Crisis, Echoes of Weimar." *New York Review of Books*, 4 December 2017, http://www.nybooks.com/daily/2017/12/04/in-merkels-crisis-echoes-of-weimar/

Marx, Karl. *The 18th Brumaire of Louis Bonaparte*. New York: International Publishers, 1852.

Matlon, Jordanna. "Black Masculinity Under Racial Capitalism," Boston Review (July 16, 2019). http://bostonreview.net/race/jordanna-matlon-black-masculinity-under-racial-capitalism

Matlon, Jordanna. "Racial Capitalism and the Crisis of Black Masculinity," *American Sociological Review*, vol. 81, no. 5: 1014–1038.

Mbembe, Achille. "The Trauma of the World and the World as Trauma." Paper delivered at the conference "Recognition, Reparation and Reconciliation," 14 December, 2018, https://www.youtube.com/watch?v=L4oYP44uc2Q

McClary, Susan. "Afterword: The Politics of Silence and Sound." In *Noise: The Political Economy of Music*, by Jacques Attali. Minneapolis: University of Minnesota Press, 1985.

McKay, Hollie. "Kanye West Told to Leave VMAs After Upsetting Taylor Swift." *Fox News*, September 14, 2009, https://www.foxnews.com/story/kanye-west-told-to-leave-vmas-after-upsetting-taylor-swift

MEERA. "Decolonising the Curriculum: What's All the Fuss About?" On the SOAS website https://www.soas.ac.uk/blogs/study/decolonising-curriculum-whats-the-fuss/

Mendez Berry, Elizabeth. "The Last Hustle." *Village Voice*, November 25, 2003, https://www.villagevoice.com/2003/11/25/the-last-hustle/3/

Moten, Fred. *In the Break: The Aesthetics of the Black Radical Tradition*. Minneapolis: University of Minnesota Press, 2003.

NAACP website. "Criminal Justice Fact Sheet," https://www.naacp.org/criminal-justice-fact-sheet/

Neal, Mark Anthony. *Looking for Leroy*. New York: NYU Press, 2013.

Neate, Rupert. "World's Witnessing a New Gilded Age as Billionaires' Wealth Swells to $6tn." *The Guardian*, 26 October 2017.

Nelson, Alondra. "Introduction: Future Texts." *Social Text* 20, no. 2 (2002).

*New York Times* editors. "Black Supporters of President Under Fire." *New York Times*, 17 October 1972: 29, https://www.nytimes.com/1972/10/17/archives/black-supporters-of-president-under-fire-sammy-davis-a-key-target.html

*New York Times Magazine* editors. "The 1619 Project." *New York Times Magazine*, August 2019, https://www.nytimes.com/interactive/2019/08/14/magazine/1619-america-slavery.html.

Okundaye, Jason Osamede. "The 'Decolonise' Cambridge Row Is Yet Another Attack on Students of Colour." *The Guardian*, 25 October 2017.

Olopade, Dayo. "How the West Was Won (interview with Cornel West)." *The Root*, 20 October 2009. https://www.theroot.com/how-the-dr-cornel-west-was-won-1790870470.

O'Malley Greenburg, Zack. *Empire State of Mind*. New York: Penguin Random House, 2011.

Ostendorf, Berndt. "Celebration or Pathology? Commodity or Art? The Dilemma of African-American Expressive Culture." *Black Music Research Journal* 20, no. 2 (Special Issue: European Perspectives on Black Music) (Autumn 2000): 217–36.

Patterson, Orlando. *Slavery and Social Death*. Cambridge, MA: Harvard University Press, 2018.

Pecknold, Diane, ed. *Hidden in the Mix: The African American Presence in Country Music*. Durham: Duke University Press, 2013.

Peralta, Dan-El Padilla. "From Damocles to Socrates: The Classics in/of Hip Hop." *Eidolon*, 8 June 2015, https://eidolon.pub/from-damocles-to-socrates-fbda6e685c26

Perry, Imani. *Prophets of the Hood: Politics and Poetics in Hip Hop*. Durham: Duke University Press, 2004.

Pickens. Therí Alyce. *Black Madness :: Mad Blackness*. Durham: Duke University Press, 2019.

Plato, *Euthyphro*. Translated by Benjamin Jowett. http://classics.mit.edu/Plato/euthyfro.html

Potter, Russell. *Spectacular Vernaculars: Hip-Hop and the Politics of Postmodernism*. New York: State University of New York Press, 1995.

Purnell, Derecka. "Jay-Z Has Crossed the Picket Line with His NFL Deal." *The Guardian, 19* August 2019, https://www.theguardian.com/commentisfree/2019/aug/19/sorry-jay-z-racial-justice-corporations-billionaires

Quinn, Eithne. *Nuthin' but a "G" Thang: The Culture and Commerce of Gangsta Rap*. New York: Columbia University Press, 2005.

Radano, Ronald. "Hot Fantasies: American Modernism and the Idea of Black Rhythm." In *Music and the Racial Imagination*, edited by Ronald M. Radano and Philip V. Bohlman. Chicago: University of Chicago Press, 2000.

Radway, Janice. *Reading the Romance: Women, Patriarchy, and Popular Literature*. Chapel Hill: University of North Carolina Press, 1984.

Redmond, Shana L. *Anthem: Social Movements and the sound of Solidarity in the African Diaspora*. New York: New York University Press, 2014.

Roazen, Ben. "Kanye West's Sunday Service—a Religious Experience or a Cult?" *OkayPlayer.com*, 19 April 2019, https://www.okayplayer.com/music/kanye-west-sunday-service-coachella-what-is-it.html

Robertson, Aaron. "The Year Afropessimism Hit the Streets?: A Conversation at the Edge of the World," *Lithub.com* (August 27, 2020). https://lithub.com/the-year-afropessimism-hit-the-streets-a-conversation-at-the-edge-of-the-world/.

Robinson, Cedric. *Black Marxism: The Making of the Black Radical Tradition*. Chapel Hill: University of North Carolina Press, 1983.

Robinson, Marilynne. "What Kind of Country Do We Want?" *New York Review of Books*, 11 June 2020, https://www.nybooks.com/articles/2020/06/11/what-kind-of-country-do-we-want/

Roediger, David R. *The Wages of Whiteness: Race and the Making of the American Working Class*. New York: Verso, 1999.

Rollefson, J. Griffith. "The Robot Voodoo Power Thesis: Afrofuturism and Anti-anti-essentialism from Sun Ra to Kool Keith." *Black Music Research Journal* 28, no. 1 (Spring 2008).

Rollefson, J. Griffith. *Flip the Script: European Hip Hop and the Politics of Postcoloniality*. Chicago: University of Chicago Press, 2017.

Rollefson, J. Griffith. CIPHER grant proposal (ERC CoG, 2018), 1–6, https://europeanhiphoporg.files.wordpress.com/2018/06/ercconsolidatorgrant-2018-rollefson-fullapp.pdf

Rollefson, J. Griffith. "'Yo Nací Caminando': Community-Engaged Scholarship, Hip Hop as Postcolonial Studies, and Rico Pabón's Knowledge of Self." *Journal of World Popular Music* 5, no. 2 (Double Special Issue: Hip Hop Activism and

Representational Politics), eds. Adam Haupt, Quentin Williams, and H. Samy Alim (Winter 2018).
Rollefson, J. Griffith. "Hip Hop as Martial Art: Towards a Political Economy of Violence in Rap Music." *Oxford Handbook of Hip Hop Music Studies*. Oxford: Oxford University Press, 2018.
*Rolling Stone* editors. "Jay-Z and Kanye West's 'Watch the Throne' Album Artwork: Preview the packaging Givenchy's Riccardo Tisci designed for the album's physical release." *Rolling Stone*, 10 August 10, 2011, https://www.rollingstone.com/music/music-lists/jay-z-and-kanye-wests-watch-the-throne-album-artwork-14035/watch-the-throne-inside-artwork-90977/
*Rolling Stone* editors. "Obama Goes on Record to Call Kanye West a 'Jackass.'" *Rolling Stone*, April 12, 2012, https://www.rollingstone.com/music/music-news/obama-goes-on-record-to-call-kanye-west-a-jackass-204727/
Rose, Jacqueline. "One Long Scream." *London Review of Books* 41, no. 10 (23 May 2019).
Rose, Tricia. *Black Noise: Rap Music and Black Culture in Contemporary America*. Hanover, NH: Wesleyan University Press, 1994.
Rosen, Jody. "Jay Z and Kanye West's *Watch the Throne*." *Rolling Stone*, 1 September 2011.
Runstedtler, Theresa. *Jack Johnson, Rebel Sojourner*. Berkeley: University of California Press, 2012.
Russo, Jean-Vincent. "Le clip branché de Hollande cartonne aux USA: Le candidat socialiste François Hollande est devenu un sujet de conversation chez les branchés américains." *20min.ch*, 12 April 2012, https://amp.20min.ch/fr/story/le-clip-branche-de-hollande-cartonne-aux-usa-746095560254
Salois, Kendra. "Forum: Religion & Hip Hop." *Performance, Religion and Spirituality* 2, no. 1.
Sandoval, Chela. *Methodology of the Oppressed*. Minneapolis: University of Minnesota Press, 2000.
Saul, Scott. *Freedom Is, Freedom Ain't: Jazz and the Making of the Sixties*. Cambridge, MA: Harvard University Press, 2005.
Schloss, Joseph G. *Making Beats: The Art of Sample-Based Hip Hop*. Middletown, CT: Wesleyan University Press, 2004.
Scott, David. "The Re-Enchantment of Humanism: An Interview with Sylvia Winter." *Small Axe: A Caribbean Journal of Criticism* 4, no. 2 (September 2000).
*Slate.fr* editors. "François Hollande en banlieue au son de Niggas in Paris (VIDEO)." *Slate.FR*, 23 April 2012, https://www.slate.fr/france/53893/francois-hollande-niggas-in-paris-video?amp
Smith, Marquita R., ed. Special Issue on Beyoncé in *Popular Music and Society* 42, no. 1 (2019).
Smith, Stephanie. "Top 'Consigliere' John Meneilly Leaves Jay Z's Team." *Page Six*, 29 May 2014, https://pagesix.com/2014/05/29/top-consigliere-john-meneilly-leaves-jay-zs-team/
Spivak, Gayatri Chakravorty. "Scattered Speculations on the Subaltern and the Popular" in *An Aesthetic Education in the Era of Globalization*. Cambridge, Mass.: Harvard University Press, 2012) 429–431.

Tate, Greg. *Everything but the Burden*. New York: Penguin/Random House, 2003.

Taylor, Astra. "Time's Up for Capitalism. But What's Next." *The Nation*, 6 May 2019.

Thurman, Kira and Alex Ross, "Alex Ross and Kira Thurman on Afro-Wagnerism for Popular Music Books in Process Series" (September 22, 2020) https://www.youtube.com/watch?v=lVA862NDiD4&ab_channel=EricWeisbard

Titon, Jeff Todd. *Worlds of Music: An Introduction to the Musics of the World's Peoples*. Belmont, CA: Cengage, 2008.

de Tocqueville, Alexis. *Democracy in America* (English edition). Edited by Eduardo Nolla, translated by James T. Schleifer. Indianapolis: Liberty Fund, 2012.

Turner, Frederick Jackson. "The Significance of the Frontier in American History." In *Annual Report of the American Historical Association* (1893), 197–227, https://www.historians.org/about-aha-and-membership/aha-history-and-archives/historical-archives/the-significance-of-the-frontier-in-american-history

Turner, Matthew Paul. "The Rapture: The Theological Idea that Inspired 'The Leftovers.'" *The Daily Beast*, 12 July, 2017, https://www.thedailybeast.com/the-rapture-the-theological-idea-that-inspired-the-leftovers?ref=scroll

Vidor, Amy, and Caroline Barta. "What on Earth Do Beyoncé, This Sphinx, and Napoleon Have in Common?" ThinkingInPublic.org, 18 June 2018, https://thinkinginpublic.org/story/what-on-earth-do-beyonce-this-sphinx-and-napoleon-have-in-common/

*Vox* editors. "Morality Tale: The Fraught Legacy of the 2009 VMAs Explained." *Vox*, 26 August 2019, https://www.vox.com/culture/2019/8/26/20828559/taylor-swift-kanye-west-2009-mtv-vmas-explained

Weheliye, Alexander. "'Feenin': Posthuman Voices in Contemporary Black Popular Music." *Social Text* 20, no. 2 (2002): 21–47.

Weheliye, Alexander. *Phonographies: Grooves in Sonic Afro-Modernity*. Durham, NC: Duke University Press, 2005.

Weiner, Jonah. "Niggas in Practice: Jay-Z, Gwyneth Paltrow, and When White People Can Say the Word." *Slate*, 12 June 2012.

West, Cornel. *Brother West: Living and Loving Out Loud*. New York: Smiley Books, 2010.

White, Miles. *From Jim Crow to Jay-Z: Race, Rap, and the Performance of Masculinity*. Urbana: University of Illinois Press, 2011.

Wilderson III, Frank B. *Afropessimism*. New York, Liveright Publishing, 2020.

Williams, Justin. *Rhymin' and Stealin': Musical Borrowing in Hip-Hop*. Ann Arbor: University of Michigan Press, 2013.

Winters, Joseph. "Contemporary Sorrow Songs: Traces of Mourning, Lament, and Vulnerability in Hip Hop." *African American Review* 46, no. 1 (Spring 2013).

Wolchover, Natalie. "'One Small Step for Man': Was Neil Armstrong Misquoted?" Space.com, 27 August, 2012, https://www.space.com/17307-neil-armstrong-one-small-step-quote.html

Woolf, Virginia. *A Room of One's Own*. New York: Harcourt Brace & Co., 1929.

Writers for the 99%. *Occupying Wall Street: The Inside Story of an Action That Changed America*. New York: Independent, 2011.

Yahr, Emily. "Billboard Said Lil Nas X's 'Old Town Road' Wasn't Country Enough. Then Billy Ray Cyrus Stepped In." *Washington Post*, 25 March 2019.
Yaszek, Lisa. "An Afrofuturist Reading of Ralph Ellison's *Invisible Man*." *Rethinking History* 9, no. 2/3 (2005).

# DISCOGRAPHY AND VIDEOGRAPHY


2 Live Crew. *As Nasty as They Wanna Be.* Luke/Atlantic Records, 1989.

A Tribe Called Quest. "We Can Get Down" on *Midnight Marauders.* Jive/RCA, 1993.

Bernstein, Elmer. "Main Title and Calvera." From *Magnificent Seven: Original Motion Picture Soundtrack.* Goldwyn Studios, 1960.

Bey, Yasiin (Mos Def). "Niggas in Poorest," https://www.youtube.com/watch?v=jfMx-miPtms

The Black Eyed Peas. "My Humps" on *Monkey Business.* A&M, 2005.

Byrd, Donald. "(Fallin' Like) Dominoes" on *Places and Spaces.* Blue Note, 1975.

Chaka Khan, "Through the Fire" on *I Feel for You.* Warner Bros., 1985.

De La Soul. "Patti Dooke" on *Buhloone Mindstate.* Tommy Boy, 1993.

Donaldson, Reverend W. A., & Congregation. "Baptizing Scene (1959)." Field recording by Alan Lomax on *Sounds of the South, Southern Folk Heritage Series.* Atlantic, 1961.

Europe, James Reese. *James Reese Europe and the 369*th *US Infantry "Hell Fighters" Band, Featuring Noble Sissle, the Complete Pathé Recordings* (IAJRC CD 1012, 1996 [1919]).

Gavras, Romain, dir. "No Church in the Wild" video (2012), https://www.youtube.com/watch?v=FJt7gNi3Nr4

Gordon, Josh, and Will Speck, dir. *Blades of Glory.* Dreamworks 2007.

Hill, Lauryn (Fugees). "Zealots" on *The Score.* Ruffhouse/Columbia, 1996.

Holy Name of Mary Choral Family. "Sermon (He'll Give Us What We Really Need)" on *He'll Give Us What We Really Need.* Delta, 1986.

Jay-Z and Kanye West. *Watch the Throne.* Roc-A-Fella Records, 2011.

Jonze, Spike. "Otis" video (2011), https://www.youtube.com/watch?v=BoEKWtgJQAU

Killer Mike. "Episode 1: Living Black," *Trigger Warning with Killer Mike.* Netflix, 2019.

Kool Moe Dee. "Wild Wild West" on *How Ya Like Me Now.* Jive, 1988.

Manzanera, Phil. "K-Scope" on *K-Scope.* Polydor, 1978.

Monáe, Janelle. "Tightrope" on *The ArchAndroid.* Wondaland Arts Society/Bad Boy Records, 2010.

Nas. "The World Is Yours" on *Illmatic.* Columbia, 1994.

Noble, Ray, and the New Mayfair Dance Orchestra. "Try a Little Tenderness—Slow Fox Trot." RCA Victor, 1933.

Olson, Mary Kate, and Ashley Olson. "You're Invited to Mary-Kate and Ashley's Sleepover Party" (1995). https://www.youtube.com/watch?v=k6DA_WwO90c

Public Enemy. *Fear of a Black Planet.* Def Jam, 1990.

Run the Jewels. "Sea Legs" on *Run the Jewels.* Fool's Gold/Big Dada, 2013.

Run the Jewels. "Ooh La La" on *RTJ4.* Jewel Runners/BMG, 2020.

Saiz, Ricky, dir. "Apeshit" video (2018), https://www.youtube.com/watch?v=kbMqWXnpXcA

Scott-Heron, Gil. "Whitey on the Moon" on *Small Talk At 125*th *and Lenox.* Flying Dutchman, 1970.

Simone, Nina. "Feeling Good" on *I Put a Spell on You.* Philips, 1965.

Sun Ra. "Outer Spaceways Incorporated" on *Pictures of Infinity.* Black Lion Records, Polydor, 1971.

Sun Ra. *It's After the End of the World: Sun Ra and His Intergalactic Research Arkestra Live at the Donauschingen and Berlin Festivals.* BASF, 1972.

Sun Ra. *Space Is the Place*, dir. John Coney. Plexifilm, 1974.

Swamp Dogg. *I'm Not Selling Out / I'm Buying In!* Sonet/Takoma, 1981.

Townsend, Robert. *The Five Heartbeats.* Twentieth Century Fox, 1991.

West, Kanye. "Amazing" on *808s & Heartbreak.* Def Jam/Roc-A-Fella, 2008.

West, Kanye. "Power" on *My Beautiful Dark Twisted Fantasy.* Def Jam/Roc-A-Fella, 2010.

West, Kanye. "Sunday Service (Week 10)" https://www.youtube.com/watch?v=rasILMsJiD0

West, Kanye. "Bush Doesn't Care About Black People" https://www.youtube.com/watch?v=zIUzLpO1kxI

West, Kanye. "Through the Wire" on *College Dropout.*

Wu-Tang Clan. "Method Man" on *Enter the Wu-Tang (36 Chambers).* Loud Records, 1993.

# INDEX